DYING TO TEACH

Other Books by the Author
Joseph Conrad: Writing as Rescue
The Talking Cure: Literary Representations of Psychoanalysis
Narcissism and the Novel
Diaries to an English Professor: Pain and Growth in the Classroom
Surviving Literary Suicide
Risky Writing: Self-Disclosure and Self-Transformation in the Classroom
Empathic Teaching: Education for Life

DYING TO TEACH
A Memoir of Love, Loss, and Learning

Jeffrey Berman

STATE UNIVERSITY OF NEW YORK PRESS

Published by
State University of New York Press, Albany

For information, address State University of New York Press,
194 Washington Avenue, Suite 305, Albany, NY 12210–2384

Production by Dana Foote
Marketing by Fran Keneston

Library of Congress Cataloging-in-Publication Data

Berman, Jeffrey, 1945–
    Dying to teach : a memoir of love, loss, and learning / Jeffrey Berman.
      p.   cm.
    Includes bibliographical references and index.
    ISBN–13: 978-0-7914-7009-1 (hardcover : alk. paper)
    ISBN–13: 978-0-7914-7010-7 (pbk. : alk. paper)
    1. Pancreas—Cancer—Patients—Biography.   2. Teacher-student relationships.
    3. Death.   4. Caregivers.   5. Eulogies.   6. Hospice care.   I. Title.

    RC280.P25B47   2007
    362.196′994370092—dc22
    [B]
                                                                2006012418

10   9   8   7   6   5   4   3   2   1

For Clark Dougan, Priscilla Claiborne, James Peltz, and Jane Bunker, My Editors and Friends

ON THE ANNIVERSARY OF HER DEATH

(in memory of Barbara Berman)

You expected she would
have been gone by March,
but instead, dying was tenacious,
and hung on, making
her belly distend, as if it was
suddenly ripe, again
with daughters.

Today, two years later,
a cruel April wind
roars and carries off the seared
blossoms that now
flood my yard,
like heaves of snow, glinting
with atomistic hooves of gold—

The earth was not ready for them, either.
It would rather toss,
and give away,
but on this day, let's think of her
not in pain, or horror,
but as this flight of ivory petals,
ferrying fro heartbeats
swift as beaming wings.

Yes, let's think she has flown away
somewhere, like them, indelibly,
where the flesh of trees no longer bleeds
and nothing left is visible,
to disappear.

      —Judith Harris

CONTENTS

Acknowledgments / xi

INTRODUCTION / 1

1
BARBARA'S CANCER DIARY / 11

2
BARBARA'S DEATH / 63

3
MY EULOGY FOR BARBARA / 99

4
AN OPTIONAL WRITING ASSIGNMENT / 117

5
THE OTHER EULOGIES / 165

6
STUDENTS READING ABOUT BARBARA'S LIFE / 185

7
LIFE AFTER BARBARA / 209

Appendix / 237

Works Cited / 263

Index / 273

ACKNOWLEDGMENTS

Many of the people who helped me write this book helped me to take care of Barbara, and so I am twice indebted to them. My greatest thanks go to my daughters and sons-in-law, Arielle and Dave Albert, Jillian Berman and Alex Willscher, and to Barbara's sister, Karen Anuar. They read enough of the book to reassure me that they did not believe I violated Barbara's privacy or their own. My cousin Glenn Dranoff, who teaches at Harvard Medical School and who led us to a clinical trial for a pancreatic cancer vaccine, helped me to understand the medical aspects of Barbara's illness. He was a godsend in so many other ways. As usual, my dear friend Jerry Eckstein read every word and was generous both in his praise and criticism. Before submitting the manuscript for publication, I gave copies to Barbara's oncologist, Fred Shapiro, her hospice nurse, Geraldine Breitenstein, and our psychotherapist, Edward Dick. Others who read the manuscript and shared their impressions with me are Barbara Adams, Judith Baskin and Warren Ginsberg, Debbie Berman, David Craig, Randy and Jane Craig, Albert and Marilyn Dranoff, Mary Ellen Elkins, Ellen Gootblatt, Judith Harris, Debra and Michael Kaufman, Janice and Howard Kozinn, Susan and Jack Kress, Ed and Ellen Lundell, Alfred and Sybil Nadel, Julie Nark, Bernard Paris, Sherman and Paula Raskin, Howard and Laura Reiter, and Karen and Peter Ryan. Special thanks to Anne Jung, whose friendship has been so important to me.

I will never forget the students who were in my fall 2004 Expository Writing course and who shared with me their impressions of hearing me read aloud my eulogy of Barbara and then reading both an early and the final draft of this book: Kunal Arora, Michael Beblowski, Dia Daley, Kristen Darling, Matthew Davis, Meagan Dicicco, Leslie DiPaolo, Amy Ferguson, Lauren Goldberg, Leanne Jwaskiewicz, Vonetta Knox, Johan Lang, Catherine Lennon, Jennifer Lonschein, Sharlene Marcano, Martha Mendrick, Matthew O'Connell, Erin Schambach, Sonia Sears, Nathaniel Terpening, Dimitra Voulkidis, Rita William, Kim Winkler, and Amanda Zifchak.

I am grateful to everyone associated with State University of New York Press for their encouragement and attention to detail. Special thanks to Anne R. Gibbons, who has now copyedited four of my books, and to Dana Foote, the production editor. I thank the two anonymous readers for their suggestions for revision. Finally, it is rare for an author to have one trusted editor: I have had four, all of whom are friends, and I dedicate this book to them.

INTRODUCTION

Most of us have a "life script," a set of assumptions, conscious or unconscious, changing or constant, publicly expressed or not, about the story of our lives, including our endings. Central to my life script, which I shared with my family and friends, was the belief that I would predecease my beloved wife, Barbara, by twenty years. I never viewed this fantasy as morbid or unrealistic, though it might have been self-centered, as fantasies often are, in that I was not only the center of attention in this dying drama but also spared from the grief of watching a loved one suffer. Barbara's gene pool was excellent, unlike mine, which is average; from this I concluded that she would outlive me by several years. Far from depressing me, the fantasy that I would predecease my wife was consoling. I wanted to believe that Barbara would die at a ripe old age, her beauty, grace, and dignity intact. Years ago I recall a colleague's wife telling me that her husband's dying words were that she meant the world to him, and in my fantasy I imagined expressing the same words to my wife, who has been the center of my universe from the moment we met in our freshman English class in 1963.

Life has a nasty way of smashing assumptions. I was right that Barbara and I would affirm our undying love for each other, for better for worse, for richer for poorer, in sickness and in health, to love and to cherish, till death do us part. I did not anticipate, however, that she would die of cancer at the age of fifty-seven.

Barbara's diagnosis shattered our "assumptive world," which Colin Murray Parkes defines as a "strongly held set of assumptions about the world and the self which is confidently maintained and used as a means of recognizing, planning and acting.... Assumptions such as these are learned and confirmed by the experience of many years" ("What Becomes" 132). Barbara and I shared several fundamental assumptions before her illness, including the three that Ronnie Janoff-Bulman proposes are "at the core of our assumptive world": the belief that the world is benevolent, the belief that the world is meaningful, and the belief that the self is worthy (6). After her diagnosis, Barbara and I could no longer believe that the world is benevolent. We knew intellectually that "bad things happen to good people," as Harold Kushner states in his best-selling book, but we did not believe that misfortune would befall us in our fifties. We were always optimistic about our future, delaying many gratifications so that we could help our children through college and professional school. Then we would "enjoy ourselves." That future never came. Barbara's diagnosis changed irrevocably our perspective on the world. It was as if we now saw life through opaque sunglasses: everything that had been luminescent was now sinister, dark, and shadowy. Suddenly the world became irrational, contingent, and unpredictable. Like Job, we couldn't understand why this had happened to us. What had we done, or not done, to deserve this catastrophe? Our own self-worth was called into question. No longer could we believe in the illusion that we were in control of our lives. We knew that we would be devoted to each other to the end, but we didn't know whether we had the strength and courage to confront a situation that struck terror in our hearts. How could we maintain hope in a hopeless situation, help each other when we each needed help?

Before Barbara's illness I never imagined I would write a memoir of our life together, nor did I envision that I would write her eulogy as she lay dying. There are many reasons why I felt compelled to write about Barbara, including the wish to memorialize her. Writing seemed the best way to do this. I have long believed in both the "talking cure" and the "writing cure." My last four books have all affirmed the value of personal writing and personal teaching: *Diaries to an English Professor* (1994), *Surviving Literary Suicide* (1999), *Risky Writing* (2001), and *Empathic Teaching* (2004). An overwhelming majority of my students have found it therapeutic to write about difficult personal issues. No subject is more difficult to write about than death, the greatest of life's mysteries, the enigma that preoccupies us increasingly as we grow older. The one experience that is impossible for us to understand, death is the "undiscover'd country," as Hamlet exclaims, "from whose bourn / No traveller returns" (3.2.56), and though we may try to imagine death, there is no way to confirm our speculations. Like my students, I turned to personal writing as a method of problem solving, in my case, to celebrate Barbara's life and to help me grieve her loss. I often share my writings with students, discussing how aspects of my life bear upon their own; consequently, it made sense to disclose my life with Barbara during her final months.

Dying to Teach explores my efforts to hold onto Barbara precisely as she was letting go of life. Her dying and death called into question all my beliefs, and I struggled to hang onto anything that would give me strength as a husband, father, caregiver, and teacher. In terms of John Bowlby's attachment theory, writing about Barbara was a way to remain close to her while I was simultaneously detaching myself from her. This paradox is, I believe, the basis of all relationships, which must inevitably end in loss. *Dying to Teach* is about my lifelong love for Barbara, the shock and horror we felt when we found out about her terminal illness, and what we both learned about love and loss from this experience. Sharing this event with my students, I was able to teach them what I was learning and to learn from their own experiences with death.

Education is reciprocal: teachers learn from their students just as students learn from their teachers. Teaching has always been less of a job to me than a calling, a way of life, a passion, and I have been fortunate that so many students have made a difference in my life, just as I have tried to make a difference in theirs. In *Dying to Teach* I pay tribute to the woman who was, and is, the love of my life, and I explore the impact of her life and death on my students, who have been the center of my work. Freud defined psychological health as the ability to love and to work; writing about my love and work kept me psychologically healthy, or at least functioning, during this dark time.

Throughout *Dying to Teach* I describe the many people who helped us during Barbara's illness, including our daughters and sons-in-law, Arielle and David Albert, Jillian and Alex Willscher, and Barbara's sister, Karen Anuar, along with the doctors and nurses who took care of her, especially her two oncologists, Fred Shapiro, and my cousin Glenn Dranoff, a Harvard researcher who led us to a clinical trial for an experimental pancreatic cancer vaccine. We were also helped by our psychotherapist, Edward Dick, and the hospice nurse, Geraldine Breitenstein.

I have been teaching for thirty-five years, and many of the stories I read with my students contain one or more characters who die. Indeed, it is difficult to find a novel or a play in which a character does not die, either on stage or off. Most of my experiences with death have come through literature, and these fictional encounters with death are both similar to and different from Barbara's experience. As soon as she was diagnosed, I began to read nonfictional books about dying and death in an effort to understand what would happen during the coming months. Many of these works can be characterized by the words that are inscribed on the medallion that Tolstoy's dying judge, Ivan Ilych, wears on his watch chain: *respice finem*: reflect on your end (132). Some of these books were classics, such as Elisabeth Kübler-Ross's *On Death and Dying*, that I had read and written upon decades earlier but that now assumed greater urgency. I also began reading memoirs, including John Bayley's *Elegy for Iris*, a moving tribute to his wife Iris Murdoch, whose literary career was cut short by Alzheimer's disease. A memorable passage describing Bayley's changing relationship to his wife foreshadowed my own shifting relationship with Barbara: "Already we were beginning that strange and beneficent process in marriage by which a couple can, in the words of A. D. Hope, the Australian poet, 'move closer and closer apart.' The apartness is a part of the closeness, perhaps a recognition of it; certainly a pledge of complete understanding" (44). Some books were too difficult to read during Barbara's illness but became valuable after her death, such as Donald Hall's *Without*, the poetry volume memorializing his wife and fellow poet, Jane Kenyon. Anna Quindlen's novel *One True*

Thing was almost too wrenching to read because it raised an issue that haunted me months after Barbara's death: euthanasia.

Chapter 1, "Barbara's Cancer Diary," records, in her own words, her responses to her illness and her efforts to make the best use of her remaining time. Physical pain brought her to the first of several physicians, culminating in the dreaded words "terminal cancer," but psychological pain was the more formidable adversary until the final months of her life. Barbara's illness created an instant divide, separating the happy years before diagnosis from the anguished months following diagnosis. And yet Barbara was unusually sensitive to the specter of death throughout her life. This can be seen in a remarkable handwritten letter—apparently to herself—that I found in one of our file cabinets after her death. Written in 1988, the letter describes her despair when our first dog, Cybele, was killed; her decision never to acquire another pet; and then her change of mind when she purchased our second dog, Pandora. Barbara's willingness to give her heart to another life, be it human or canine, reveals her acceptance of the inevitability of loss and grief—an acceptance that Arielle, Jillian, and I similarly reached at the close of her life.

Chapter 2, "Barbara's Death," explores the similarities and differences between real and fictional representations of death. Literature often shapes our understanding, or misunderstanding, of death; my own knowledge of dying and death before Barbara's illness was influenced more by literature than by real life. Many of the novels and plays that I taught or read immediately before or after Barbara's diagnosis took on new meaning for me after her death. Margaret Edson's 1999 Pulitzer Prize–winning play *Wit*, Ernest Hemingway's *Farewell to Arms*, and Anna Quindlen's *One True Thing* all focus on an aspect of dying or death that casts light on Barbara's ordeal. After her death I found myself "talking back" to the authors of these texts, telling them what they had grasped, or failed to grasp, about our experience.

Chapter 3, "My Eulogy for Barbara," opens with the first draft of my eulogy of Barbara, which I wrote in January 2004, when we were told that she did not have much time left. The eulogy describes how we met, the kind of person she was, our marriage, and how we responded to her diagnosis. Writing the eulogy was my first attempt to make her into a "character," explaining why she was so important to her relatives, friends, and colleagues, as well as describing how we were similar and different. I also discuss the eulogy as a literary genre, with its own formulaic characteristics. Eulogists confront many challenges: they must speak for the dead without falsifying their characters, exploiting their lives, or rendering them into narcissistic versions of themselves. The eulogist has only a few moments to do this. Maintaining composure is itself a daunting challenge, especially in the case of premature death.

Chapter 4, "An Optional Writing Assignment," discusses my students' responses to hearing the first draft of the eulogy, which I read aloud to my writing class in March, a month before Barbara died. The eulogy had a profound impact on my students, intellectually and emotionally. Several stated that it was the most powerful classroom experience in their lives. They not only viewed me differently after hearing the eulogy but they also felt that my self-disclosure encouraged them to write about their own experiences with death. The eulogy narrowed the distance between teacher and student, allowing everyone to learn from each other. With this heightened self-understanding came increased empathy for others.

Chapter 5, "The Other Eulogies," contains the final draft of the eulogy that I read during Barbara's funeral on April 9 along with four other eulogies. There are important differences between the first and final draft of my eulogy, differences caused by the relentless metastasis of the disease. Some of these changes, which I could not anticipate months earlier, were so agonizing that I could not acknowledge them, not even to myself, until after Barbara's death. The other eulogies, written by Jillian, Arielle, Karen, and my dear friend Jerry Eckstein, are not only revelations about Barbara's life but also fascinating to read: funny, serious, truthful, and heartfelt.

Chapter 6, "Students Reading about Barbara's Life," focuses on my students' responses to reading an early draft of this book containing their reactions to hearing the eulogy. Students now learned about their classmates' reactions to the eulogy. Some students were more affected by my daughters' eulogies than by my own, probably because they were closer to my daughters' ages and could imagine losing a parent but not a spouse. Just as writing became a form of grief work for me, so did several students predict that my eulogy would help them to mourn future losses. They became more aware of the fragility of life, pondering the implications of my statement that our family's attitude toward death changed from regarding it as a dreaded antagonist to welcoming it as an ally. As one remarked, "Reading [this essay] has made me face some of my fears." And yet not all students wanted to face their fears—one, in fact, objected to hearing the eulogy and then reading about it. Teachers must be careful when discussing traumatic subjects in the classroom, lest students be themselves traumatized. The teacher's challenge to students, like the writer's challenge to readers, is to narrate stories that are not *too* painful.

Chapter 7, "Life after Barbara," describes how our family has grieved her loss, which remains the most catastrophic event in our lives. The chapter opens with a discussion of the "language of condolence," the difficulty of finding the right words to express sorrow. "After great pain a formal feeling comes— / The nerves sit ceremonious like tombs"(Dickinson 365). After Barbara's death I began to understand, for the first time, Emily Dickinson's poetics of grief in her poem "After Great Pain." That formal feeling was of numbness, not quite an indifference to life, nor simply an acceptance of death, but a feeling of death-in-life. Time is not a healer, as most people believe, but working through grief takes time. Barbara's death subverted my assumptive world, and I needed to discover a new set of assumptions. I wanted not to "move on" with my life or to "achieve closure"—two popular descriptions of the bereavement process that strike me as glib—but to learn to live with Barbara's death. Living with death allows us to acknowledge the continuing presence of absent people, the ways in which they remain alive to us. They have left us, but we have not left them.

Upon completing *Dying to Teach*, I sent the manuscript to the students in Expository Writing who heard me read my eulogy for Barbara in March 2004. The appendix contains their responses to the completed book.

Why would anyone write about the most wrenching experience in life? Dave Eggers explores this question in his highly autobiographical novel *A Heartbreaking Work of Staggering Genius*. After describing how his father died of lung cancer and, a few weeks later, how his mother died of stomach cancer, Eggers uses a self-interview format to reveal the writer's conflicting sides:

So why are you here?
I want you to share my suffering.
You don't seem to be suffering.
I don't?
You seem happy.
Well, sure. But not always. Sometimes it's hard. Yeah. Sometimes it's so hard. I mean, you can't always suffer. It's hard to suffer all the time. But I suffer enough. I suffer sometimes.
Why do you want to share your suffering?
By sharing it I will dilute it.
But it seems like it might be just the opposite—by sharing it you might be amplifying it.
How do you mean?
Well, by telling everyone about it, you purge yourself, but then, because everyone knows this thing about you, everyone knows your story, won't you be constantly reminded of it, unable to escape it?
Maybe. But look at it this way: stomach cancer is genetic, passed more down the female side of our family than otherwise, but because according to [my sister] Beth and me my mother was done in by dyspepsia, the dyspepsia caused by swallowing too much of our tumult and cruelty, we are determined not to swallow anything, to not keep anything putrefying down there, soaking in its juices, bile eating bile . . . we are purgers, Beth and I. I don't hold on to anything anymore. Pain comes at me and I take it, chew it for a few minutes, and spit it back out. It's just not my thing anymore. (209–10)

Eggers's theory of the origins of his mother's stomach cancer is questionable, but what is beyond question is that he affirms what may be called a purgative theory of writing, in which artistic expression brings with it psychological relief—what I have called in my book on Joseph Conrad the idea of "writing as rescue." Eggers must convince himself throughout his postmodernist novel that he is not exploiting his parents' deaths for the sake of art, a fear that anyone who writes about a real person's suffering or death must similarly confront.

One of the paradoxes of writing a book about a spouse's recent death is that the writer must not only bring the deceased back to life, in the process re-experiencing the trauma associated with dying and death, but the writer must then rebury the dead at the end of the book, thus repeating the loss. Reading Barbara's cancer diary in its entirety for the first time after her death, I felt acutely again how much she and our entire family suffered throughout the twenty-month ordeal. Why, then, would any writer go through such a painful process again? Simply because writing about Barbara's life and death was more helpful than harmful for me. I needed to recall as many details of her life and death as possible both to honor her memory and to help me grieve her loss. "Mothers typically are the chroniclers of a family's narrative history," states Hope Edelman (200), and this was especially true of Barbara, who rarely forgot anything. As I revise these words, eighteen months after her death, I struggle with two conflicting fears. The first is that for the rest of my life I will remain obsessed with Barbara, thinking about her from the moment I wake up to the moment I fall asleep—not to mention dreaming of her at night. The second fear is that I will forget about Barbara as time passes, and that such forgetting will constitute a betrayal of her memory. I suspect that many bereaved experience these conflicting fears.

Words, no matter how loving or consoling, cannot bring a dying person back to life, nor can they by themselves diminish suffering, but words are finally all that we have, and they can rescue a person from oblivion. *Dying to Teach* demonstrates how all the members of our family used language not only to express our devotion to Barbara but also to keep her memory alive. I have vivid memories of only one of my grandparents; the other three died when I was very young. Our grandson, Nate, was seven months old when Barbara died, and his only knowledge of her will come from our spoken and written words. Perhaps the most heartbreaking moment of Barbara's illness occurred when she held Nate for the first time. There is no word in the English language that captures our conflicting feelings—those of sorrowfuljoy, a neologism that is more accurate than "bittersweet." The more we speak and write about Barbara, the more Nate and our future grandchildren will learn about their grandmother's life.

The title "dying to teach" captures many of the ambiguities of this book. How much agency does one have when one feels compelled to do something almost against one's will? I have resolved, on the one hand, to tell the story of Barbara's life and death and her impact on my family and work. Yet I have felt driven, on the other hand, by an inner force that I cannot resist. Control is important to me, and therefore it is wrenching to give up all control when watching a beloved spouse die. I want to believe that I have controlled every aspect of this book, but it would also be true to say that this book has controlled me. I wrote it, but it wrote me. I can't recall the moment or day when I started this book. Its existence is both an act of will and an example of following one's obsession. I did not feel the same joy that I experienced writing my earlier books, but I did feel, surprisingly, pleasure, along with the satisfaction that I was honoring Barbara's memory and perhaps helping readers understand her life and death. *Dying to Teach* is not a "how-to" book, but I hope that it will enable readers to understand how our family's experience with death may help other families when they find themselves in our situation.

Dying to Teach reflects a caregiver's need to explain to others and to himself the mystery of death. I needed to learn as much as possible about what was happening to our family. I needed to know. It is impossible, however, not to feel ambivalent about certain kinds of knowledge. As I write in *Empathic Teaching*, "The central ambiguity in Robert Penn Warren's novel *All the Kings Men*—'The end of man is knowledge'(9)—can be read in antithetical ways: knowledge is the goal of life but certain types of knowledge may be fatal" (15). The greatest terror we felt during Barbara's illness was at the beginning, waiting with our children for the telephone to ring with the results of her liver biopsy. It was a time of pure dread, when we both thought we would die literally of fright.

Barbara knew exactly what was happening to her, and no one withheld anything from her, but unlike me, shortly after her diagnosis she did not want to know the specifics of her disease. She wanted to hear only survivor stories, of which there are almost none, and it became increasingly difficult for her to read, which had been a lifelong passion. From the beginning, however, she made a heroic effort to teach her husband and children everything they would need for life without her. She was, in a terrifyingly literal way, dying to teach us everything she could for our survival. We were simultaneously caring for and teaching each other until the day of her death.

I was also dying to teach my students about what was happening. I have long believed that one must teach a subject to understand it. Nowhere is this more evident than the subject of dying and death. Anything that does not kill you, strengthens you, Nietzsche observed wryly, and for many people, the thought of death is paralyzing. Virginia Morris quotes the British sociologist Geoffrey Gorer as saying that the subject of death has become as unmentionable today as sex was during the Victorian age (112). In an age that is obsessed with youth, and in which, unlike in previous ages, 80 percent of people die in hospitals, nursing homes, or other institutions, we have become divorced from the reality of death and its centrality to life. As Howard Spiro remarks, "Once, when grandparents, parents, and sometimes children—too often children— died at home, everyone knew death first hand. Death is as common as birth, but it went into hiding in our twentieth-century hospitals" (xv). Countless stories focus on love and loss, but surprisingly few books explore how college teachers can help students survive and record their own unavoidable losses. Such books need not be depressing or morbid; they may, indeed, be life affirming.

I
BARBARA'S CANCER DIARY

Throughout her life Barbara enjoyed excellent health, and she had none of the risk factors for pancreatic cancer except being over the age of fifty. She appeared decades younger than her age; when our daughters were in college, she looked like their older sister rather than their mother. She never abused her body: never smoked, never drank excessively, exercised regularly, had annual physical exams, and always maintained a healthy weight. Perhaps equally important, there was no history of cancer on either side of her family: nearly all her relatives lived to their eighties or nineties, including her parents and their many siblings. Given her health history, we were not worried at first when she began to experience minor stomach discomfort, which we assumed was caused by indigestion or acid reflux. Our concern changed to alarm, however, when she felt a mass in her abdomen a few days before her appointment with a gastroenterologist, to whom she had been referred by her primary care physician.

That was the moment when we began to fear that her illness might be serious, even life threatening. The gastroenterologist was also troubled, and he ordered a biopsy of her liver. And so when Barbara was diagnosed with metastatic pancreatic cancer—a redundancy since nearly all pancreatic cancer is metastatic by the time it is detected—on August 12, 2002, one day after our thirty-fourth wedding anniversary, she was given less than a year to live.

Fear, shock, and horror followed Barbara's grim diagnosis, and for the next several months we were in and out of the hospital, undergoing tests, consultations, and treatments. There is no cure for pancreatic cancer—it is one of the most virulent cancers, with a 99 percent mortality rate, and the standard treatment, chemotherapy, works only for a few months, if that long. As a colleague from another department told me after learning of Barbara's diagnosis, "everyone dies of pancreatic cancer," a statement that we knew too well and did not need to hear again. From the moment of her diagnosis we were on a roller coaster—there is no avoiding this overused metaphor. Unlike amusement roller coasters, in which thrill-seekers know in advance that they are paying for the illusion of danger, we knew that this ride would plunge Barbara lower and lower until its final crash. Barney Glaser and Anselm Strauss use the term "dying trajectories" to describe the duration of a terminally ill patient's disease. Barbara's situation contained elements of two of the three categories used: expected quick death trajectory and lingering trajectory. (The third category is the unexpected quick death trajectory.)

There were, to be sure, a few unexpected highs, when the disease seemed to be retreating, thanks to an experimental pancreatic cancer vaccine that Barbara took for eighteen weeks. The vaccine supercharged the chemotherapy, giving her several additional months of life; but when she was forced to end the chemotherapy after six months, due to a dangerously low white blood cell count, the cancer spread with a vengeance throughout her pancreas, liver, and abdomen. All hope of remission vanished. Slowly and almost imperceptibly our attitude toward death changed from regarding it as a dreaded adversary, to be avoided at all cost, to welcoming it as an ally, signaling the end of the nearly twenty-month ordeal. Ironically, during the final weeks of her life, when all of us were embracing death, the roller coaster inexplicably stopped short of its final destination, leaving us suspended in air.

Barbara did not keep a diary when she was well, except when we were traveling or to record special events, but she began one early in November 2002, shortly after starting the experimental eighteen-week pancreatic cancer vaccine treatment. Her cancer diary records the physical and psychological state of her health along with the day's activities: what she did, where she went, whom she saw, when she took her medications, and how she felt. The diary contains few psychological, existential, or spiritual ruminations, but it offers us insight into her personality—her love for life, her willingness to pursue any treatment that might offer hope, her connection with relatives and friends, her desire not to burden others, her mystical relationship to dogs, and her delight in the quotidian events of existence. She continued the diary until early January 2004, when, close to the end, she found it impossible to write. Her last entries list her pain level, which much of the time was high. We continued the diary until her death, noting the ever-increasing amounts of morphine during the last weeks.

Nearly every diary entry documents Barbara's suffering, but her words fail to convey the intensity of her pain. As Elaine Scarry remarks, "Whatever pain achieves, it achieves in part through its unsharability, and it ensures this unsharability through its resistance to language" (4). Scarry quotes a passage from Virginia Woolf's essay "On Being Ill" in which the novelist acknowledges that although the English language can express Hamlet's thoughts and Lear's tragedy, it has "no words for the shiver or the headache": "The merest schoolgirl when she falls in love has Shakespeare or Keats to speak her mind for her, but let a sufferer try to describe a pain in his head to a doctor and language at once runs dry" (Woolf, "On Being Ill" 194). Scarry also notes that "physical pain does not simply resist language but actively destroys it, bringing about an immediate reversion to a state anterior to language, to the sounds and cries a human makes before language is learned" (4). Scarry makes one more observation that is worth quoting, and which describes my role as Barbara's editor—others must speak for the person in pain: "Because the person in pain is ordinarily so bereft of the resources of speech, it is not surprising that the language for pain should sometimes be brought into being by those who are not themselves in pain but who speak *on behalf of* those who are. Though there are very great impediments to expressing another's sentient distress, so are there also very great reasons why one might want to do so, and thus there come to be avenues by which this most radically private of experiences begins to enter the realm of public discourse" (6; emphasis in original).

Barbara's life changed from the moment of her diagnosis. Her suffering began the moment of her diagnosis despite the fact, paradoxically, that she felt little pain at the time, only slight discomfort. As Eric Cassell points out, suffering and pain are not identical. "Suffering is an affliction of the *person*, not the body" (xii). Moreover, some pain, like childbirth, can be severe but not considered suffering, while suffering can be relieved in the presence of continued pain "by making the source of the pain known, changing its meaning, and by demonstrating that it can be controlled and that an end is in sight" (35). Relieving Barbara's suffering was always a more daunting challenge than relieving her pain. Pain and suffering are subjective phenomena, and, as Cassell explains, "anxiety, depression, and fear increase the experience of pain. It is important to understand that anxiety and its physiologic correlates do not cause the increase in pain; the increased or altered pain is part of the meaning of which the anxiety is also a part" (268). Cassell notes additionally that "suffering always involves self-conflict even when the source appears as external" (287).

Why did Barbara begin the diary? She knew that she was one of a handful of patients receiving the experimental treatment, and she may have felt compelled to keep a record of her responses to the vaccinations. She knew she was living in the shadow of death, but she tried as hard as possible to enjoy her remaining days. Her diary records both the dying of the light and the approach of darkness. She did not agree to have an autopsy after death, as she was asked to do when she signed the medical consent form for the vaccine, but she may have felt that a diary would serve a similar purpose. It is likely that she wanted to leave an account of the ending of her life for those who would be interested in learning more about her. She loved anything associated with the past—antiquing, restoring furniture, looking through old newspapers and magazines, saving childhood treasures—and she may have felt that her diary would one day be a reminder of her own brief existence. As Jason Tougaw remarks in his chapter on AIDS memoirs, silence equals death, and one of the "antonyms" for silence is writing (168). Chekhov's observation in his short story "Lights" supports Tougaw's argument: "You know, when a man of melancholy disposition is on his own by the sea, or contemplates any scenery that impresses him with its grandeur, his sadness is always combined with a conviction that he'll live and die in obscurity, and his automatic reaction is to reach for a pencil and hasten to write his name in the first place that comes handy" (208).

By writing in her diary, Barbara was keeping alive her memory for those who read her daily entries. Writing is an affirmation of existence, one that we knew would end too quickly. As Robert Nash says, "To write is to demonstrate with a degree of certainty that we truly matter. Is it too extravagant to say, paraphrasing Descartes, that I write, therefore I exist?" (22). Margaret Atwood suggests, in a book aptly called *Negotiating with the Dead*, that "*all* writing of the narrative kind, and perhaps all writing, is motivated, deep down, by a fear of and a fascination with mortality—by a desire to make the risky trip to the Underworld, and to bring something or someone back from the dead" (156; emphasis in original). She mentions in particular the "quest for a lost beloved" (170) as an important motivation for writing. Writing is a bridge connecting past, present, and future, a way to maintain connection, continuity, and community.

Toward the end of her life, the diary reminded us when Barbara needed the next medication. I skimmed the diary briefly, before her death, hoping to find a passage that I could use for my eulogy; her comments regarding Arielle's wedding gown were perfectly in character. It was only after her death that I read the diary in its entirety. Nearly every entry describes daily suffering, but she tried her best to ignore the pain so that she could enjoy her remaining time.

Barbara did not know that I would use her diary entries in a book about her, but I doubt that such knowledge would have altered the contents of her entries. There is little in the diary that she would have considered private. With one exception, all her comments about relatives, friends, and colleagues were uniformly positive and appreciative. The exception occurred when she visited her elderly parents in Florida for the last time in June 2003. She loved her parents deeply, and was loved deeply by them, but she found it difficult to be with them at times—a reaction with which most "grown-up" children would surely identify. We often said jokingly to each other and to our children, "Shoot me if I ever become like my parents." As I grow older, I have become an easy target for our children, but they would have taken few shots at their mother. David Cook's observation is relevant here: "The perfect mother and the perfect father do not exist in this life, and I am glad for that. No child could stand them or get free from them" (qtd. in Theroux, 248).

To add to her woes, Barbara had a paralyzed vocal cord, which arose mysteriously following the September 11 terrorist attack. This was a stressful time for her, especially because it was during this period that we had to put to sleep our dog Ebony, who developed cancer. The death of a beloved pet was always devastating to Barbara, and I suggested that we purchase another dog, which helped cheer her up despite her difficulty speaking. We learned that paralyzed vocal chords are caused by throat or lung tumors about 60 percent of the time; the rest of the time, as in Barbara's case, they arise from a virus, which generally disappears after six months. She needed repeatedly to clear her throat to speak, causing her much discomfort, and she could not be heard in noisy places such as restaurants or stores. Her throat surgery in late January 2003 was successful, but her vocal cord once again stopped working normally as soon as she returned to chemotherapy. "Voice has immediately been affected," she writes in the February 14 entry. "Feel like phlegm in throat. Sometimes when swallowing doesn't feel like things can go down quickly. Need to take small sips." After the diagnosis of pancreatic cancer, a radiologist looked at the CT scan taken shortly after she lost the ability to speak normally, and he could see, on the lower bottom of the scan, a suspicious mass in the liver. That mass did not cause the paralyzed vocal cord, but its appearance confirms that the pancreatic cancer predated the loss of her voice.

To understand the cancer diary, one must recognize that all Barbara's assumptions about a benevolent, meaningful existence were, in a single diagnosis, shattered forever. Ronnie Janoff-Bulman captures the shock and bewilderment that accompany a traumatic event: "Nothing seems to be as they had thought; their inner world is in turmoil. Suddenly, the self- and worldviews they had taken for granted are unreliable. They can no longer assume that the world is a good place or that other people are kind and trustworthy. They can no longer assume that the world is meaningful or what happens makes sense. They can no longer assume that they have control over negative outcomes or will reap benefits because they are good people. The very nature of the world and self seems to have changed; neither can be trusted, neither guarantees security" (62).

Existential Anxiety

"The idea of death," Ernest Becker states at the beginning of his landmark book on the subject, "the fear of it, haunts the human animal like nothing else; it is a mainspring of human activity—activity designed largely to avoid the fatality of death, to overcome it by denying in some way that it is the final destiny for man" (ix). What makes death so paradoxical, Becker adds, is that we are "out of nature and hopelessly in it"; this dualism remains a terrifying dilemma: "Man is literally split in two: he has an awareness of his own splendid uniqueness in that he sticks out of nature with a towering majesty, and yet he goes back into the ground a few feet in order blindly and dumbly to rot and disappear forever" (26).

Barbara's existential anxiety was intense, but it never overpowered her courage. "Courage does not remove anxiety," Paul Tillich remarks. "Since anxiety is existential, it cannot be removed. But courage takes the anxiety of non-being into itself. Courage is self-affirmation 'in spite of,' namely in spite of nonbeing. He who acts courageously takes, in his self-affirmation, the anxiety of nonbeing upon himself" (66). Barbara's "courage to be" faltered but never disappeared. "Courage always includes a risk," Tillich continues, "it is always threatened by nonbeing, whether the risk of losing oneself and becoming a thing within the whole of things or of losing one's world in an empty self-relatededness" (155).

I often felt like I was dying during Barbara's illness. Many times I wished I could have died instead of her. One encounters wrenching existential survivor guilt: why her instead of me? A stark description of survivor guilt appears in *Cancer in Two Voices*, in which Sandra Butler reveals how she felt while caring for her partner, Barbara Rosenblum, who died of breast cancer at the age of forty-four. "The guilt of survival. The guilt of comparison. The guilt of randomness—being selected out as the one of us who will outlast the other. The one of us who will live beyond the 'us' that has been the foundation of my life. The guilt of the relief that it is not me" (142).

In *The Gift of Death*, Derrida highlights the impossibility of saving another person from death. "Because I cannot take death away from the other who can no more take it from me in return, it remains for everyone to take his own death *upon himself*. Everyone must assume his own death, that is to say the one thing in the world that no one else can *either give or take*: therein resides freedom and responsibility" (44; emphasis in original).

Barbara and I were fortunate that, with the exception of our freshman English professor and close friend Len Port, who committed suicide two weeks after our wedding, few of our immediate relatives and close friends died during our marriage. Until my father's death in 1998, all four of our children's grandparents were alive and in excellent health. One of the deaths that had the greatest impact on our family was not that of a person but of a dog, Cybele, who was run over by a truck in front of our house in 1977. It would be hard to exaggerate the traumatic implications of this loss both for Barbara and for Arielle. Barbara was so devastated that she vowed never to own another pet. She felt depressed for months, and it was only with the greatest reluctance that she eventually changed her mind.

Cybele's death had a greater effect on Arielle, who was only four at the time. Neither she nor her younger sister Jillian had experienced a major loss before our dog's death, and they did not understand what I was doing when I buried her in the backyard. They looked on curiously as I dug a hole and placed Cybele, who was wrapped in a blanket, in it. Barbara's tears distressed them, but they must have thought that they were observing a game, for they began laughing, and a few minutes later, as we were walking away, Arielle asked me when we would dig up Cybele so that they could play with her again. Following Barbara's death, when I reread Kübler-Ross's *On Death and Dying*, I was struck by a passage that described Arielle's response to Cybele's death: "Many a parent will remember remarks of their children such as, 'I will bury my doggy now and next spring when the flowers come up again, he will get up'" (3).

A few months after Cybele's death, Arielle began to "shake," at first only slightly, then more noticeably. One day, when we thought she was having a seizure, we rushed her to our pediatrician, who tested her neurologically and then told us, reassuringly, that she was experiencing "separation anxiety," a response, he thought, to our dog's death. The nervous tics continued throughout kindergarten, elementary school, and middle school, intensifying during periods of stress. About a month after Cybele's death, Barbara told me about a conversation she had with Arielle, who began by asking her whether people die, just as our dog did. When she was told "yes," her next question was whether her mother would die, to which Barbara responded, "yes, but not until I'm very old." Barbara told Arielle what most parents tell their children, the unwritten law of nature that children bury their parents, but as Philip Roth observes in *The Dying Animal*, "The loveliest fairy tale of childhood is that everything happens in order. Your grandparents go long before your parents, and your parents go long before you. If you're lucky it can work out that way, people aging and dying in order, so that at the funeral you ease your pain by thinking that the person had a long life. It hardly makes extinction less monstrous, that thought, but it's the trick that we use to keep the metronomic illusion intact and the time torture at bay: 'So-and-so lived a long life'" (148–49).

Arielle's third question was whether she too would die one day, which Barbara answered in the same way. I was not present when this conversation took place, but I recall how distressed Barbara was when she reported it to me. Curiously, although she experienced a variety of nervous tics throughout her childhood and adolescence, Arielle no longer remembers them: she was amazed a few years ago when we brought up the subject. (Jillian remembers this clearly.) About a year after Cybele's death we bought another Belgian sheepdog, Pandora, who, like our next dog, Ebony, died of cancer. The deaths of the three dogs were almost too painful for Barbara to bear; she could not accompany me to our veterinarian when it was time to put them to sleep.

"We Had Absolute Trust in Each Other"

After Barbara's death, I came across a three-page essay in a manilla folder in our file cabinet that reveals both her grief following Cybele's death and her decision to acquire a new dog, Pandora, nine months later. Barbara wrote the essay, which I had never seen before, in 1988, and it can be understood fully only by other dog lovers. The letter describes not only love and the inevitability of loss but also the strength of attachment bonds:

It was almost ten years ago when we went to New Jersey to get Pandora, and as I took her in my arms into the car to drive home, I cried, but then they were tears of happiness. That was June 1978. On September 7, 1977, Cybele had been killed. The shock and pain was so great that I told myself that I could never get another dog. The hurt was more than I could bear again. But as the months wore on, although the pain continued, I felt the need that perhaps only a dog lover can understand, to start all over again. I had to say goodbye yesterday to an animal, some would say, but to me she was a beloved friend and soul mate. So now I feel the need to write down my memories of her, some few isolated memories out of so many years to convince myself that her presence was real, that she was here for me to touch, to smell, to care for, and that having her with us was not just a dream. I could look into her eyes and as corny as it might sound we could communicate. We had absolute trust in each other. On our walks I would tell her she was the best dog. She was loving, affectionate, and trusting.

When we brought her home she was six weeks old and a little black fluff ball. We picked her up on the way back from Florida visiting my parents, and when we arrived in Albany our grass hadn't been mowed in weeks. She romped in the grass that towered over her. I remember, soon after we got her, taking a walk in the woods down behind Kraus Road. She was lumbering along, tripped, and did a complete somersault. We laughed watching a new beginning.

I vowed that I would stay detached this time, that this would be an outside dog. She slept on an old yellow blanket in the garage which she took great pleasure in chewing. Spread out, it looked like Swiss cheese. She didn't come into the house. I'd sit in the garage talking to her and she would lift her paw. It was her way of communicating. The plan of detachment lasted until December 1978. Until then the days were busy running back and forth along the back and side fences with [our neighbors' dogs] Ralph, Daisy, Duchess, and Gaby. All the running, though, eroded the sandy soil and uncovered fill which had probably been dumped and covered when the house was built. It remained undisturbed until now. It contained broken glass which we discovered only after Pandora seriously cut the pad on her foot. The first night after her surgery she slept in the house. I remember a fitful night of sleep listening for her every move. The next night she was back in the garage. The following morning I found the bandage partially chewed off and some of the stitches removed. She slept the rest of the convalescent period in the house. I treated the healing pad with peroxide, and I became emotionally connected.

Barbara's statement that she could look into Pandora's eyes and communicate confirms an observation made by Alina Luna, a former doctoral student of mine, about the adage that eyes are the window to the soul: "Those whom I suspect desire to see the ultimate unseen, the soul, look to the eye as the window into which they may peer to gain knowledge of it. The eye becomes that through which one may glimpse a spiritual plane as well as a physical manifestation of the condition of one's soul" (2). There was nothing corny about Barbara's mystical kinship with her beloved companions; she would do anything for them, and they for her.

Barbara's cancer diary affirms the importance of connection, human and canine. Emotional connection is a theme of women's autobiography, as Judy Long explains in *Telling Women's Lives*. "The female subject often situates herself in a web of relationships, or tells her history in terms of relationships. Relationships are important in women's developmental trajectories, as well as at the point of self-writing. This female emphasis on connectivity is more than a narrative stance. The discourse of connectivity does not arise only in response to the challenge of autobiography; it has deep roots in female culture" (49). Female connection and relatedness lie at the center of feminist theories of development, and two influential books—Carol Gilligan's *In a Different Voice* and Nancy Chodorow's *Reproduction of Mothering*—argue that attachment plays a key role in women's lives. "The basic feminine sense of self is connected to the world," writes Chodorow, while "the basic masculine sense of self is separate" (169). Many empirical studies have demonstrated that women tend to be more empathic than men, and Mary Field Belenky and her associates believe that this greater empathy is the basis for women's "connected knowledge." Judith Jordan and her associates suggest in *Women's Growth in Connection* that empathic attunement and mutual intersubjectivity play a greater role in women's lives than in men's. Throughout her life Barbara was attuned to her family and friends, and her diary entries reveal this connection.

Barbara was always aware, however, of the inevitability of loss, and it made no difference to her whether loss involved a person or an animal; she felt the same grief, the same shock, the same trauma. She knew that she would have to experience the same process of bereavement for every dog we acquired—though she had no way of knowing that she would predecease our present dogs, Caleb and Sabrina. Just as she turned to writing to preserve her feelings of love, loss, and memories of the past, so, too, have I turned to writing for the same reasons—to capture her own special qualities. The most poignant aspect of her letter for me is the sentence, "So now I feel the need to write down my memories of her, some few isolated memories out of so many years to convince myself that her presence was real, that she was here for me to touch, to smell, to care for, and that having her with us was not just a dream." This sentence characterizes my own efforts to write down my memories of *Barbara*, to convince myself that her presence was real and not just a dream.

I recall thinking when our dogs died that Barbara's grief would not have been greater had one of our children died. This was only a slight exaggeration. But Barbara's diagnosis was of another magnitude, like comparing a storm to an earthquake. From the moment of her diagnosis, we began researching experimental treatments. We knew that the disease is almost always fatal, but we hoped that she would be the exception. A pancreatic cancer Web site states that "pancreatic cancer is the fourth leading cause of cancer death in the United States. According to the American Cancer Society, in 2002, an estimated 30,300 Americans will be diagnosed with pancreatic cancer and approximately 29,700 Americans will die from the disease. Because symptoms are nonspecific, cancer of the pancreas is rarely diagnosed at an early stage leaving surgical removal of the tumor as a treatment option for only approximately 20 to 30 percent of pancreatic cancer patients. The average survival time following diagnosis of patients with metastatic cancer of the pancreas is three to seven months."

Barbara and I agreed, immediately after her diagnosis, to share with each other whatever information we learned about pancreatic cancer, but within a few days she told me that she wanted to hear only "survivor stories," of which there were practically none. She could not bear to read anything about cancer, cancer treatment, or death. I did all the research, using the Internet every day as well as reading articles in newspapers and in cancer magazines. Relatives and friends kept us informed of their own research. There are advantages and disadvantages to patients (or their caregivers) researching their diseases. As a metastatic cancer patient observed in a cancer guide, the advantages are that "it could save your life," "it's empowering," and "you can make a more informed decision." The disadvantages are that "it can be difficult and intimidating," "you might make the wrong decision," "you will have to confront the statistics," which, in the case of pancreatic cancer, are relentlessly grim, and "there might not be any better treatment." During Barbara's illness, I accumulated so many photocopies of articles on pancreatic cancer that they filled the top drawer of my two-foot file case. Each week I asked Barbara's oncologist, Fred Shapiro, about his response to whatever new and exotic treatment I had come across in my reading. We were fortunate that Fred always gave us as much time as we needed, and he patiently answered all our questions. The problem was that the cancer was so advanced that there were no good treatment options.

Throughout her illness Barbara was treated at St. Peter's Hospital, a Catholic facility in which the images of Jesus, Mary, and the crucifixion were ubiquitous. Most of the nurses and staff wore crosses, and they always told us that Barbara was in their thoughts and prayers. At first the religious atmosphere seemed foreign to us, but we soon felt comfortable there. Fred Shapiro was, like Barbara, a New York City Jew, and perhaps for that reason we both felt close to him culturally and temperamentally. Fred was, in his appearance and mannerisms, iconoclastic: patients called him by his first name; he had a completely shaved head; he often wore outrageous ties; he played electric harmonica in his own blues band, "MoJo Lightning," whose concerts we attended when Barbara was still feeling well; and he was adored by his nurses and staff. Though he told us early on that he was not a "touchy-feely" doctor, meaning, he elaborated, that his patients do not walk away from him believing that they will all be cured, he was never too busy to answer our many questions or to offer his opinions on the new experimental treatments for pancreatic cancer that I had researched on the Internet. Fred would call us day or night, weekdays or weekends, with the results of the latest CT scans and blood tests, and he empathized with Barbara when she began experiencing disabling anxiety and panic attacks. "I would be a basket case if I were in your situation," he told her, a comment that brought a rueful smile to her face.

Immunotherapy

Much has been learned about this deadly killer, but progress is agonizingly slow. We became aware of immunotherapy through my cousin Glenn Dranoff, a Harvard University Medical School professor who is doing pioneering work on vaccines for melanoma and lung cancer. Glenn is a gentle, kind, and modest person, the rare individual who is both extraordinarily brilliant and self-effacing. Immediately after Barbara's diagnosis, he spoke to a colleague at Johns Hopkins University, Elizabeth Jaffee, who is working on a pancreatic cancer vaccine. Glenn called me up within a few days and said: "I have some news for you, which might cause you to reevaluate your disbelief in God." The news was that a clinical trial of Jaffee's vaccine was being tested at five sites in the country, one of which was at St. Peter's Hospital in Albany—on the same floor that Barbara was receiving weekly chemotherapy. There is so much research going on that even conscientious and devoted oncologists like Fred cannot keep up with all the new developments, and he was unaware that a clinical trial was occurring just a few feet away from his office. The Albany site was treating five patients and was closed, but Barbara was accepted into the clinical trial through Glenn's influence. His news did not convert me into a believer, but he was a godsend to us.

At the time Barbara was accepted into the trial, a patient could not be on any other active treatment, including chemotherapy, since researchers would not be able to determine whether the patient's progress, if any, was due to the vaccine. Fred was initially skeptical of the vaccine, mainly because he had no experience with it and because he was reluctant to take Barbara off chemotherapy for several months, but he deferred to Glenn's judgment. Barbara and I grasped at any hope for remission, if not cure, and Glenn told us that he thought the vaccine offered the most promising experimental treatment. Both Fred and Glenn consulted with each other and agreed that Barbara would have six weeks of chemotherapy, which might result in a modest shrinking of the tumors, and then begin the eighteen-week vaccine trial, after which she would return to chemotherapy. Throughout this time she would be closely monitored.

The phase II clinical trial into which Barbara was accepted was for patients with inoperable metastatic pancreatic cancer. The theory behind immunotherapy is simple: if the patient's immune system can be heightened, and if cancer cells, which somehow are invisible to the body's immune system, can be clearly marked and targeted, then the body's white blood cells can destroy the cancer. The devil lies in the details. Barbara's vaccine, known as GVAX , is non–patient specific, developed by a private bioengineering firm, Cell Genesys, as an "off-the-shelf" pharmaceutical product. The vaccine consists of pancreatic cancer cells that are irradiated, so that they cannot reproduce, and then genetically altered to secrete granulocyte-macrophage colony stimulating factor, GM-CSF, a hormone that increases the immune system's white blood cells and makes them more active. Because the gene for GM-CSF is inserted into the pancreatic cancer cells, the vaccine is a form of gene therapy. As Glenn notes about GM-CSF-based cancer vaccines on his Dana Farber Cancer Institute home page, "We have shown that vaccination with irradiated tumor cells engineered to secrete granulocyte-macrophage colony stimulating factor (GM-CSF) stimulates potent, specific, and long-lasting anti-tumor immunity in multiple murine tumor model systems. . . . The mechanism underlying the stimulation of anti-tumor immunity likely involves improved tumor antigen presentation by dendritic cells and macrophages recruited to the site of immunization."

Barbara's vaccine treatment called for sixteen injections every three weeks, over a period of eighteen weeks, for a total of ninety-six injections. There were thus six treatments of sixteen injections; the treatment sites alternated between arms and thighs. The vaccine trial would be daunting to most people, not only because of the injections themselves, which felt like bee stings, but also because of the immediate skin rashes they produced, which lasted for days and became inflamed and itchy. Throughout her life Barbara was squeamish about blood, needles, and pain—she had never donated blood for this reason—but she displayed no reluctance to receive the shots. Michele Butler, the nurse and research coordinator in charge of the vaccine trial, told us that Barbara was her best patient, both in terms of her ability to withstand pain and, as it turned out, her body's strong immunological response to the injections.

We never found out the national results of the GVAX pancreatic cancer vaccine trial, though we were told a few months after Barbara ended the vaccine treatment that she was the only Albany patient still alive. In fact, only one of the five Albany patients lived long enough to complete the trial, after which he soon died. Later we learned that subsequent clinical trials allowed patients to remain on chemotherapy while receiving immunotherapy, a recognition that the vaccine in its present form works best in combination with other active treatments.

Barbara felt increasingly ill during the clinical trial. We assumed at the time that the steady growth of the cancer in her liver made her sick, but Glenn told us when the treatment was over that Barbara's nausea, fatigue, and weakness were caused not mainly by the cancer but by her supercharged immune system. "When people become ill with the flu," he explained, "it's not because of the illness but because of the immune system, which is fighting the flu." He did not tell us this during the treatment for fear that it might raise false hope. Scarcely a day went by during this period without Barbara feeling abdominal pains, bloating, anxiety, fatigue, and depression. She generally did not reveal the extent of this discomfort to anyone except to me and, to a lesser extent, our children, but the diary makes clear that she seldom had more than a few hours of relief. During her illness I could see Barbara's fierce determination to live, but this became even more striking as I read her diary.

Barbara was always keenly aware of her body, and during her illness she recorded in detail how the injections affected her health. Her opening entry, dated November 5, 2002, describes her reactions to the first series of injections. "Oct. 25—received the first of 16 injections of vaccine—8 per arm. By the next Friday when Arielle came they were all hard welts which were extremely itchy. Now, the following Tuesday, it looks like 2 on the left are reduced in size. Saturday Arielle and I raked, then went shopping & I was exhausted by 5:00. The next day we drove to Alfred & Sybil [Nadel] in Rhinebeck and I felt uncomfortable—stomach ache—most of the day. Monday slept late, rested after walk & worked about 11:30–2:30—then dinner at the Mankes [our next-door neighbors]. Today feeling very tired from right after breakfast. Is it the vaccine working?" On November 19 she notes her father's eighty-ninth birthday. "Woke up feeling optimistic but then the fear creeps in—feeling well. Legs not too uncomfortable—just a little itchy."

Barbara's body responded immediately to the first set of sixteen injections and to all subsequent injections. This was encouraging because it indicated a strong immunological response. She received the second series of injections on November 15, this time on her thighs, and the November 18 entry summarizes how she felt. "By Friday night thighs became very hot & inflamed. Then by Saturday it was painful to walk. Spent the day lying down. In the evening applied cold wash cloth to thighs to draw off the heat. Saturday night while sleeping the area became very itchy. Sunday was better, not so painful but was listless and listened to Marylynn's [healing] tape for a few hours & slept a few hours. Went to dinner at the Ryans [dear Albany friends] after taking a shower at 4:45 pm. Felt better there. Had a hard time falling asleep—maybe the decaffeinated tea still had some caffeine. Slept late—almost to 10:00. Went to work about 11:30. Very fatigued & nauseated. Took a Promethazine, which helped nausea. Home about 2:30—after meditation and nap had intense itching on my legs. Took two Benadryls & used cold wash cloths which made it bearable."

The first CT scan during the vaccine treatment, in December 2002, indicated relatively good results: one of the liver tumors increased only slightly, while the other tumors remained the same size. Barbara and I were disappointed because we were hoping for a miracle—remission—but Fred and Glenn nevertheless were encouraged. From the beginning of Barbara's diagnosis, and until near the end of her life, the detectable cancer was confined to her liver. The August 2002 CT scans indicated a tiny shadow in her pancreas, the presumed primary site, where the cancer had first developed. The first diagnosis was pancreatic cancer, because of the slight shadow in that organ, but when the radiologist, pathologist, and oncologist looked at all the tests, they concluded that the suspicious shadow in the pancreas was too small to be definitively judged cancerous, and so they changed the diagnosis to "primary unknown." We sent the CT scans to Glenn, who showed them to his colleagues. They concurred with the Albany physicians. The disappearance of the primary tumor is unusual, occurring in only about 1 percent of patients. No one knows precisely why primary tumors disappear spontaneously; it might be, Fred speculated, that the cancer's blood supply dries up.

A smile broke out on my face when Fred informed us, in the middle of August 2002, that the diagnosis was now "primary unknown." I assumed that any cancer had to be better than the dreaded pancreatic cancer. Unfortunately, neither Fred nor Glenn shared my excitement. They told us that once the primary cancer spreads to the liver, as it had done in Barbara's case, the presumption is that cancer cells are circulating throughout the body, even though they may not be detected by CT and PET scans or blood tumor markers. (Barbara's blood tumor markers were negative every time they were checked, even at the end of her life, when the cancer had spread throughout her abdomen.) When we asked about the possibility of a liver transplant, Fred told us that there were too many tumors, in too large an area, for a liver transplant to be successful. And besides, Fred added, by the time cancer spreads to the liver, the presumption is that it is everywhere. I recall reading an article by a pancreatic cancer patient who used the analogy of placing a chicken in a pot of boiling water and then removing the chicken after an hour or two: what's left in the pot is chicken soup. Presumably, that deadly chicken soup was circulating throughout Barbara's body. Her final CT scan, in December 2003, revealed that a large mass was now in the pancreas, confirming the doctors' initial suspicion that the cancer began in that organ.

Barbara and I continued to assume, despite the doctors' statements to the contrary, that a diagnosis of "primary unknown" is better than that of pancreatic cancer. We took hope wherever we could find it. We wanted and needed to believe that her immune system momentarily had laid down its guard but now was strong again, battling the secondary cancer in her liver. The initial chemotherapy stabilized Barbara's condition. The CT scans taken in the middle of January 2003 indicated that one tumor continued to grow modestly, increasing from 2 × 2.5 to 3.5 × 4cm, while the other tumors remained the same size. Relative stability was the next best result if we could not have remission.

Until near the end of her life, the psychological challenge of cancer was more daunting than the physical challenge. "Awoke feeling well," she writes on January 2, 2003, "but was afraid to get out of bed"—a fear that she battled daily. Whereas many terminally ill cancer patients are afraid to go to sleep at night, fearing they might not awake, Barbara had the opposite fear, as the January 8 entry confirms: "Woke about 9:30. Felt good and was afraid to get out of bed for fear of feeling badly once up." She expressed this fear in many entries. Nevertheless, she did not let this fear stop her from continuing her life.

Barbara was exposed throughout the twenty months of her illness to a barrage of tests and examinations, including blood tests, liver function tests, CT scans, MRIs, and PET scans. The preparations for these tests sometimes made her ill—the fluid she drank preceding the CT scan invariably produced diarrhea—but she never complained about any of these tests. Sometimes we would laugh dryly when we came across a word whose meaning was counterintuitive, as when a radiologist described her brain as "unremarkable," meaning, that it showed no evidence of cancer. Words that would ordinarily have transparent meaning suddenly assumed portentous significance, as Janet Hobhouse describes at the end of her novel *The Furies*, when she discovers she has ovarian cancer: "All words were scanned for some double entendre, some secret message from out there. Taxis passed many street signs and you read them, sometimes with irony, sometimes not: Passenger Terminal, No Exit, No Through Road, Road Narrows, Dead End, Complete Stop Ahead" (287).

Maintaining Hope

Maintaining hope in a hopeless situation is perhaps the ultimate challenge for a terminally ill patient. It is a psychological and existential challenge. For the first sixteen months of Barbara's illness, I felt that one of my major roles was to be her cheerleader, and each day I did everything I could to convince her— and myself—that she might be one of the exceptions. "The disease is confined to your liver," I would tell her, though we both knew that cancer cells were circulating throughout her body. "You're holding your weight, and that's a very good sign," I reminded her nearly every day. "You have excellent genes, and you've always been healthy," I repeated, like a mantra. "You're still feeling well, and Fred and Glenn say that's the best indication of how you're doing clinically," I said truthfully. "You're taking a new pancreatic cancer vaccine, and you've been doing great," I added. She was helping herself in every way possible. She was an exemplary patient, just as she was exemplary in every other way.

Barbara and I both knew about the importance of maintaining hope— hopeful patients do better than hopeless ones. There is growing evidence that the immune system is controlled, directly or indirectly, by the brain. "One of the most widely accepted explanations of cancer," Bernie Siegel writes in *Love, Medicine, and Miracles*, "the 'surveillance' theory, states that cancer cells are developing in our bodies all the time but are normally destroyed by white blood cells before they can develop into dangerous tumors. Cancer appears when the immune system becomes suppressed and can no longer deal with this routine threat. It follows that whatever upsets the brain's control of the immune system will foster malignancy" (68). Many studies demonstrate a link between patients' hopefulness and positive outcomes. Daniel Goleman, a contributing science writer to the *New York Times*, has written extensively on the growing scientific evidence supporting the mind-body connection. In "Afflictive and Nourishing Emotions," he describes a classic research study conducted by Dr. David Spiegel at Stanford University. Women with advanced breast cancer were divided into two groups, both of which received the standard medical treatment. Unlike patients in the control group, those in the experimental group also met for group therapy once a week for a year:

> They talked about their feelings concerning the cancer and what it meant for their families. They became very close as a group, with a lot of love being generated in these meetings. They also learned a self-hypnosis technique for pain control.
> The researchers then studied the death rate of both groups over the next ten years. After two or three years, the groups started to show differences. The women who had participated in group therapy died less rapidly than those who got only the regular medical treatment. After ten years, the death rate was twice as great in the group that only had medical treatment. (42–43)

The mind-body connection is maddening to catastrophizers, especially when they realize, as Barbara and I did, the self-fulfilling nature of pessimistic thinking. Martin Seligman's theory of depression is that it arises not mainly from genetic or biochemical forces but from "learned helplessness," the belief that one has no control over his or her life. Seligman concedes that depressed people tend to see reality more accurately than nondepressed people; nevertheless, the latter tend to feel heathier and to be more successful in a wide variety of areas than the former: "Life inflicts the same setbacks and tragedies on the optimist as on the pessimist, but the optimist weathers them better. . . . The optimist bounces back from defeat, and, with his life somewhat poorer, he picks up and starts again. The pessimist gives up and falls into depression. Because of his resilience, the optimist achieves more at work, at school, and on the playing field. The optimist has better physical health and may even live longer. Americans want optimists to lead them. Even when things go well for the pessimist, he is haunted by forebodings of catastrophe" (207).

Seligman suggests that optimism heightens the immune system, encourages people to seek medical help and maintain treatment, and helps them remain connected to others. He devotes the last chapter of his book *Learned Optimism* to a discussion of effective cognitive "talking back" strategies to pessimistic thinking, including "disputation," finding a positive explanatory system for adversity. He concludes by admitting that pessimism has a role to play in life. We must have the "courage to endure pessimism when its perspective is valuable. What we want is not blind optimism but flexible optimism—with its eyes open" (292).

Seligman would doubtlessly acknowledge the grimness of Barbara's situation and the difficulty of maintaining flexible optimism. From the beginning of her diagnosis, Barbara struggled with anxiety, depression, and panic attacks. Apart from seeing our psychotherapist, she was treated by a psychiatrist, who prescribed powerful medications: Ativan and Klonopin for anxiety and panic attacks, Paxil and then Lexapro for depression. She became increasingly dependent on these medications, as she did on morphine, but "dependency" and "addiction" are not problems about which terminally ill patients need to worry. Beginning in December 2003, our physicians told us that we had run out of treatment options, and for the remaining four months of her life, the nature of our hope changed, from hope for remission to hope for a speedy and merciful death.

Barbara was still working in the winter of 2003, though only a few hours each day, waiting for a retirement incentive that soon came. She worked throughout her life, first as an elementary school teacher and then as a computer analyst. She looked forward before her illness to retiring in her early sixties, so that she could devote herself to her many interests and talents, but fate proved otherwise. "I retired as of February 22, 2003," she wrote, trying to be as optimistic as possible. "I hope this is the beginning of an uphill [fight]." She was disappointed that she had to retire but grateful for the farewell party that her colleagues made for her three months later, when she was feeling better: "Today at 10:30 my coworkers made a party for my retirement in-house on the fifth floor. Jeff and I were escorted up by Pat through the orange alert [a period of heightened national security]. Everyone entering the building had to be pre-approved. A few months ago I couldn't have imagined doing this—between not feeling well and the emotions involved. But now I was prepared and although I was teary eyed the good feelings of all were very special. Ted Hallman [the deputy commissioner of the New York State Department of Criminal Justice Services and himself a cancer survivor] came in especially for it. We shared some hugs—Hugs with everyone! It was a giant receiving line and every hug was positive energy flowing into my body. Jeff spoke to all about my progress. He was wonderful and articulate as always. Tom Meyer presented me with a certificate and spoke very tenderly about my presence on the team. Dawn, Dave O, Cathie Bryant, & Leslie Robbins were there from OTDA—my first 17 years. They presented me with a beautiful Waterford Vase & gift certificate to Joanne's [a fabric store], which will be wonderful therapy!"

Each day in the late winter and early spring was occupied with treat-ment, medical and otherwise. In addition to the sixteen injections she received every three weeks, she took advantage of other healing techniques. Like a grow-ing number of cancer patients, Barbara availed herself not only of standard and experimental medical treatments but also alternative healing practices, includ-ing the complementary therapies that seek to mobilize the body's vital energy. She thus enlisted the help of both "vigorous science," with its Western-based assumptions, and "energy healing," growing out of an ancient Eastern spiritual tradition. She went regularly for acupuncture and massage therapy. She vis-ited our friend Herb Weisburgh whenever possible so that he could mobilize her energy fields through the art of therapeutic touch. Central to Hindu and Eastern religion and philosophy is the belief that there are seven chakras, or energy centers, in the body. These energy fields can be stimulated by the use of mantras during silent meditation. There are seven single-syllable Sanskrit words that correspond to the seven chakras, including the two on which Bar-bara concentrated, *vam*, the solar plexus, which was the area of the cancer, and *ham*, the throat, the region of the paralyzed vocal chord. "To Herb's for healing touch at 1:00," she writes on April 22. "He had me practice turning on 'switch' & off for energy in top of head chakra & showed me the difference in energy levels of the heart chakra depending on whether I thought of a happy rather than a sad thought which slowed energy." A week later she adds, "Herb creates such a supportive & positive environment. He has the ability to relax me and make me feel that I can conquer this." Every morning and evening she practiced mindfulness meditation, which, as defined by Sharon Salzberg and Jon Kabat-Zinn, is "simply learning to have an open accepting attitude toward whatever arises in one's mind, while watching the movements of the mind. This very simplicity makes it useful as a stress-reducing technique" (107). She also practiced "visualization," a technique in which she tried to mobilize her immune system. She spent several minutes of each day visualizing white blood cells destroying cancer cells or, alternatively, visualizing serene images such as waterfalls.

Friends did Internet research for her and alerted us to new experimental treatments. "[Our friend] Joyce [Weiss] received an article from Roswell Park [a cancer hospital in Buffalo, New York] about Radio Frequency Ablation—will bring it over." The next day she read the article and was visibly distressed. "It freaked me out reading it." She also began "juicing"—drinking large amounts of carrot juice, which she extracted from an electric juicer that we had bought immediately after her diagnosis. She drank so much juice that within a few weeks her skin turned orange. "Everything in moderation," both Fred and Glenn told us, in gently reproving voices. But moderation in an extreme situation is nearly impossible.

The Healing Power of Music

We also attended as many classical music concerts as possible. Music has always been one of our great passions, and we have spent countless hours listening to classical records, compact disks, and National Public Radio. A stately baby grand piano sits in our living room, bequeathed to us by Barbara's parents when they moved from Brooklyn, New York, to Florida in 1975. Music's healing power is legendary. As Maureen McCarthy Draper observes, "A woman I know who survived pancreatic cancer said that after trying everything else, she turned to Beethoven's last string quartets for consolation. Finally, with this music, she was led to an acceptance and understanding that were necessary to her healing. In addition to inner healing, it happened that her cancer went into remission, and she now works in a hospital as a music therapist" (152). Kay Redfield Jamison writes in her book *Exuberance* that "music activates the same reward systems in the brain that are activated by play, laughter, sex, and drugs of abuse. Brain imaging studies show that pleasurable music creates patterns of change in the dopamine and opioid systems similar to those seen during drug induced euphoric states. . . . Music not only activates the reward system, it decreases activity in brain structures associated with negative emotions" (160).

Bernie Siegel plays classical music in the operating room: "Music opens a spiritual window. When I first brought a tape recorder into the O.R., it was considered an explosion hazard. But we ran it on batteries, and then the nurses and anesthesiologists felt so much better that, if I forgot my music, they'd ask for it. Now there are tape recorders in almost all the operating rooms in New Haven" (50). William Styron reports in *Darkness Visible* that when he had reached the bleakest moment of suicidal depression, prepared to end his life, he was saved by hearing a soaring passage from Brahms's *Alto Rhapsody*. "This sound, which like all music—indeed, like all pleasure—I had been numbly unresponsive to for months, pierced my heart like a dagger." The music helped him to realize that he "could not commit this desecration" on himself (66–67).

Why is music so powerfully therapeutic? Draper's explanation is that music has an "uncanny capacity to suggest . . . universal narrative patterns of exploration and discovery, loss and triumph" (57). Invoking Rainer Maria Rilke's *Sonnet to Orpheus*, she observes that "grief should walk only in the footsteps of praise, for joy already understands what grief is still learning—life is to be praised" (81). The Greeks, Draper reminds us, knew about the healing power of music—"In the Greek mind, medicine and music were so intertwined that Apollo presided over both realms" (187). As much as I love literature, only music can transport me to otherworldly realms. I feel something akin to an out-of-body experience when listening to the choral movement of Beethoven's Ninth Symphony or Bach's Orchestral Suites. I do not experience religious awe upon entering a church or synagogue, but I never fail to be spiritually moved when listening to Bach's Mass in B Minor, Beethoven's *Missa Solemnis*, and the glorious requiem masses by Mozart, Brahms, Faure, and Verdi. Barbara experienced the same musical joy that I do, but unlike me—I cannot read a note of music—she had extensive musical training, even performing in a piano recital at Carnegie Hall when she was a teenager, and so her passion for music was enhanced by technical understanding.

One of the books in Draper's bibliography, Mitchell Gaynor's *Sounds of Healing*, piqued my interest, and I was fascinated to learn about the growing scientific evidence of music therapy. A medical oncologist trained in mainstream medicine, Gaynor also uses complementary modalities in his approach to healing and wellness, particularly the medium of sound. "I have long since come to accept nontraditional, holistic approaches as necessities, rather than personal options, that must be integrated with the care and treatment of my patients" (4). The sounds of healing include not only music but also silent chanting during meditation and visualization through guided imagery, all of which, Gaynor notes, have been demonstrated, through the new field of psychoneuroimmunology, to strengthen the body's immune system. I was intrigued by his discussion of *entrainment*, the tendency in the universe toward harmony:

> The seventeenth-century Dutch scientist Christian Huygens noticed that the pendulums of two clocks, hung side by side, would begin of their own accord to swing to the same identical rhythm. The reason that entrainment occurs is that the more powerful rhythmic vibrations of one object, when projected upon a second object with a similar frequency, will cause that object to begin to vibrate in *resonance* with the first object. We human beings also react in resonance with the vibrations and fluctuations in our surroundings, so it follows that our physiological function-

ing may be altered by the impact of sound waves, whether produced by our own voices or by objects or instruments in our environment. (49)

If the phenomenon of entrainment may be used to describe two people who have lived together for two-thirds of their lives, and who could almost read each other's mind, Barbara and I were striking examples of such harmony—for better and for worse. We rejoiced in each other's happiness and suffered in each other's despair. Throughout her illness we were on the same wavelength, each devoted to the other's well-being. Just as, in Gaynor's words, "part of what promotes healing in a therapy situation is the entrainment that occurs between therapist and patient" (70), so did Barbara and I know that we needed to synchronize our energies. Each of us felt incomplete without the other.

A diary entry on February 2 indicates how music affected Barbara's body. "Arielle and Dave left at 8:00 am for a party in Boston. I felt well while in bed & not so good waking up. Felt like it was hard to take a deep breath in lungs. Walked the dogs—felt tired & walked slowly. Breakfast, then did fix the toilet in upstairs bathroom. Rested before Union College concert. Noticed that I felt poorly before and after music but when music is playing my body feels well as if the vibration of the instruments is calming to the body. After the concert back to feeling poorly—burning sensation (not bloating today). Sometimes the sensation wraps around & kidney area feels uncomfortable." Even when she was in pain, Barbara derived comfort from music, which has the power to affirm life amid tragedy and loss.

Barbara received the final series of injections on February 7. One day later she writes: "Woke up & for a few seconds, felt so well that I forgot I was ill. But then it hit." A week later she returned to chemotherapy and had another CT scan, which indicated that the liver cancer was largely under control. Slowly she began to feel better physically, despite the fact that she was now taking two potent chemotherapeutic agents, gemcitabine, the standard treatment for pancreatic cancer, and irinotecan (CPT-11), used for colon cancer. Fred told us that new research indicated that a combination of these two drugs is more effective for pancreatic cancer than either of them alone. (I thanked Fred immediately for being aware of this new research, after which Barbara scolded me in private for making what she thought was a patronizing comment.) She tolerated both chemotherapeutic agents remarkably well. The April 18 entry records that the cancer, while not in remission, seemed to have stabilized. "Jeff woke me about 8:15, have 9:45 appt with doctor, then chemo—Dr. Shapiro said I'm withstanding the test of time—no spread of disease." She felt even better physically in early May, but we were disappointed that the CT scan did not indicate a dramatic improvement, as we expected. "Was surprised to find that CT scan was unchanged from last time," she writes in the May 9 entry. "But all liver function tests are normal except for one. Dr. scheduled me for a PET scan on May 18 to see if possible scar tissue. Test sees which cells are absorbing glucose. Had chemo. Left hospital about 3:00. Felt the best I have after any chemo. Didn't need to lie down. Didn't feel sick."

Unlike a CT scan, which shows a mass in the body, PET scans record metabolic activity—what's happening inside the mass. It is possible, we were told, that the CT scans were reporting "empty" masses in Barbara's liver, scar tissue formed by the cancerous mass that is now destroyed, like an empty tenement. As Glenn wrote to me in an email, "It is unlikely that vaccines will produce substantial tumor shrinkage over a relatively short time (several months). When vaccines work, they usually involve changing the composition of the tumor mass from uncontrolled tumor growth to a mixture of immune cells, scarring, and dying tumor cells. These changes cannot be easily followed by CT scans, and would require a biopsy of the tumor and then evaluation by a pathologist. (I don't think another biopsy would be appropriate here, though.)" The good news came on May 23: "Up at 9:00. Balanced chakras & wrote about the past 2 days. Showered—feeling anxious & shaky inside—took Klonopin at 10:30. Had breakfast, took a long walk with the dogs. Worked outside in the garden for hours. Fred called about PET scan—very good news—only some spots in liver showed mild to moderate activity—others showed no activity. This is the best news since Aug. 12th—Will continue to do everything I need to do & have been doing to heal! Jeff was ecstatic—jumping up & down. I'm going to beat this!" Fred told us the next time we saw him that the PET scan showed that nearly all of Barbara's liver cancer had disappeared, an "amazing" development, he added, which became more astonishing in light of his usual cautiousness. Now Barbara was beginning to believe that the worst might be over. "May 30. Had an 11:15 visit with Dr. Shapiro—Great news—PET scan showed only 10% of tumors mild to moderate activity—explains why I'm feeling so much better. Now I really believe a cure is in sight." Fred and Glenn agreed that this extraordinary improvement was due almost certainly to the vaccine, which by itself could not halt the cancer's growth, but which made the chemotherapy far more effective than it would have been otherwise.

Physically Better, Psychologically Worse

Ironically, once Barbara started to feel better physically, she began to feel worse psychologically, as the March 30 and 31 entries suggest. "Sunday, March 30— Woke up very panicky—did chakras balance—took long walk—still panicky— took Ativan at 9:20 to calm me. Drove to Boston for Rachael [Arielle's sister-in-law] and Phil's wedding—dozed most of the day—Raining—got sandwiches at Brueggers & then drove to Claire's [Alex's sister] apartment with Jill and Alex. Lynn [Alex's mother] was there—visited a while—went to pick up rental car for Jill and Alex—then went over to Phil and Rachael's house—anxiety intense—so took another Ativan. Went over to Walden Grill for the wedding—Felt not so good—got there before 5—ceremony started probably 5:45—after that I was nauseous & took a Promethazine. We stopped overnight at the Best Western—I couldn't fall asleep & was afraid of waking Jeff [by] tossing and turning—woke about 7:00—so anxious I could feel my heart pounding in my chest, took an Ativan about 8:00. Drove home about 11:30. Message on machine from Dr. Shapiro. Blood liver tests look good—one is now normal—Now I need to deal with this anxiety."

As the preceding entries suggest, Barbara came to rely on an increasing number of psychopharmacological drugs to help her with anxiety and depression, both of which she had experienced before her illness in mild to moderate form, but which now became severe and constant. She also experienced for the first time panic attacks, which continued throughout March and April. One early spring day we drove to the Clark Museum in Williamstown, Massachusetts, but as soon as we arrived there, she felt so panicky that she thought she was going to die, and we immediately turned around and left. I was so distressed that I received a speeding ticket on the way home. I couldn't help recalling at the time that April is the cruellest month, the opening line from T. S. Eliot's poem *The Waste Land*. Nevertheless, April has always been one of our most joyous months, and Barbara begins the April 12 entry by noting that it is a special day for our family. "Arielle's 30th birthday—Got an excited call from her this morning—they're in Woodstock, Vermont & Dave gave her a beautiful watch." In the next sentences, however, she returns to feeling unwell. "Terrible sleeping last night—stomach feels bloated—had some bad dreams & sweats—took an Ativan at 5:10 am—woke up around 10—stayed in bed till after 11—feeling anxious." And on the next day she writes that she "cannot go through another night like this trying to fall asleep."

Illness did not prevent Barbara from writing a memorable letter to Arielle on her thirtieth birthday. Arielle was pregnant at the time, and Barbara recalled how excited she was thirty years earlier when she gave birth to our first child:

April 12, 2003

Dear Arielle,

This is a momentous birthday for you. You are beginning a new decade, and so many exciting beginnings will be occurring in this special year. I know how thrilled you and Dave are about the new baby. And the completion of your degree and start of a post-doc are important milestones for you. But you also have to share this day of celebration with me, for April 12, 2003, was the 30th anniversary of the first of the two most spectacular and miraculous days of my life, the days my children were born.

When your day comes in August, you will understand how much it is your special day as well as the birthday of your child. When his first birthday comes, it will be an anniversary for you and Dave as well, as will all his future birthdays.

Though 30 years sounds like a long time, I can visualize all the events of that time as if they had just happened. I had stopped teaching at the end of December, 1971, knowing that we would like to have a family. Teaching twenty-five six-year-olds every day, I knew that I had to be away from children for a while before I could take that step. I enjoyed my freedom, the first time in my life that I wasn't working or going to school. I took many different classes: pottery, silver jewelry making, leather craft, and weaving lessons. In March we brought our puppy Cybele home, and I took long walks with her in the fields behind Lansing Apartments on Triphammer Road. Loving the puppy brought out all my maternal feelings.

During my pregnancy I threw up only once. It happened the day before I went to the doctor to get tested. Our friends Trudy and Ron Buxembaum (she taught kindergarten with me and he had been a Cornell Ag student from Brooklyn that married Trudy, and now ran his own dairy farm) called and asked if we wanted to fly to Rochester that day to visit a former teacher, Ella Porter, her husband Judd, and their new baby. Ron had taken up flying since his free time was limited to between 5 AM and 5 PM milkings. We said we'd love to go. I had eaten breakfast consisting of a BLT and orange juice. While in the air, I felt myself becoming nauseated. I was trying to concentrate on not getting sick. Jeff pointed out something from the plane window, and when I shifted my gaze, I lost it. That was the last time they invited us to fly with them.

Only one time did I have possible regrets about being pregnant. We were visiting Ed and Ellen [Lundell] for dinner. Eva was about 2 years old and sitting in her high chair—an antique reproduction with a caned seat. Suddenly while sitting in her chair, she started to pee, and when the urine hit the floor, I was repulsed, but I knew I couldn't turn back!

You were due on March 28th. When I went for my March 16th appointment, the doctor told me I had begun to dilate and that it could be anytime. Immediately after the appointment, I went to get yarn to make you a sweater to wear when leaving the hospital. I finished the sweater, and we still waited. Each week at the doctor's office I would meet a woman named Linda Cole. She also was waiting patiently past her due date.

On the night of Wednesday, April 11th I took Cybele to our weekly obedience class. I came home, and during the night I felt stomach pains.

Since I was two weeks overdue, I concluded that this must be the real thing. We called the doctor at 6:30 AM and were told to rush to the hospital. The medical practice I had been going to had five doctors. I was unfamiliar with Dr. Hayes, who was to deliver you, but he was great. They prepared me and gave me a paracervical block, which took away the pain but still left me feeling the contractions. They broke my water, which started the process moving quickly. They started to roll me into the delivery room, but I told them I had to go to the bathroom. I realized when I had Jillian, and experienced the same sensation, that the feeling of having to urinate is due to the baby putting pressure on the bladder. The doctor, nurse, dad and I were all in the delivery room. There was a window, and the room was light and bright. In a short time you emerged, wet and crying. Dad was yelling, "It's a girl, it's a girl!" You had so much hair! We were so excited. Both the nurse and doctor had told us before your birth that based on the fetal heart rate, you were probably a boy. Wouldn't Dave have been disappointed! They put you into a crib-like cart, and I had to strain over to look at you. Now they immediately give babies to their mothers. When Jillian was born they gave her to me without delay. The thrill of seeing you was indescribable: a new creation, a new miracle.

They rolled me into a room, and I was ravenous. You were born at 11:58 AM, and I was ready for lunch. I hadn't eaten since the night before. The feeling of elation never left. I had brought a book to read in the hospital, *Them*, by Joyce Carol Oates, but I couldn't get past the first paragraph. I couldn't think of anything but you. The day after you were born, a nurse came in to tell me that Linda Cole had just had a baby boy and had asked if I were in the hospital. Linda and I had waited patiently together in the doctor's office while we were pregnant, and now we were in the hospital together.

You and I spent 5 days in the hospital together because you had jaundice and needed to lie under a special light. Lying naked under the light, you looked like a roasting duck with a black blindfold.

When we arrived home, Dad and I watched you adoringly in your crib, and from nowhere came our salutation: "Ga bu lu, Sir od nee, wi ch ch, wi ch ch, wich ch ch!" I don't know from where it came. I'm not sure if you still remember it. But it was an expression of our joy in having you.

We are so proud of the person you have become. So today we gaze at you, and with the same joy we felt 30 years ago, we say: "Ga bu lu, Sir od nee, wi ch ch, wi ch ch, wich ch ch!"

I Love You Always,
Mom

P.S. I think you were also Dad's lucky charm. He had received his Ph.D. in May 1971. Between the years of 1967 when he began and 1971, the job market for English professors had dried up. Dad had been applying for jobs for two years without success. 1973 was the third year of job hunting. Cornell had been very good to him by giving him lectureships each year while he was looking for jobs. Within a few weeks after you were born, he had three job offers: Ithaca College, Nassau Community College, and SUNY Albany. He had to postpone his interview here at Albany because I still hadn't given birth.

Barbara could have included a less positive memory of her husband during Arielle's birth. Photography was one of my hobbies at the time, and she gave me permission, albeit reluctantly, to photograph the birth. I had just bought a Nikon 35-mm camera, with several lenses, and I was allowed to use a Cornell darkroom to develop black-and-white negatives and prints. I knew that my main role in the delivery room was to help Barbara, but I was more intent on photographing the miraculous event. For his part, the obstetrician seemed more interested in my camera than in his patient, asking me endless questions about the film, lens, shutter speed, and aperture opening. With each question, Barbara became increasingly annoyed with both of us. I discovered to my dismay, when I later developed the film, that I had loaded the camera with a roll of exposed film: every shot of Barbara and Arielle was double exposed. "Poetic justice" was Barbara's sardonic response.

Not even a clueless husband could destroy Barbara's happy memories of Arielle's birth, and her letter is perfectly in character. Reading it, one could not tell that she was terminally ill. Every sentence conveys her humor and joy, her awareness of the past and hopefulness for the future, her celebration of life's miraculous renewal and rebirth. The vivid details that she recalls thirty years earlier seem as if they occurred yesterday. Only Barbara could remember that her infant baby looked like a "roasting duck with a black blindfold." She feels a connection not only with the past but with the future—despite the knowledge that she will not be around in the future to watch her grandchild grow up. There is no hint of anger, sadness, bitterness, or self-pity in the letter, nothing that would darken her daughter's thirtieth birthday. The April 12 diary entry reveals the intense anxiety she was feeling on Arielle's birthday, but nowhere does this appear in the letter. She was also writing for consolation. As Wendy Bishop and Amy Hodges remark, letter-writing becomes "our genre of choice during moments of challenge, complexity or loss. . . . As we use letters to investigate the conditions of daily life, we make meaning of our worlds via the written word" (142).

Barbara's letter also reveals that love is at the heart of family life. Love is a miracle that cannot be described fully or analyzed completely. One of my

favorite songs, "Some Enchanted Evening," from the Rodgers and Hammerstein musical *South Pacific*, affirms the mystery of love: "Who can explain it,
who can tell you why / Fools give you reasons, wise men never try." For some
novelists, like Thomas Hardy, love is a catastrophe: blinding, irrational, and
self-destructive. Eustacia Vye embodies this form of love in *The Return of the
Native*: "To be loved to madness—such was her great desire. Love was to her
the one cordial which could drive away the eating loneliness of her days. And
she seemed to long for the abstraction called passionate love more than for any
particular lover" (56). For other novelists, like D. H. Lawrence, love is a constant, irresolvable struggle against engulfment; for Virginia Woolf, love remains
a solitary experience, requiring a room of one's own; for still other novelists,
like Ernest Hemingway, love is always hopeless or short-lived. Barbara and I
were fortunate in that our love for each other was deep, constant, and unconditional. We expressed our love for each other differently, however. She was
less demonstrative than I. She did not feel the need to affirm her love on a
daily basis, as I did. Her birthday letter to Arielle captures her spontaneous,
heartfelt, unselfconscious love, which resembled her physical beauty: it was
always there, for everyone to see and appreciate, but she did not call attention
to it. She could convey her love in a letter but felt no need to make speeches
or write books about it.

A Wedding Toast

Barbara was emotionally more self-contained than I am; perhaps that is one of
the reasons she was worried about me when she was dying. I cried far more
during her illness than she did, especially during our psychotherapy sessions.
Many times I broke down and wept in front of relatives and friends while Barbara remained dry-eyed. I try to control this emotionality by adopting a scholarly persona, which gives me a degree of self-control and ironic self-mockery.
For example, Jillian and Alex's wedding took place in early October 2002, less
than two months after Barbara's diagnosis. The speech I delivered, invoking,
of all people, the iconoclastic German philosopher Friedrich Nietzsche, surely
must rank as one of the more bizarre wedding toasts:

> As many of you know, our older daughter Arielle was married exactly
> two years ago. A few days before her wedding, I asked her whether she
> wanted me to offer a toast to her and her husband Dave, and without
> hesitation she said, "no!" "Fine," I said, recalling King Lear's words to his
> beloved daughter Cordelia: "nothing will come of nothing." And so you
> can imagine my delight when Jillian asked me to speak at her wedding.
> Since I was reading at the time Nietzsche, the great nineteenth-century

German philosopher, I thought it would be interesting to see how his comments on love, marriage, and friendship may apply to Jillian and Alex.

Prefiguring Freud, Nietzsche knew the importance of mothers. "Everyone carries inside himself an image of woman drawn from his mother: this determines whether he will revere women or despise them or generally be indifferent to them" (219). Since Jillian and Alex have extraordinary mothers—both Barbara and Lynn are smart, strong, and multitalented—our newlyweds are off to a great start. Nietzsche also recognizes the importance of fathers: "If someone does not have a good father, he should provide himself with one." I never had the pleasure of meeting Dr. Max Willscher, but I have heard from several people how much his family, friends, and patients admired him. I won't comment on Jillian's father, except to say that we should all mistrust a person who quotes Nietzsche at a wedding. Nietzsche believed that a man should be able to answer the following question before entering marriage: "do you believe that you will enjoy conversing with this woman all the way into old age? Everything else in marriage is transitory, but most of the time together is spent in conversation" (223). Jillian and Alex are excellent conversationalists, both inside and outside the courtroom, and they thus pass this crucial test. Since they have been best friends for several years, they pass another Nietzschean test: "The best friend will probably obtain the best wife, because a good marriage rests upon the talent for friendship" (219).

Nietzsche had some cynical advice to newlyweds that may apply to Jillian and Alex. "If spouses did not live together, good marriages would be more frequent" (221)—an observation with which our dear friends Jack and Susan Kress would surely agree. Jillian and Alex are both nearsighted, and they may agree with the following Nietzschean insight: "Sometimes simply having stronger eyeglasses suffices to cure someone smitten with love" (226). Let's hope that their eyes will never become that sharp. As they grow older and find their memory weakening, they may also agree with Nietzsche's statement that "the advantage of a bad memory is that we can enjoy the same good things for the first time several times" (279).

I want to end by disagreeing with Nietzsche. He is surely wrong when he claims that "there is not enough love and goodness in the world to allow us to give any of it away" (98). The more love and goodness that Jillian and Alex give to their family and friends, the more their own love and goodness will be replenished. For all his brilliance, Nietzsche never married and could not imagine a marriage based on mutual love, respect, devotion, and equality. Nor could he imagine how much joy Jillian and Alex—along with their siblings—have provided their parents and friends.

One need not be a student of philosophy to predict that Jillian and Alex will have a loving and enduring marriage.

In retrospect, the wedding toast strikes me as arty and pretentious. I have a Woody Allenesque humor—Jewish wry—that can be embarrassing and off-putting, something that was never true of Barbara's humor, which immediately put people at ease. I can also be, as Barbara never was, eccentric, odd, and weird, which perhaps explains why Arielle did not want me to give a wedding toast. I often embarrassed our children, as Barbara rarely did. She knew instinctively how to relate to people, both when she was well and when she was ill. She loved reading books, but she did not need to rely on book knowledge to express love.

Barbara looked radiant during Jillian's wedding, singing, dancing, talking, laughing, enjoying every moment of the event, while I struggled to hold back a torrent of tears. Looking at Jillian's wedding video, one would never suspect that Barbara was dying. Her joy was genuine, not forced. I was hardly able to think about my daughter's wedding without returning to my wife's terminal illness. I was so preoccupied with grief that I initially included a line in the wedding toast that Arielle advised me to omit: that love can survive anything, including death, an idea that struck her as alluding too strongly to her mother's illness. It was hard for me not to be overwhelmed by grief during the wedding, but as happened so often during our marriage, Barbara's inner strength gave me courage. Throughout our marriage we each took turns being strong; if one of us was worried about something, the other pretended not to worry. This was true when Barbara was well, and it was true when she was ill. We almost never cried at the same time. We were so attuned to each other's emotions and moods that each became the other's therapist. When that worked no longer, we turned to a real therapist.

Psychotherapy

Psychotherapy was helpful precisely because it enabled us to talk about our fears of death, a subject that we rarely discussed when we were alone. Our therapist, Ed Dick, a gentle, soft-spoken, insightful man, was interested in a wide variety of healing techniques, both psychological and spiritual, including meditation, the belief that there is an inner space within the mind that embodies serenity. Ed's presence alone was calming, and he consistently gave us excellent advice, as the April 8 entry shows: "Have meeting with therapist at 10:30. Visit went well. He suggested adding positives to journal. Suggested breathing techniques to bring me back to 'now.'" A week later she writes, "Had a 12:00 appt with Ed Dick. He suggested I was fighting the medication last night thinking I would have a reaction—tonight I will be more trusting." The advice helped. Ed asked us to verbalize our fears of death, and in doing so, we were able to gain a degree of control. The April 30 diary entry reveals Barbara's first reference to this fear. "Slept well. Woke at 8:00 anxious—have meeting with Ed Dick. He had me take the Ativan right then. I was pretty low during the session. The fears of death came up. I don't know if I can deal with them." A week later we had another therapy session. "Talked about the good week I was having—then why I feel the way I do about death. Still very difficult to deal [with]—but feeling better. I can put it out of my mind more." In early June she conveyed the good news about the CT and PET scans to Ed. "He had me centered again by analogy—I'm now 20 feet from edge of cliff instead of 2 feet. I still have to deal with my anxiety in all aspects of life & calm myself—get rid of anxiety as first reaction to situations."

I, too, had to deal with rising anxiety. For several years I had been taking a small dose of an antidepressant, amitriptyline (Elavil), to help me sleep, but with my physician's approval I raised the dose immediately following Barbara's diagnosis. We were so close emotionally that I seemed to experience in my own body all of her anxiety. I struggled to distance myself enough so that I could help her without feeling overwhelmed by her fears. Barbara's stomach pains often became my stomach pains, her depression, mine. Clarissa Dalloway's imaginative identification with the news of Septimus Warren Smith's suicide in Virginia Woolf's novel—"Always her body went through it first, when she was told, suddenly, of an accident; her dress flamed, her body burnt" (163)—describes the intensity of my involvement with Barbara's pain. Ed was valuable here, reminding me that I could not help Barbara without first helping myself.

Psychotherapy focused on the here-and-now rather than on the distant past, but we explored the probable origin of one of Barbara's fears of death, which she traced back to her father's frequent "disappearances" when she was growing up. Morris would often be late for dinner without calling, or he would take long walks without telling anyone where he was going, and Barbara's mother, Jean, would worry incessantly, sometimes telling her children that he was probably "lying face down in an alley somewhere." As Karen, Barbara's sister, later recalled, after making this statement, her mother would sit on the foyer couch "knitting feverishly while telling me to go to sleep. It's very hard to fall asleep feeling scared that your father was dead in an alley." These stories, and the screaming that accompanied them, terrified Barbara and her sister. Morris never realized how upsetting his disappearances were to his family, and Jean never realized how her children associated his lateness with death.

Barbara visited her parents in Florida twice during her illness, and the first visit occasioned a memorable letter from her mother describing not only her strong religious faith but the belief that Barbara was a "miracle child":

September 24, 2002

Dear Barbara,

It is now 7:30 AM & I had to get out of bed to write this letter. It was wonderful to have you visit this past weekend. These visits don't happen very often. However, listening to your present problem gave me the reason for this letter.

I want to go back in time to remember what happens, good, bad and whatever. I had a wonderful childhood. My father was the one who always had something to do to enjoy life at its best, and I remember a lot of it. We were not a religious family, but were taught to live honestly & be good to others. This is how I have lived all my life. However there are many times when I had to worry if things were not going smoothly. And that is why I am writing this note.

When my father died on February 24, 1931, I suddenly became head of the family. It was nothing I knew & it was frightening. The first thing was that there was no money. My mother must have been scared to death. But my uncle Paul Lederman gave me a job for $8 a week in the Bronx, in a wholesale drug company. His accountant taught me "Bookkeeping." Traveling by train 3 hours a day gave me exercise changing 4 times each way. I graduated high school 4 months after losing my father, so college was put aside. I already was going with Morris & he helped by being around. So, what did I do? I was active in the temple & did some volunteering. I went to a Saturday service & found a "Friend," Mr. GOD. When I had a problem, I talked to "Mr. GOD." It made me feel better & I eventually listened to "HIM, " all worried out. I seemed to "hear" how I was to manage my life, to the present time. Believe me when I say that plenty of things came up during the 70 years I [have known] Morris and I survived. He is "His Royal Highness, " and I have spoiled him. But I love him and always will. I get angry & scream, but I get over it very quickly. I don't hold a grudge. He is the most important person in my life. A problem came to us. We had decided to have children. I was not regular. Doctors had given me injections to regulate, but nothing happened. We thought of adopting & would have had not "Mr. GOD" thought of us. On our ninth anniversary, we were blessed with a lovely girl named "Barbara." No doctor & there were many were able to do anything for us. Only "Mr. GOD" was able to make us a family, and I have thanked "HIM" every moment of every day since her birth for her, because she was the most perfect child in the world.

Now, let's come to the present. She is now a Mother herself & has a problem. Now her mother & father & all the others close to her are joining to solve this problem. Who to talk to—"Mr. GOD." Faith has always worked for me and I am certain that "Mr. GOD" will be there for all of us. I don't believe I could survive without it. I am thankful for everything and everyone and I can promise you that faith will protect you & make you all better sooner than you think.

So, with love, and everything else that we can offer, please believe me and try it.

Love & more love,
Mother Jean

Barbara felt well for the six months she was on chemotherapy following the completion of immunotherapy, from February through July 2003, though there were minutes or hours of most days when she felt physical discomfort or anxiety. The frightening panic attacks she experienced in the early spring were now largely under control, thanks to both psychotherapy and medication. We were able to enjoy this time. Alex's family invited us for Easter dinner on April 20, as Barbara records: "Left for Nyack [New York] at 10:30—arrived about 1:00. It's a beautiful warm sunny day. All the relatives were sitting out front when we arrived, basking in the sun. Alex's whole family is so warm & friendly. Had an Easter egg hunt for the kids. And a wonderful dinner crowded into the dining room—a real feast." On May 25 we attended our niece Court-ney's graduation at Cornell, where we had spent so many happy years. "I walked through the Arts Quad & to the suspension bridge—so many wonder-ful memories of Ithaca & our life there." In early June we drove to Cambridge to attend Arielle's baby shower and then proceeded to Newport, Rhode Island, where we toured the palatial mansions. "Incredible how ornate these mansions are & only used for 8 weeks at most each year—like European palaces." On June 27 we attended a reception in honor of Arielle's graduation from her clinical psychology internship. "Took the T to Harvard Faculty Club—it was a super reception. Got to meet colleagues of Dave & Arielle & could see the warmth toward them. It was a privilege to share the evening with them." On the Fourth of July weekend we visited Alex's family at their summer home in Wolfeboro, New Hampshire:

Woke up about 8:30 feeling well. Waffles, fruit, juice & tea at B&B. Then over to Lynn's where we spent the day. It was very hot—Dave got up on the water ski board today & Jillian succeeded in getting up on 2 skis & then dropping 1 & skied on 1. Jeff and Dave went on tube pulled by the boat—Quite a workout. Yesterday both Gayle and Jeff swam across the lake to the island—about ½ mile. Alex & Jillian, Garth & Claire kept busy with different water sports—kayaking, sailing, boating. We had a big lunch about 2:30. I didn't eat too much—stomach felt overstuffed from yesterday & breakfast. In the evening Jeff & Lynn volunteered at a concert by the Heifetz Institute—a program for young musicians. I saved seats & sat in the 2nd row. Jeff joined me after handing out programs, Lynn after the intermission. Both students & instructors participated in a program of American music. Not up to the quality of the Union College concerts, but it was very enjoyable. The singer was particularly good. Lynn, Jeff, & I went for ice cream sundaes after the concert. Got back to the B&B about 11:45. A great day!

July was Barbara's best month. She completed a lovely quilt for Arielle's baby, and each day she was able to walk the dogs and converse with friends. On July 16 she records her growing excitement about the baby: "Dreamt Arielle's baby could be held through her stomach even though it wasn't yet born. It was a beautiful baby—it's exciting & getting so close." We went swimming nearly every day at the local YMCA, which we had joined, and we went to Tanglewood as often as possible. We had lunch at the Red Lion Inn in Stockbridge, Massachusetts, and saw plays performed by Shakespeare and Company in nearby Lenox. We drove to Saratoga to see the New York City Ballet. We met our dear friends Alfred and Sybil Nadel at Tanglewood on July 12; a friend of theirs had died recently of cancer, and Barbara tried not to interpret the death as an omen. "A little anxious but didn't take any medication. Their friend Dick who was diagnosed with pancreatic cancer had died. But I talked to myself—I am me, not Dick—what happens to him does not reflect what happens to me—I am feeling well."

We met Glenn at Tanglewood on Sunday, July 20, and he slept over at our house that night, as he had done the preceding summers. The Monday entry shows Barbara's continuing physical health but psychological struggle: "Jeff and Glenn were up when I came down. We spoke about treatment options after chemotherapy. I am feeling physically very well—did need to take a Klonopin to get rid of anxiety that discussing my life as a patient created." Her July 26 entry is unique in that it describes an idyllic day without a hint of illness:

Slept well—Jeff woke me to go to Tanglewood. Beautiful day. Met Randy, Jane, nephew Bill & Cheryl (Randy's mother). Great rehearsal with a young South American composer—Songs by Oswaldo Golijov sung by Dawn Upshaw. He spoke during the pre-concert talk. Later we saw him on the grounds & spoke to him about our admiration for his work. After rehearsal of his song he got up on stage with conductor & both were directing musicians at the same time—he knew just how he wanted it—something we've never seen but fascinating to watch him unable to control himself from directing. No time to play William Tell

Overture without going into overtime—will listen tomorrow on the radio. Followed by fabulous lunch. A photographer came by & took a shot of our table with all the great food—was doing an article on picnics at Tanglewood.

The End of Chemotherapy

Barbara was forced to end chemotherapy in the middle of July 2003, when her white blood cell count became dangerously low, making her susceptible to infection. She had been on active chemotherapy for six months, which oncologists consider a very long time. We then found ourselves confronting a new dilemma: what type of treatment to pursue, if any. As far as we knew, no one in the phase II GVAX pancreatic cancer trial was receiving a second round of injections. Like many cancer patients, Barbara felt more anxious when she was off chemotherapy than when she was on it—patients tend to feel "abandoned" when treatment ends. In early August, Fred and Glenn decided that Barbara should begin taking thalidomide. The horror drug of the 1960s, when it produced severe birth defects in pregnant women, thalidomide has recently been used successfully to block the blood supply of solid tumors. Barbara began the thalidomide on August 9, the same day Arielle gave birth to her son, Nate. The diary entry records Barbara's joy over seeing our first grandchild despite feeling ill from the new medication: "Left for Boston about 2:45. Arrived about 6:00—found the hospital without too much trouble. What a thrill to see the new baby—he's beautiful, definitely has Dave's mouth. Had a little hat on covering his hair. Arielle & Dave are ecstatic with the new baby. The thalidomide made me feel very shaky—dizzy & nauseous feeling." The entries during the next few days convey rising anxiety and panic along with increased dizziness, grogginess, and nausea. On August 11, the day of our thirty-fifth wedding anniversary, and exactly one year and a day since Barbara's diagnosis, Fred recommended that she lower the dosage of the drug. "Felt bad—dizzy, shaky, nauseous—called the doctor. He said to cut back from 4 pills per day to 2 pills. It's our 35th anniversary—didn't do anything special. Just being together is enough." Finally, on August 21, Fred told Barbara to stop the thalidomide treatment. "Woke feeling scared," she writes the next day, "thought of no medication is scary. Worry about Jeff alone—try to put these thoughts out of my head & think of the positive—in much better position than a year ago."

    We did not know it at the time, but the cancer began to spread as soon as Barbara ended chemotherapy. She continued to feel ill throughout the late summer and early fall of 2003. For much of this time we believed, or rather hoped, that her feeling of illness was due to the lingering effects of the thalidomide. It slowly became clear, however, that the abdominal pains, nausea, and weakness were caused by the spread of the disease in the liver. She tried to do as much as possible despite feeling sick. We spent many hours planning to remodel our kitchen, which we had decided to do before her diagnosis. Our children and their husbands came nearly every weekend, which delighted both of us. Barbara's sister began to visit us, and we all enjoyed the spectacular autumnal bursts of color when we went to Indian Ladder Apple Orchard. I started teaching again, the beginning of my thirty-first year at the University at Albany.

In late September we drove to visit Alex's grandmother in Portland, Maine. "We walked along the beach with Lynn—I had been feeling not that well after the ride. After the walk I felt better. Pat had us over to dinner—flounder & potato & vegetables & cookies & ice cream. What a gracious and wonderful woman she is. Her home on the ocean is so peaceful. After dinner Pat, Jan, Lynn, Jeff, & I went to the art museum. The most important thing—Arielle called from Chicago just as we were about to eat to let us know she passed her defense of her dissertation. Now she is a PhD doctor!"

The next morning we walked around Portland and visited the Longfellow House, where we went on a tour conducted by Gemma Cannon. Afterward we struck up a conversation with Gemma—I told her that she was the most articulate and knowledgeable guide I had met. We continued talking, and Barbara disclosed to her that she was struggling with pancreatic cancer. Gemma, who had received a master's in social work from Columbia University, reminded Barbara about the importance of positive thinking, and in November she sent Barbara a long letter filled with clinical and practical advice:

> Limit your "worry time" to one half-hour per day. Identify a time, 1:00 PM, for example, and, throughout the day, when a worry pops into your head, write it into your "worry notebook." Then, tell yourself, "Self, I'm going to stop worrying until 1:00 PM, and then I'll address everything." At 1:00 PM, sit down with your "worry notebook," pen in hand, and go through each worry, one at a time. With each worry, ask yourself the following important questions, and answer each one: *Is my worry really true, or is it irrational?* (Remember, just because we think something doesn't make it true; we can waste a lot of our energy on realities that exist only in our heads. Our immune system needs us to protect our energy—it isn't infinite—and focus only on what's real. To help identify irrational thoughts, I always refer to David Burns' brilliant book and workbook— the workbook is excellent—*Feeling Good: The New Mood Therapy*.) If you recognize the worry as real, then ask yourself the next question: *What action can I take to address this worry?* This is the place to brainstorm. Edit nothing out. Write down all possible angles to address your worry. This is a very important question to answer because it returns self-control.

One of my professors at Columbia always said, "Activity alleviates anxiety." In my years of professional practice, as well as in my personal life, I've found her words the most accurate [information] passed on from teacher to pupil. "Activity alleviates anxiety." Make it your mantra as you formulate an action plan from your worry list. Then follow through with it. Let your "worry list" become your "to do list." This is a very effective tool in minimizing generalized anxiety. The key is to get specific—name your fear—and identify how you plan to address that fear. Spell everything out. Write everything down. Believe me, Barbara, this has a "ricochet" effect that will amaze you.

Gemma's letter is filled with other excellent advice. She urges Barbara to make an "existential laundry list" that includes our fear of death and aloneness, and she offers an example of how to do this in language consistent with eighteenth-century colonial America. "Mentally, imagine yourself immersing these realities in cleansing water, the way the Wadsworths and Longfellows did their wash in the set kettle of the 18th century. Meditate on them as you give that wash a good swirl with an imaginary wooden rod, then haul out these wet thoughts, one by one, for a good rinsing in a good tin tub. Then, wring out each thought, give it a decent wringing, and then, air it out to dry." She then encourages Barbara to search actively for consolation. "I have learned that loss is the shadow and consolation is its light. All losses have their consolation. Search for yours in books, biographies, poetry, stories, your spiritual heritage, and nature. Look everywhere for food to nourish your soul. Let your mind and heart rest in the deep still waters of consolation, and not the turbulent whirlpool of anxiety." She ends the letter by telling Barbara to make each day count. "One of my friends with cancer said to me, 'Gemma, the last years [since diagnosis] have been the best two years of my life. I've learned how much I love, and how much I am loved.' She went on to say, 'Every one should get cancer when they're twenty-one, and be cured when they're twenty-two.' To live life deliberately is a great gift to ourselves, and to others."

From Portland we drove to Acadia National Park, where it rained constantly. We drove instead of hiked through the national park, and the gloomy weather reflected our melancholy. Barbara felt ill most of the time in Maine, but she managed to enjoy a lobster dinner. It was our last vacation together.

The turning point came in early October 2003, when we found out that all Barbara's liver function tests, which had been normal for several months, were now elevated. On October 3 she writes that she is scared and depressed: "I feel like everything is starting all over again." Three days later she taught me how to make lentil soup: "I felt too nauseous to do it myself." On October 7 she comments upon our growing pessimism: "Jeff has been getting up earlier & earlier—We are both being tortured by this." She had a CT scan that day and received the results the next day: "Drs appt—Fred saw CT scans—I knew something was happening & very anxious. It turned out that one of the tumors is enlarging & causing the bile duct not to drain causing jaundice & the sickness I am feeling."

Fred referred us to a surgeon when Barbara became severely jaundiced, which occurs when bilirubin, a product of dead blood cells, cannot drain into the duodenum and builds up in the bloodstream, causing yellow skin and acute itching. The surgeon looked at the CT scans and told us in an impersonal voice that the tumor surrounding the blocked bile duct was inoperable. He was the only physician we encountered who seemed abrupt and cold, so different from Fred and Glenn. I recall that the surgeon was dressed impeccably, wearing expensive shoes and a Rolex watch—dressed very differently from Fred and Glenn. Barbara's only option was to have two stents inserted surgically to open up her bile duct, but the gastroenterologist, Dr. Orris, who was the father of one of Jillian's high school friends, was able to insert only one, which proved inadequate. Dr. Orris told Jillian and me that Barbara's cancer was "very aggressive." We found ourselves in a Catch-22 situation: there was the possibility that a return to chemotherapy might lower Barbara's bilirubin level, thus ending the jaundice, but chemotherapy could not be used safely until the bilirubin level returned to normal.

The decision was made to insert an external catheter into the liver, which might allow the bilirubin to drain. A urologist performed the surgical procedure, in which a catheter was inserted, using ultrasound guidance, into the liver, allowing the bile to drain into a removable bag taped to Barbara's skin. The procedure was initially successful, but she developed a high fever and had to remain hospitalized for five days. When she returned home, a nurse came to show us how to flush the catheter every day. Twice the catheter stopped working, which required additional surgical procedures in the hospital. The external catheter proved difficult, physically and psychologically, for Barbara. No longer was she able to go swimming, nor could she easily take a shower. She could not sleep on her stomach or the left side of her body. She became frightened whenever the dogs jumped on the bed, fearing they would dislodge the catheter, which was taped onto her body. Each day she felt worse than the preceding one. On October 21 she needed to have the external catheter replaced again. "Surgery scheduled for tomorrow. Len's birthday. Day Phyllis [Len's wife] died. Are they watching over me?"

We were now desperate, and everyone knew that time was running out. To use Ed Dick's analogy, we found ourselves once again two feet from the edge of the cliff. Glenn suggested a new immunological treatment that he was using successfully with one person: a vaccine "booster" consisting of two drugs, GM-CSF and interferon gamma, both of which had been FDA approved for other treatments, but which Glenn was now using for the first time in combination with each other. Fred agreed, and he was able to persuade our insurance company to pay for the expensive drugs, which otherwise would have cost us over five thousand dollars a week. I learned how to inject both drugs into Barbara's arms and thighs. The new experimental treatment offered a ray of hope in an otherwise bleak situation.

"My Favorite Memories"

Despite feeling increasingly ill, Barbara wrote a long and moving letter to her father in November 2003 on the occasion of his ninetieth birthday. The letter evokes not only the happy times she had with them in childhood but also her delight in the simple pleasures of life. I suspect that she was writing the letter not only for her father but also for her future grandchildren, who will want to learn more about their grandmother's life:

> Dear Dad,
>
> Next Wednesday, November 19, will be your 90th birthday, and there is nothing I would rather do than to be with you and mom in Florida celebrating this special occasion. But right now I just can't travel. So instead I thought I'd write this letter with memories that pop into my mind. If it's anything like the memories Jillian and Arielle and I share, they may remember things I do not, and I can remember things they do not and on rare occasion we all remember together.
>
> One of my favorite memories is when you and mom brought Karen home from the hospital. You put her in the crib in the bedroom that all of us shared in 1320-51st street. I remember looking at her, and her eyes were so bright I said, "Look, she has stars in her eyes!"
>
> When we were a little older we used to have great fun with you when you would be lying on the bed trying to take a nap. We found that we could ask you for anything and you would agree just to get rid of us. Karen and I would ask for the most outrageous things including a mink coat for mom and you would always agree! You probably have no memory of this.
>
> Do you remember how Karen and I would come into your bed in the mornings and mom would make a mountain with her knees? We would sit on them and then she would surprise us by quickly lowering her legs and we would tumble down and laugh. That was one of my most favorite games. Do you remember one time that you let us put one of those suction cup toys on your forehead—the kind that kids put on high-chair trays—and it made a big hickey on your head? I'll bet you have no memory of that one.

One of my most pleasant memories is of taking car rides and returning home in the evening when I had either fallen asleep in the car or was close to sleep. Living in an apartment house, there was no predicting how close the parking spot would be to the building. So whether I was asleep or not, I always pretended to be asleep so that you would have to carry me upstairs and put me to bed. I felt so comforted being carried, and I loved the feeling of being slid into the cool blankets on the bed and being tucked in. I felt completely safe.

Both Karen and I used to love going to "the place" with you. It's funny how it got to be called "the place" as if everyone would understand what "the place" was. It was a loft on the 4th floor in 125 Fifth Avenue in Manhattan. The loft extended from the front to the back of the building, but the only windows were the ceiling to floor windows facing Fifth Avenue. When you stood on the street looking up, you could see the window that said "Philmor Clothes," and I felt proud because I knew that was yours.

The building itself was an experience. The elevator was old and rickety with a gate as a door so as it went up you could see the floors you were passing. The door into The Place was heavy metal—almost like a bank vault. You would give us tasks to do. We could be kept busy for hours on the typewriter. They were the old uprights—one was missing the space bar. So a piece of wood from a cigar box was used to replace the missing bar. There were so many interesting things up there on the desks and in the back—shelves stocked with pants patterns hanging on the walls and the smell of mothballs. I never did care for the bathroom up there with the single light bulb and the toilet that flushed by pulling a chain. Sometimes we would take packages of pants and drop them off at customers. We were having a fine time, but mom was at home never knowing where we were and when we would be home. Too bad they didn't have cell phones then. That would have saved mom a lot of aggravation.

I have particularly fond memories of the summers we spent in the Catskills. Karen and I couldn't wait until Friday night when you came up. We would go down to the main road and watch the headlights of approaching cars hoping that each would be turning into the bungalow colony and be you. And always your car would come. Then over the weekend we would drive the country roads into Kaneonga from White Lake. In the back seat of the car was a cord—a handle to grasp for people sitting in the back seat. This was a long time before seat belts and other safety features that really served a purpose. Karen and I would stand in the back seat holding onto that cord and pretend we were water skiing—you would drive over hills and we would have a ball!

Do you remember the time in Lapidus when they had newly tarred a road? You, Karen, and I were walking and Karen fell face down in the tar. What a mess she was to clean up!

We used to have great food stores in Borough Park. I remember the time before we had the Waldbaum's supermarket built on the corner of 13th Avenue and 51st Street. But even after that we still had the wonderful assortment of stores. Do you remember the wonderful aromas of Miller's appetizing? Those big barrels of sour pickles smelled so wonderful you almost wanted to drink the brine! You would bring home lox (and the little fins we called "fliegels"), white fish, chopped herring, and carp. On Saturdays we would bring in bologna and knishes from the 55th Street deli for lunch. We had so many choices of good knishes—the square ones at the 55th Street deli (along with the tubes of mustard in wax paper), the thinner crusted square knishes from Edelman's on thirteenth avenue, and the round knishes from Hershi's near the entrance to the 50th street train station. I must say I gave up on Hershi early on because I found a dead fly in my knish—mom tried to convince me it was an onion, but I never believed that. Then all the great bakeries. You would go down shopping and brought back the greatest treats—black and white cookies, onion rolls, Ebinger cakes, and delicious rolls from Gottlieb's on 18th avenue. The list was endless.

And then there were the wonderful places we used to love to go to have dinner out. Probably my favorite restaurant was Horn & Hardart, and always the same food—hamburger, mashed potatoes, and creamed spinach. I think you remember the time that they were out of hamburger and you got me the chopped sirloin steak instead. My mouth had been anticipating that hamburger, and I was so angry when I couldn't get it. Fortunately that only happened once! It's too bad the automats are gone— the gleaming walls of glass, marble, and brass were just beautiful.

Then there were our two favorite Chinese restaurants—the one on Flatbush Avenue, which we later replaced with Taeng Fong on Borough Parkway. We used to get that huge bowl of wonton soup with lots of bok choy (the green stuff which I used to think was lettuce). Karen and I would eat the shells of the egg roll, and you and mom ate the filling. Karen and I learned to like lobster in the Chinese restaurant because it was cut up and in sauce. We never saw how repulsive a real lobster was—otherwise I doubt we would ever have tasted it. Mom always sacrificed herself and gave Karen and me the best sections of lobster. Do you remember that one evening after dinner at 711 we went across the street to a little pet store. You and mom bought me a little turtle. I named him "Kimosabe" after that term that the Lone Ranger used for his friend Tonto meaning "friend." Not having any expertise in caring for animals, I don't think Kimosabe lasted too long, but just getting him was a thrill for me. Then when you found Taeng Fong and their delicious roast pork, that became the Chinese restaurant of choice.

Another of the favorites was going to Nathan's in Coney Island and eating in the small sit-down room at the back. Red tables and dark wood—there was one booth in the whole restaurant. I can still see the waiter's face—they all wore white aprons. My absolute favorite food was their fried shrimp sandwich on a bun with tartar sauce—it was sublime. But then there was always a hard choice to go with the shrimp or get a hamburger piled high with onions or their delicious chow mein sandwich. Not to mention the clam chowder (manhattan), french fries, and hot dogs. After eating we would go next door to the candy shop and choose between cotton candy and jelly apple. I think I went with cotton candy more often since it wasn't as messy. Then we would walk back toward the beach along the row of rides and games, and we always got to throw darts at balloons. If you broke one, you would get a prize. I can't remember if I ever won, but I loved playing the game.

One day after eating at Nathan's, you told me you had a special surprise for me. We walked back along the row of rides until we got, to my surprise, a pony ride. I was absolutely thrilled. I had always adored horses I had seen on TV shows—from Roy Rogers' palomino "Trigger" to "Fury." I had never seen a real horse up close, and I was shocked when I mounted the black and white pony. It had so much hair! I never realized that horses had hair—I just thought it was shiny skin. I couldn't have asked for a better surprise.

Once in Coney Island I can't forget the wonderful memories of going to the beach, of meeting the Browns there, Helen, Mal, and Linda, and the salty smell and the waves and the knishes sold by vendors on the beach. The sand under the boardwalk was so cool on your feet—if you found any soda bottles, you would get 2 cents deposit for each. The only unpleasant part was driving home all sandy and fighting to be the first into the shower.

Visiting Grandma Paulie and Grandpa Louis in their house in Coney Island was always an adventure. That house seems huge to me now with a huge garden with hydrangeas on one side and the two wrap around porches—one for each flat. Grandma and Grandpa lived upstairs, and I remember walking up the stairs into the pink light. I think Grandma must have had sheer pink curtains. There were lots of things in that house to keep Karen and me entertained. In Grandma and Grandpa's bedroom was a drawer filled with odd photographs which we were allowed to take out. We particularly enjoyed seeing you and Uncle Phil, Aunt Hilda, and Uncle Irwin as children, and the horses and buggies. Then Grandma had these fur collars which were whole animals like little foxes. They had heads and tails and legs and a clamp on the mouth so that it could encircle your neck and grasp the tail. Pretty grotesque now to think about but in our fantasy world they were live animals.

Grandma always made us great egg creams, cherry heering for the adults, sponge cake, sliced peeled apples, and packages of candy charms. I remember sitting in their living room enjoying spinning their globe and explaining the cartoons I was watching to grandpa. They had a dog named Rexie—a white spitz—I loved dogs but was a bit afraid so I never did get too close.

Right across the street was Aunt Hilda and Uncle Aaron's house—now they had a scary dog! Flash was a vicious, curly German shepherd who lived outside in the space between Uncle Aaron's and his brother Uncle Eddie's house—a guard dog who could kill two birds with one stone. I was pretty shy on those visits and just kind of sat around listening and taking things in.

There are just some of the good memories that flow through my mind at this time. I hope you enjoyed sharing them with me.
Happy 90th Birthday.

I love you always,
Your daughter Barbara

I find it remarkable that Barbara was able to conjure up in the letter the tantalizing ethnic foods of the distant past precisely at a time when she was hardly able to eat anything solid. It was as if she were relying solely on memory rather than on appetite: indeed, the desire for food had long vanished.

Around this time Barbara began taking two synthetic morphine painkillers, OxyContin, a powerful narcotic pain reliever designed for slow release over twelve hours, and Oxycodone, for "breakthrough" pain. Only after I read *Truth and Beauty*, Ann Patchett's memoir of her friendship with Lucy Grealy, whose death in 2002 is widely regarded as a suicide, did I learn that heroin addicts view OxyContin as a popular street drug: "All you had to do to change OxyContin into something sweeter than heroin was crush it up. That destroyed the time-release mechanism, thus giving you twelve hours of pain relief in one startling, beautiful minute" (231). Pain management became an urgent issue. Barbara's stomach became increasingly distended, both from the growth of the disease and from the retention of fluids, and her ankles and legs became swollen from edema, the accumulation of fluids. Her skin, which used to be so taut from working out at the gym, now hung loosely from her arms. I didn't notice that the color of her skin had turned yellow, but relatives and friends who had not seen her in a few weeks were struck by the change. The diary entries during the late fall and early winter became shorter, preoccupied now mostly with recording her hourly pain medications. She was reporting intense liver pain, soaking night sweats, and crushing fatigue. One of the side effects of morphine is constipation, which became painful and required daily laxatives and stool softeners. She was still able to leave the house occasionally, to meet friends, walk the dogs, or see a movie, but she was sleeping increasingly. This was a time for leave-taking. Dear friends came to visit for the last time, to say goodbye. She became increasingly worried about me, as the December 9 entry reveals: "Jeff getting very depressed watching me. I don't know what to do."

Barbara completed several weeks of the vaccine booster at the end of December, and she was able to return briefly to chemotherapy, taking one agent instead of two, at a reduced dosage. She was accepted into home-care hospice. Normally patients who are receiving active treatment for a terminal illness do not qualify for hospice, but an exception was made because her case was "experimental" as a result of the GVAX pancreatic cancer vaccine. Twice she went to the hospital to have fluid removed from her abdomen; more than two liters were removed on both occasions. The procedures provided temporary relief, but the fluid built up again in a few days. She began eating less and relying more on a high-caloric liquid shake, Ensure. Her weight began to drop until finally she stopped weighing herself. She was scheduled for chemotherapy on December 22, but we were told that her bilirubin level had jumped alarmingly. "Bad news," she writes tersely, "bilirubin back to 6.3. No chemo." On that day we were told, finally, that we had run out of treatment options.

Approaching the End

Most of our therapy sessions in the fall and early winter focused on the fear of death. One of Barbara's longest therapy entries occurs on October 1. "Got up late—a little trouble falling asleep. [Took] trazadone, then took an aspirin. Head feels uncomfortable lying on my back but that's how I prefer to fall asleep. Woke less nervous than usual. Gloomy rainy day—appt. with Ed Dick today. Difficult session—we spoke about death & how I feel about leaving Jeff alone & how Jeff felt—it was so painful. I want to heal so much so that we can be together for a very long time." This was Barbara's last extended entry about psychotherapy. Her anxiety and depression increased as she felt more and more tender spots in her abdomen. We continued seeing Ed in his office until she could no longer get out of bed, at which point he visited us in our home.

Barbara believed that she "passed" her anxiety onto the children, but two late October 2003 entries, written in the hospital, where she was undergoing a surgical procedure, indicate otherwise. "Sweated like crazy in the hospital even with light blanket and hospital gown. Jillian came to Albany on Friday morning—she & Jeff were with me watching me suffer that day, Jillian came over Saturday—we did a lot of talking about family and childhood memories. Sunday. Arielle and Nate drove down Sunday afternoon. Came to the hospital after dinner. We had a good talk about how she felt growing up—I felt I had passed my anxieties on to her & Jillian but found out that I had done a good job hiding my anxious nature from them. Had a good evening exchanging stories & mostly me related stories of my childhood & growing up in Brooklyn."

There were no sudden breakthroughs or epiphanies in Barbara's cancer diary, nothing that remotely approaches what we see in *The Death of Ivan Ilych*, when Tolstoy's dying judge, who has never previously engaged in self-reflection, achieves self-understanding and finds darkness transformed into light. Rather, our acceptance of death was slow, gradual, and incomplete. Psychological progress was usually followed by renewed fear and worry, until the final weeks, when we were all emotionally prepared for death. Though therapy sessions were often wrenching, we invariably felt better as we drove home. Ed's psychological orientation was Jungian rather than Freudian, but it didn't matter, since he brought a lifetime of clinical experience, wisdom, and empathy into therapy. I am reminded of Doris Lessing's observation, in her autobiographical work *A Small Personal Voice*, that she based the psychotherapist Mrs. Marks in her novel *The Golden Notebook* on her own psychotherapist: "My own psychotherapist was somewhat like Mrs. Marks. She was everything I disliked. I was then aggressively rational, antireligious, and a radical. She was Roman Catholic, Jungian, and conservative. It was very upsetting to me at the time, but I found out it didn't matter a damn. I couldn't stand her terminology, but she was a marvelous person. She was one of those rare individuals who know how to help others. If she had used another set of words, if she had talked Freud talk, or aggressive atheism, it wouldn't have made a difference" (68).

The subject of death never scared Ed, as it scared us; the calmness of his voice helped to calm us, and he convinced us that the idea of death is more terrifying than the process of dying. Most of his questions were directed toward Barbara. Yet if she spoke more than I did, I cried more, and on several occasions I would suddenly explode into tears, without warning, an eruption that would startle all three of us. I recall one session in particular when Ed and Barbara spoke for about forty-five minutes. I was listening carefully but remained silent. Finally, with about five minutes left, Ed turned to me and asked, "How are you doing, Jeff?" and just as I was about to say "fine," I burst into tears and began sobbing uncontrollably. My tears were a more accurate indication of my feelings than my unverbalized language. As psychoanalyst Christopher Bollas says, the body speaks "that which is known but not yet thought"

(4). Or in Martha Nussbaum's words, my tears were "geological upheavals of thought," emotions that people cannot fully control (90).

Contrary to gender stereotypes, throughout Barbara's illness I cried far more often, longer, and more violently than she did, and this pattern continued in the presence of our children. Indeed, it seems that I have become a weeper, which can be embarrassing when I'm struggling to avoid bursting into tears when watching a film in a theater. In *Men Don't Cry . . . Women Do*, Terry Martin and Kenneth Doka identify two major types of grieving patterns, an "intuitive pattern where individuals experience and express grief in an affective way," and an "instrumental" pattern where "grief is experienced physically such as in a restlessness or cognition" (2). The former is traditionally defined as feminine while the latter is seen as masculine. Both types of grieving, Martin and Doka argue, are influenced but not determined by gender, and both have advantages and disadvantages. Viewed in these terms, my own grieving pattern would fall into the intuitive pattern. The authors' observation that "intuitive grievers gain strength and solace from openly sharing their inner experiences with others—especially grievers" (35) accurately characterizes my own feelings. Perhaps this explains my belief in the "talking cure"—and in the "writing cure" and "teaching cure."

The most important therapy session came toward the end, when Barbara said that her worst fear was that I wouldn't be okay without her, and when I said that my worst fear was that she was still terrified of death. Each of us reassured the other: she said that she had now accepted death and was ready to die, and I said that the closeness of our family would allow us to cope with her death.

I suspect that Barbara's acceptance of death occurred only during the last few weeks of her life. Depression still accompanied earlier "acceptances." The five stages that Elisabeth Kübler-Ross discusses—denial and isolation, anger, bargaining, depression, and acceptance—were never clear cut. As Gemma Cannon observes, these five stages reflect not the grief process but the ways in which we react to bad news. Barbara never went through the "bargaining" stage—although we said to each other many times that our suffering would have been greater had one of our daughters been dying instead of one of us. The "anger" stage—"When the first stage of denial cannot be maintained any longer, it is replaced by feelings of anger, rage, envy, and resentment. The logical next question becomes: 'Why me?'" (50)—was not pronounced. No hint of these emotions appears in her diary.

Barbara was sleeping during Ed's last home visit, and we spoke about whether I should continue to see him after her death. We both agreed that I was sad, not depressed, and that grief should not be treated as an illness but as a normal process. After Barbara's death, I began studying cross-cultural attitudes toward bereavement, and I was not surprised to discover vast differences in mourning. "Grief is expressed so differently from culture to culture," writes Paul Rosenblatt, "that it is absurd to use notions of pathology derived from one culture to evaluate people from another. In some cultures, for example, self-mutilation is common in grief, and in others the anger of bereavement is expressed in the suspicion that some person was responsible for the death. An Egyptian mother who for seven years after the death of a child remains withdrawn, mute, inactive, and self-absorbed is behaving normally by the standards of her own culture, as is the Balinese mother who in the same situation remains calm and cheerful, even though the behavior of both would be judged pathological by U.S. standards" (18). Bereavement involves in some cultures ancient practices that appear barbaric in other cultures. Though now outlawed, suttee— the Hindu practice of widow-burning—is practiced periodically in parts of India. As V. N. Datta notes with horror, "Suttee has still the power to thrill Hindus with reverence and many continue to have sympathy for it. Some of the leading Hindu intellectuals admire the courage and heroism of the widow who dies for the love of her husband" (231). Glaser and Strauss assert that ethnicity influences the way in which relatives react to newly deceased kinsmen in a hospital: "Italians and Greeks tend to be considered [by the hospital staff] as very expressive and it is feared they will create scenes. Scots and English are considered stoic and to be depended upon for composure even though they may be breaking down inside" (205). Ed and I agreed that I would resume therapy with him if I found myself becoming depressed in the future.

Hospice was also a great comfort to Barbara and me. Without their aid, it would have been much more difficult to care for Barbara in our home. They also helped us to accept Barbara's death. Our primary hospice nurse-aide, Gerry Breitenstein, a warm and caring person, often stayed with us longer than the scheduled ninety minutes per day. She sometimes called us on her off-duty weekends to find out how we were doing. No one could have given Barbara better care than Gerry. In *Time for Dying* Glaser and Strauss make an observation that is *not* true about Gerry: "On the whole, American nurses seem to find it difficult to carry on conversations about death or dying with patients. Only if a patient has already come to terms with death, or if they can honestly assure him he will die 'easily,' if he is elderly, do they find it relatively easy to talk about such topics with him" (165). Gerry had no difficulty talking about dying and death to Barbara and me. This may have been, however, due to her hospice training. Colin Murray Parkes's statement about hospice characterizes our own experience:

> Experience in hospices suggests that it is sometimes possible for a husband and wife to work together towards an acceptance of the approaching death of one of them. If the circumstances are right . . . , they can share some of the anticipatory grief which each needs to feel. The

striking thing about such cases is that, despite the sadness which is an inevitable component of anticipatory grieving, couples who choose to face the future in this way often seem to win through to a period of contentment and calm which persists to the end. After bereavement has occurred, the surviving spouse is likely to look back on this period with a satisfaction that contrasts with the dissatisfaction expressed by many who have chosen to hide the truth. (*Bereavement* 131)

There were many times during our twenty-month ordeal when I found myself wishing that Barbara or I had been run over and killed by a truck rather than tortured slowly, but in retrospect I agree with Parkes that, despite the sadness of anticipatory grief, our time together was the most important of our marriage. I cannot say that we felt contentment or calmness—most of the time we felt dread—but I can say that it was the period of our greatest love, understanding, and devotion. I cannot be certain that, were the situation reversed, I would have demonstrated Barbara's strength and courage, but I am certain that she would have cared for me as I cared for her.

The diary entries in December 2003 record Barbara's medications and pain level. The entries become shorter, more disorganized, harder to decipher. Pain became her constant companion, recalling Emily Dickinson's lines: "Pain has an element of blank; / It cannot recollect / When it began, or if there were / A day when it was not" (12). Without the increasing dosages of morphine, the pain level would have remained at 10, the highest; even with the morphine, the pain level was often 8 or 9 during certain hours of the day and night. Most of the doctors and nurses reassured us that Barbara's pain would be controlled through medication. A book called *Myths and Facts about Pancreatic Cancer*, written by two physicians, James Abbruzzese and Ben Ebrahimi, reflects the statements we received from most health professionals:

> Pain is a common problem for patients with pancreatic cancer, especially when the cancer grows outside the pancreas and presses against nerves and other organs, but it can and should be controlled. Inadequately treated pain can have negative effects on the psychosocial functioning of an individual and can contribute to depression. Uncontrolled pain may even contribute to reduced survival. It is important for patients to report their pain so the doctor can take steps to relieve it. There are many options for good pain relief, and in the vast majority of cases, excellent pain control can be maintained through cooperation between patients and their health-care team. (39)

I don't doubt the truth of this statement, but Barbara was not among the "vast majority of cases." Hospice is superb at pain management, and we followed their recommendations faithfully. Nevertheless, we could not eliminate Barbara's pain entirely, despite ever-increasing doses of morphine. I recall vaguely a hospice nurse suggesting the possibility of a morphine pump, but no one pursued the suggestion. A pump might have done away with the hourly morphine drops that we squirted into Barbara's mouth. Kierkegaard's observation—we can understand our life only backward, but must live it forward—comes to mind here. In retrospect, I should have insisted on a morphine pump. A hospice nurse told me privately that there are a few patients like Barbara whose pain remains high no matter how much medication they receive. The same person later told me that despite our best efforts, Barbara's death was "very difficult." Watching her suffer was unbearable.

Barbara's protracted struggle was the opposite of the "perfect death" that the social worker Lily Pincus describes in her book *Death and the Family* when she recalls her husband's cheerful departure after an eleven-year battle with cancer: "When Fritz's last night came, he made sure that I shared with him the full awareness of it, and when I could give him this assurance, he said with a smile, 'Then all is well.' He died a few hours later in complete peace. The night nurse, who had kept watch with me, had mercifully left the room to make her breakfast, so that I was alone with Fritz in his last, peaceful hour, for which I shall be eternally grateful" (5). My father was in great pain from prostate cancer that had spread to his spine, but his suffering was much shorter than Barbara's. And a friend whose wife had breast cancer was feeling well enough to go for a drive with her husband a couple of days before her death. My point is simply that Barbara's suffering was intense and interminably long.

Barbara's only comment on the Christmas day entry, apart from listing her medications and pain level, is the following: "Quiet day home—disappointed Jeff by not wanting to go out." She writes on December 27, "Before dinner had time to watch Nate in Johnny Jumper. So adorable. Caleb [one of our dogs] terrified by swing." The only comment on the December 31 entry is "Jillian's birthday." On January 2 she writes, "Jeff telling me about [eulogy] speech he is writing." It was around this time that she stopped writing diary entries; she had come to the end of the diary book just as she was losing the ability to write. Many of her diary entries contain the words, "the WORST Pain." Shakespeare's observation in *King Lear* comes to mind: "The worst is not / So long as we can say, 'This is the worst'" (4.1.27). Leon Wieseltier's remark about Kafka is no less apt: "If you can write about the wreckage, the wreckage is not complete. You are intact. Here is a rule: the despairing writer is never the most despairing person in the world" (210–11). Barbara's worst pain, her most despairing moments, came when she could no longer write. Her cancer diary reveals one of the paradoxes of illness narratives: she was finally too ill to write about illness. As her physical pain increased, her psychological pain decreased, recalling Karl Marx's bitter aphorism, as quoted by Stanley Edgar Hyman: "There is only one antidote to mental suffering, and that is physical pain" (118).

Barbara had filled 131 double-sided pages of a 9½-inch × 6-inch spiral notebook. The last page of the notebook, which must have been written months earlier when her handwriting was still clear, contains a list of novels she had wanted to read: Irvin Yalom's *When Nietzsche Wept*, Jonathan Franzen's *Corrections*, Ann Patchett's *Bel Canto*, Ann Lamott's *Blue Sky*, A. S. Byatt's *Possession*, and Richard Russo's *Empire Falls*. The imminent prospect of death, Dr. Johnson said, wonderfully concentrates the mind. Perhaps, but Barbara stopped reading serious literature nearly a year earlier because she had lost her concentration. Her last diary entry is January 8 and begins and ends with references to bowel pain. Writing was her connection to life, and finally the only connection she could record was pain. When that ended, so did her life.

Barbara's twenty-month ordeal resulted in the wasting away of her body, as usually happens with pancreatic cancer, particularly when someone is relatively young and in otherwise excellent health, as she was. Had she been older and sicker when she developed the disease, with a weaker heart, she would have died more quickly—and more mercifully. It could be that the experimental pancreatic cancer vaccine, which almost certainly prolonged the length and quality of her life, inadvertently prolonged her suffering at the end. Yet what I try to remember is not Barbara's final suffering but how determined she was to seek out any treatment that would prolong the quality of her life. She suffered from all the usual side effects of prolonged chemotherapy, including nausea, fatigue, diarrhea, fever, chills, and hair loss. She endured the severe flulike symptoms associated with immunotherapy. The thalidomide produced dizziness, fogginess, and nausea. The vaccine "booster" elicited sharp, stitchlike pains. Then there were the special tortures of the cancer itself: consistent bloating and abdominal pain, severe bowel pain, drenching night sweats, and, when her biliary duct became blocked, jaundice. The painkillers caused constipation, confusion, disorientation, terrifying nightmares, and paranoia. She frequently became dehydrated and required IV fluids in the hospital.

Despite these physical and psychological horrors, Barbara did everything possible to remain alive. The woman who was terrified throughout her life of blood and needles willingly endured countless needle pricks and transfusions without complaint. A nurse who gave Barbara the final IV injection said that there were no more good veins to use—all had collapsed. Nor did Barbara complain when her hair thinned, when her stomach became so distended that she had to wear maternity pants, when she had an external catheter inserted into her body, and when finally she had to wear a diaper. *She never complained.* Her statements to me that she was "being tortured" were not so much complaints as factual statements of her condition.

Barbara looked the picture of health on the day of her diagnosis, and her vitality only heightened our shock upon learning of her terminal illness. She not only looked well but she also felt generally well; the stomach discomfort did not seem particularly worrisome until she felt a mass in her abdomen.

Countless novels and films portray healthy-looking people receiving dire news, but melodrama became truth in her case.

Barbara took pride in her body for as long as she could. She went to the gym for months after her diagnosis, swam as often as possible, went walking with the dogs, visited a dentist in the late fall of 2003 to repair a chipped tooth, had her annual gynecological exam, brushed her teeth daily, and continued to comb her hair. All these details reveal her courage, strength, and dignity.

The diary entries also reveal Barbara's delight in friendship. Love for friends reflects healthy self-love; we cannot love others without loving ourselves. Barbara's cancer diary abounds in references to dear friends. "Jack and Susan [Kress] came over about 4:00 & we had a great visit," she writes in April; "I love seeing them." In May she went to her hairdresser, a young vibrant woman who never failed to lift Barbara's spirits. "Went to Jodi for a haircut at 11:30. I love Jodi—she's a wonderful person." Many friends invited us to dinner, and she especially enjoyed these events in the spring and summer, when she was feeling well. "To Randy and Jane for dinner. Gareth [my departmental chair] and Caroline [Griffiths] were there & we had a wonderful time with fantastic food. We ate for over 3 hours continuously. Good friends & good conversation. Didn't get home until after 11:00." In June we went to our friends Anna and Jon Rosen for dinner. "We brought pie & ice cream. Their life is happy and chaotic with 3 children."

Later that month we drove to Newton, Massachusetts, to be with our friends Mike and Debby Kaufman, whom we have known since my graduate school days. "This is the first time we saw them since Jillian's wedding. Debby made a fabulous dinner—baked trout & we had as always a great time talking to them." She was especially grateful to friends who had "positive energy," which she tried to absorb. "Met Shirley Daniels on walk. She's a remarkable person—so positive and centered. Live for each day." Barbara gave quilting lessons to our oldest Albany friend, which occasioned the following wry entry: "Karen Ryan over at 10:00 for quilting lesson. We spent 3 hours cutting & sewing. She's a good student. Our friendship is not in jeopardy!" In August we visited Barbara's cousins Howard and Janice Kozinn and Barbara's uncle Phil, her father's ninety-three-year-old brother. "Arrived in CT about 2 o'clock— Uncle Phil looks great—same as when we saw him almost three years ago. Howie and Janis have a beautiful home with beautiful furnishings. They're warm & good to be around. Good vibrations with everyone. We had a wonderful afternoon with them & saw pictures of Sela [Howie and Janice's new granddaughter]. She's absolutely beautiful. Her lips are so beautifully shaped & so pink, a little angel." My brother, Elliot, and sister-in-law, Debbie, came for a tearful goodbye.

Barbara's diary contains several references to Ellen Gootblatt, her oldest and closest friend, whom she had known since the third grade. Ellen began her career as a teacher in Harlem and then had her own radio talk show on ABC News in New York City. She now gives motivational talks on college campuses. During Barbara's illness, Ellen called almost daily, often from different parts of the country, and she was one of our many friends who would tell us about new treatments for pancreatic cancer. I was working in my office during Ellen's last visit on January 25, and when I heard her scream, I raced into our bedroom, where she and her boyfriend of several decades, Murray Koenigsberg, were kneeling beside Barbara. For the past year they had planned to get married, but Murray had just formally proposed to the flabbergasted Ellen, who couldn't contain her surprise and delight. Had she been able to write, Barbara would have recorded her great pleasure in being witness to this unique marriage proposal.

I was with Barbara every time she was examined in the hospital, and I was struck by the gentle and respectful way in which her physicians and nurses palpated her body. After she died, I began reading books and articles written by cancer survivors about their own experiences. Judith Hooper, a breast cancer patient, writes: "At the doctor's office, I noticed, there are two castes of people, those with cancer—the patients—and those without—the doctors, nurses, secretaries, and receptionists. The latter gossip among themselves and treat the patients with the mild contempt reserved for those on the other side of the glass, the diseased ones" (113). That was not Barbara's experience.

Barbara never commented on the act of writing itself, and so I don't know how she felt about her cancer diary. She stopped writing more than two months before her death, and we have no way of knowing what her final weeks were like. Perhaps she experienced the same growing darkness and dissolution that Harold Brodkey describes in his haunting memoir *This Wild Darkness: The Story of My Death*: "At times I cannot entirely believe I ever was alive, that I ever was another self, and wrote—and loved or failed to love. I do not really understand this erasure" (172).

Until I read her cancer diary, I did not realize how much writing she did during her illness. She must have known, at the end if not at the beginning of the diary, that she was writing for others, and that she would never be able to reread her words. She wrote for as long as she could, believing in a future in which only her words and spirit would exist. She never asked me to preserve or destroy the diary, but it was not in her nature to destroy anything, and I am certain that she would have wanted me to save it for her children and grandchildren. When Karen's son Gabe was hugging Barbara and expressing his love for her, she returned the sentiment and responded, "talk to your children about me." One way to do this is to read her diary, where she speaks in her own eloquent voice.

2

BARBARA'S DEATH

L iterature abounds in death scenes, some violent and wrenching, like *The Death of Ivan Ilych*, others cloying and sentimental, like Little Nell's death in Dickens's *Old Curiosity Shop*, about which Oscar Wilde wickedly exclaimed that one would need a heart of stone not to laugh. As Garrett Stewart points out, death is the only event in life that novelists can only imagine rather than know. "Despite its brutal factuality at the close of life, dying is by nature the one inevitably fictional matter in prose fiction. Death for the self exists only as nonexistence, is not a topic so much as a voiding event, has no vocabulary native to it, would leave us mute before its impenetrable fact" (4). As she lay dying, I was conscious of the many similarities and differences between Barbara's experiences and those of the fictional characters I discuss in class. After her death, I felt like "talking back" to the authors of these works, telling them what they had grasped, or failed to grasp, about our experience.

Wit: Making a "Significant Contribution" to Knowledge

Barbara and I saw Margaret Edson's Pulitzer Prize–winning play *Wit* shortly after it opened at the Union Square Theatre in New York City in 1999. The play moved both of us, but it had a greater impact on me, largely because a decade earlier my mother had been diagnosed with ovarian cancer, the same type of cancer that afflicts Edson's heroine, Professor Vivian Bearing, played by Kathleen Chalfant in the original production. Like that of Professor Bearing, my mother's tumor was, according to the surgeon who removed it, the size of a grapefruit; unlike the fictional character, and unlike most people in real life, who do not usually survive this deadly cancer, my mother has been cancer free since her surgery. Another reason the play affected me more than Barbara was because, as I note in the introduction, I have long assumed that I will die of cancer whereas she did not have this fear before her diagnosis. *Wit* also touched me deeply because the play is about an English professor in her fifties, the same age I was when we saw the play. Neither Barbara nor I imagined that less than five years after viewing the play, she, too, like Edson's character, would be diagnosed with stage four adenocarcinoma; as Professor Bearing reminds us grimly, there is no stage five. Barbara's physicians told us that her disease developed slowly over a period of years, so it's possible that she had cancer while we were watching the play.

The play opens with Vivian wondering how she should respond to the question "How are you feeling today?" It is a complicated question both for the dying and their caregivers. One wonders not only how much information to reveal but also how much information the questioner wants to receive. As Barbara and I both discovered, sometimes it is too emotionally exhausting to answer the question in anything other than a perfunctory way. Other times one does not wish to answer the question fully since it might require the dying person or caregiver to serve as the questioner's therapist, especially if one is *not* feeling well and does not want to depress others. As Eve Kosofsky Sedgwick remarks wryly about her experience with breast cancer, "Often people want you to 'think positive' so they won't have to deal with their own feelings about your (or their own) vulnerability to grave illness. Lots of times, 'Think positive' is polite-speak for 'Shut up about it already'" (188–89). Vivian's uncertainty over how to answer the question demonstrates her tendency to escape pedantically into language. "Should one reply 'I feel good,' using 'feel' as a copulative to link the subject, 'I,' to its subjective complement, 'good'; or 'I feel well,' modifying with an adverb the subject's state of being?" (7).

As the play's title implies, Vivian's approach to literature emphasizes wit, the play of mind, associated with metaphysical poetry, in which unexpected meanings and paradoxes arise from verbal expression. Once cancer strikes, she becomes keenly aware of the "ironic significance" of many of the details of her changed life, including the fact that she has become an "unwitting accomplice" in a play that will end two hours later with her own death. The play sparkles— or bristles—with acerbic puns that Vivian makes at her own expense. She prefers to be cast in the "mythic-heroic-pastoral mode" (8), but she knows that her grim ending makes this impossible. Despite the play's many references to its own performativity, which has the effect of subverting verisimilitude, *Wit* is frighteningly realistic in its portrayal of the ravages of cancer.

Vivian encounters a dark double in the form of Dr. Harvey Kelekian, an arrogant physician who sees his patients only as scientific experiments, medical "problems" to be solved. The similarity of his name to "Doctor Death, Jack Kevorkian" may be unintentional, but both physicians are or have been perceived as chillingly detached from their patients. He is as dismissive of his patients' needs as Vivian has been of her students' needs. Until her illness Vivian privileges intellect over feeling and aspires, like her mentor and Dr. Kelekian, to be a "scholar of distinction" (17), which she believes she has achieved as a result of her many scholarly books and articles. Writing about Donne's Holy

Sonnets has conferred prestige on Vivian. Only when she is reduced to an object of examination does she recognize that she has lost her bearing on life. She finds the teacher-student role reversed when a former undergraduate, Jason Posner, now one of Dr. Kelekian's clinical fellows in oncology, performs an examination on her. Jason's pelvic exam embarrasses them both; when he feels the large mass in her abdomen, the stage directions indicate that he is "amazed and fascinated" (27), but he is unable to offer any words of hope or comfort. Later in the play Jason waxes poetic over his fascination with cancer, describing it almost hypnotically as "immortality in culture" (46) and affirming, without irony, that "cancer's the only thing I ever wanted" (45). "I can imagine," Vivian responds dryly, perhaps thinking that one should be careful about what one wishes.

Jason's fascination with "immortality in culture" may conceal fear of his own mortality. David Wendell Moller reports in his sociological study *Confronting Death* that physicians have a heightened fear of death and that they enter the profession partly for counterphobic reasons: the need to master their own anxiety. He cites a research study that compared physicians with two groups, healthy people and sick people: the physicians were "significantly more fearful of death than either group of nonphysicians." The researchers found that a "self-perpetuating cycle of fear is created: Exposure to death spawns a fear of death that is both unrelieved and intensified by the absence of meaningful support systems to assist physicians in responding to dying and death with openness and compassion" (30). Moller makes another observation that bears upon the doctors' efforts to resuscitate the dead Vivian at the end of the play. "Technology is the primary weapon that physicians use to fight death"—so much so that "preliminary research into varying degrees of the fear of death among physicians indicates that doctors with higher death anxiety are more likely to use technology aggressively to prolong dying. In fact, the patients of physicians with high death anxiety are in the hospital an average of five days longer before dying than patients treated by physicians with medium and lower death anxiety" (30–31).

In contrast to doctors, who are generally anxious about death and who tend to have relatively little contact with dying patients, nurses, according to Moller, "have a more positive attitude toward death" and "are more likely to provide emotional support for the dying patient and are less likely to support the use of heroics to prolong terminal existence" (34). This helps to explain why only Susie Monaham, the attending nurse, is capable of understanding Vivian's growing terror. Susie is the moral center of the play, and though she lacks an extensive vocabulary—she does not know what the word "soporific" means—she alone treats Vivian with dignity and compassion. Susie alone sees death, in Moller's words, as "safe," a "rebirth," and a "form of victory" (34).

Wit is a cautionary tale for young and old alike, for those who are healthy and for those who are not. In the end, Vivian leaves no legacy from which she can draw strength. She has no relatives or friends to comfort her, and she cannot reflect on her teaching career without feeling guilt and shame for the many students whom she has humiliated. She has not made a difference in her students' lives, nor have they made a difference in her own life. She has denied to them the kindness she now seeks. Nor can she take pleasure in her publications, which now strike her as cerebral and self-indulgent. She has spent her career in hiding behind wit, which now offers her cold comfort. Reading John Donne's poems only heightens her regret and terror, leaving her at a dead end.

If Vivian learns too late the adage what goes around, comes around, the play dramatizes powerfully the need for human connection. Susie is Vivian's guiding light, and her personal and professional commitment to her patient affirms an observation made by Alan Mermann, a clinical professor of pediatrics and chaplain of the Yale University School of Medicine: "If we are fortunate, we are exposed to love as a child and begin our journey through this life knowledgeable in the ways and means of loving: the awareness that others have needs; the willingness to make sacrifices for others; the concept of nurture; and that strange and astounding revelation that the more we give of ourselves, the more we receive" (53). Susie cannot cure her patient's disease, but she can offer her compassion and empathic understanding, both of which are indispensable. Susie's unconditional support and approval have far greater significance to Vivian's life than the erudite discussions of seventeenth-century views of forgiveness that have dominated her scholarly thinking. She values Susie's honest appraisal of her patient's failing health as much as she appreciates the refreshing Popsicle Susie gives her to cool her burning mouth. Amid the cold impersonality of the hospital setting, such acts of loving kindness take on greater meaning.

Medical Research

The main weakness of *Wit* is that it presents a stereotypical portrait of medical researchers and research professors. Dr. Kelekian and his protege, Jason Posner, are more interested in furthering their careers through scientific publications than in easing their patient's suffering. The play endorses Vivian's cynical belief that her doctors "foresee celebrity status for themselves upon the appearance of the journal article they will no doubt write about me" (43). Throughout the play "research"—whether it is in medical science or in literary studies—is associated with arrogance, egotism, and blind ambition. Jason's fascination with cancer is monstrous because of his failure to recognize the human suffering associated with it. In dramatizing the tension between medical researchers and clinicians, literary researchers and teachers, *Wit* never imagines that physicians and professors can be interested in *both* the advancement of knowledge *and* its humane application. Another weakness is the play's implication that patients who receive experimental treatment are "guinea pigs," whereas the truth is that they are monitored more closely than are those receiving conventional treatment. Nor are research and teaching always antithetical, as the play implies. Margaret Edson researched her play by working in a cancer ward of a teaching hospital, but she nevertheless oversimplifies the relationship between medical scientists and clinicians.

One can envision a different play in which a dying professor is committed to both scholarship and teaching, and who is treated by physicians who are also devoted both to medical science and compassionate clinical care. Such a play might also explore the larger aspects of the human experience: life, death, and God. Like Donne's Holy Sonnets and Edson's *Wit*, the play might address existential and spiritual quandaries without resolving them. How does one come to terms with premature death? How does a terminally ill patient maintain hope in a hopeless situation? How does one overcome fear and dread to achieve final acceptance of death? The antagonist in such a play might not be uncaring research oncologists but the dying patient's understandable terror of death, which produces an anxiety and depression so severe that they become a more formidable challenge than metastasizing cancer.

Such a play, indeed, would describe Barbara's life. She was fortunate to have two oncologists, one "clinical," Fred Shapiro, the other "research-oriented," Glenn Dranoff, who worked together to give her both compassionate care and the latest experimental treatment. My experience with oncologists is obviously limited, and so I cannot generalize about the profession. I can say, however, that Fred was always interested in experimental treatments of cancer and that Glenn always spoke admiringly about the important work done by clinicians. Fred and Glenn never met, but each valued the other's work and conferred several times on the telephone. Jason's statement that "clinicians are such troglodytes" (46) was the opposite of Barbara's own clinical oncologist, just as Dr. Kelekian's arrogance was the opposite of Glenn's humility. And we were fortunate to have nurses who were as caring and empathic as Susie.

Vivian's statement that she "distinguished" herself in illness was even more true of Barbara, who was proud of the fact that she was making a contribution to medical knowledge. The main issue of dying for Vivian is receiving forgiveness for being a cold, arrogant person and teacher; the main issue of dying for Barbara was confronting and accepting the loss of everything she loved in and about life. Medical science gave us a degree of hope that otherwise we would not have had. The experimental pancreatic cancer vaccine almost certainly gave Barbara several additional months of life. Even when that hope came to an end, replaced with a different kind of hope, for merciful death, we were grateful for the opportunity to participate in a clinical trial. She often spoke about "being in a medical textbook" one day. Even when the vaccine could no longer prevent the growth of the disease, Barbara benefitted from research: all the medications she took were themselves products of research. The success of cancer vaccine is still uncertain—in an article published in the November 12, 2004, issue of the *Chronicle of Higher Education*, Steven Rosenberg, chief of surgery at the National Cancer Institute, remarked that "as of now, we haven't figured out how to make it work" (A26). Nevertheless, immunologists have made great progress in the last few years, and Barbara was proud that she made a contribution to knowledge.

Vivian slips into a coma toward the end of the play, and Jason and Susie insert a catheter into her to collect urine. "It's not going to hurt, don't you worry" (59), Susie says soothingly. Barbara also had a catheter inserted near the end of her life, when she was in a coma, by a male hospice nurse. I remember thinking how difficult it would ordinarily be for Barbara, who was extremely modest about her body, to be in this situation. I also wondered how my daughters felt when they, along with Karen and I, witnessed this procedure. I knew every inch of Barbara's body, but until the final stages of her illness, I'm not sure whether Arielle and Jillian had seen their mother naked. I suspect that this situation was more difficult for them than for me. It is not something I feel comfortable speaking about to them, nor writing about here, but I recall thinking that nothing is shameful when done to mitigate suffering. We did everything possible to alleviate Barbara's pain, and though we could not make it disappear—her face grimaced throughout the procedure—the catheter helped to dry up the urine in her diaper, thus preventing the nasty bedsores from worsening. I know that if the situation were reversed—if I were having a catheter inserted in the presence of my wife and daughters—they would be as respectful of my privacy as we were of Barbara's.

A Farewell to Arms: "It Was Like Saying Good-by to a Statue"

Ernest Hemingway's *Farewell to Arms* is not a novel to give to a pregnant woman or to her family, nor to the dying or their caregivers. Published in 1929, the story is about Frederic Henry's farewell both to the arms of war and to the arms of the woman whom he professes to adore, Catherine Barkley, who dies while giving birth to a stillborn son. Like Maria in *For Whom the Bell Tolls*, Catherine declares repeatedly that she wishes to merge her identity with that of her lover, to obliterate her own individuality, but the fantasy of union coexists with more powerful fantasies of alienation, persecution, and separation. Frederic's response to loss and bereavement at the end could not be more different from my own.

Hemingway dramatizes Catherine's rising fear and dread during childbirth, her sense of being "broken." Despite her willingness to do anything to escape from intolerable pain, including ending her life—"I don't care if I die if it will only stop" (322)—she remains heroic, destroyed but not defeated, like the elderly fisherman in *The Old Man and the Sea*. Frederic intuits that something will go wrong with the childbirth even before she goes into labor; her bravery occasions one of his most striking observations: "If people bring so much courage to this world the world has to kill them to break them, so of course it kills them. The world breaks every one and afterward many are strong at the broken places. But those that will not break it kills. It kills the very good and the very gentle and the very brave impartially. If you are none of these you can be sure it will kill you too but there will be no special hurry" (249). The novel's plot enacts the paranoid fantasy of a malevolent force singling out for early destruction those rare individuals like Catherine who embody extraordinary qualities. It is not clear whether Frederic, who survives at the end to narrate the story, is one of the "many [who] are strong at the broken places."

Hemingway's words have proven inspirational to some readers. Eulogizing his twenty-four-year-old son Alex, who died in a car accident, the Rev. William Sloane Coffin cites the line (slightly misquoted), "The world breaks everyone, then some become strong at the broken places," which appeared in a "healing" letter from a well-wisher. "My own broken heart is mending," muses Coffin, "and largely thanks to so many of you, my dear parishioners; for if in the last week I have relearned one lesson, it is that love not only begets love, it transmits strength" (qtd. in Theroux, 344). In the full context of Hemingway's passage, however, it is hard to take comfort in the existence of a cosmic sadist who destroys the best and brightest. Coffin might have chosen a different novelist from whom to draw comfort amid suffering. Henry James's letter to his friend Grace Norton affirms, like Hemingway's war story, the belief that strength may arise from tragic loss, but without the later novelist's paranoid vision: "Sorrow comes in great waves—no one can know that better than you— but it rolls over us, and though it may almost smother us it leaves us on the spot and we know that if it is strong we are stronger inasmuch as it passes and we remain. It wears us, uses us, but we wear it and use it in return; and it is blind, whereas we after a manner see" (qtd. in Theroux, 336). Without invoking Hemingway, Colin Murray Parkes uses a Hemingwayesque metaphor that Coffin might have used: "Just as broken bones may end up stronger than unbroken ones, so the experience of grieving can strengthen and bring maturity to those who have previously been protected from misfortune. The pain of grief is just as much a part of life as the joy of love; it is, perhaps, the price we pay for love, the cost of commitment" (*Bereavement* 6).

Frederic agrees with Catherine's dying words that life is "just a dirty trick" (331), and he seems incapable of holding onto anything positive about their brief life together. He tells us, in the last paragraph of the novel, that seeing

her lifeless body is "like saying good-by to a statue" (332), and we recall his statement earlier that unlike a bronze, which "looked like something," marble busts
"all looked like a cemetery" (28).

How will Frederic remember Catherine? If we can speculate on the
future life of an imaginary character, it appears unlikely that he will recall
anything positive about his stony remembrances of her death. It is impossible
to imagine that he will be able to internalize the lost love object, a process that
may be the most important task in mourning. Seeing Catherine only as a cold
statue suggests that he cannot make her part of his inner world. There is little
evidence in the story to intimate that he remembers anything of value about
his past, and he is not the kind of person who can keep alive the memory of a
loved one. It is as if, to reverse the Ovid myth, Galatea comes to life, upon Pyg-
malion's desire, but then turns into stone again, without a trace of having lived.

One cannot imagine Frederic reconnecting with the world of the living.
As Pamela Boker remarks in *The Grief Taboo in American Literature*, "Because
Frederic Henry cannot openly express or acknowledge his grief, he must suffer the more devastating loss to the self that results from repressing one's emotions, and mourn eternally, not only for the beloved whom he has lost, but for
the *nada* of his own inner emotional emptiness" (201). The three factors that
impede recovery from conjugal bereavement, according to Colin Murray Parkes
and Robert Weiss—sudden, unexpected death; a conflicted, ambivalent relationship; and excessive dependency (52)—all characterize Frederic's situation.
Ann Kaiser Stearns's metaphor of "frozen emotion" bodes ill for Hemingway's
hero: "Water, as it freezes and the molecules expand, has the power to burst
steel pipes wide open. Likewise, frozen emotion assumes a power out of pro-
portion to its original nature. In the middle of a very harsh winter it's wise to see
to it that the water flows fairly regularly through your home plumbing system.
Similarly, during the harsh seasons of grief, it is best to keep the channels open
so that hurtful feelings are freely expressed. Frozen emotion, like a frozen pipe,
has the potential for causing unexpected problems" (60–61).

Those who die dwell in the memories of the living, but this consolation may be problematic, as C. S. Lewis writes in *A Grief Observed*, his moving reflection on the death of his wife, Joy Davidman, whom he referred to as
"H." when he published the memoir under a pseudonym (the film *Shadowlands* was based on their relationship): "What pitiable cant to say, 'She will live
forever in my memory?' *Live*? That is exactly what she won't do. You might as
well think like the old Egyptians that you can keep the dead by embalming
them. Will nothing persuade us that they are gone? What's left? A corpse, a
memory, and (in some versions) a ghost. All mockeries or horrors. Three more
ways of spelling the word *dead*. It was H. I loved. As if I wanted to fall in love
with my memory of her, an image in my own mind! It would be a sort of in-
cest" (20).

Lewis is right to suggest that a loving remembrance of the deceased may be cold comfort to the bereaved; there is a world of difference between a living person and a memory of her. Yet such remembrances may not be false, as Lewis admits later, and they need not be frozen in time: memory changes over time, and our recollection of lost love may also change. We do not fall into sentimentality when we say that we make the dead part of our lives.

Barbara would not have agreed with Catherine that life is nothing but a "dirty trick," nor would she have agreed that the "good," the "gentle," and the "brave" are singled out for early death. That she was good, gentle, and brave was evident to all who knew her. Unlike Catherine, she never offered to give up her identity for me or to subordinate herself to me, nor would I have wanted her to do so. I loved her for the ways we were *different*. Although her belief in God and the afterlife was as vague as Catherine's, she would have smiled wryly at the idea that I was her "religion." She knew that she meant the world to me, and I to her, but unlike Catherine and Frederic, she remained connected with her relatives and friends. Her children were the center of her life.

Barbara's modesty prevented her from believing she was courageous and strong, but her suffering lasted not for hours, as with Catherine, but for months, and despite increasing amounts of morphine, she was in constant pain until the day of her death. The morphine relieved some but not all of her pain. She developed festering bedsores, which required us to turn her from one side to another every few hours, which brought her further distress. A hospice nurse told me that pancreatic cancer is one of the most painful forms of cancer, second only to primary bone cancer. The pain may have "broken" her body but not her belief that life was meaningful. Unlike Catherine and Frederic, Barbara maintained hope for the next generations of life, in which her children and grandchildren will continue her legacy.

Peaceful Death

Barbara did not look like a statue on the day she died. As good luck would have it, we were all with her at the end. It must seem odd to invoke "good luck" here, but two hospice nurses told us weeks before her death that terminally ill patients usually "pass" when no one is around, even when family and friends maintain a bedside vigil. Virginia Morris makes the same observation, noting that "people often die when their loved ones are out of the room. Family members and friends are at the bedside around the clock and then, during that one moment when they are gone, the person up and dies. Loved ones feel cheated because they weren't there, and they feel sad that this person was alone at the moment of death" (120). People generally die, we were told, late at night or early in the morning, before sunrise. From the moment of her diagnosis until the day of her death, I was with Barbara nearly twenty-four hours a day, except when I was teaching or running errands. (We were separated for two weekends, the first time when she visited her parents in Florida, and the second time when I attended a professional conference.) Based on the information from the hospice nurses, I thought it likely that one morning I would wake up to find Barbara alongside me, no longer breathing. We slept next to each other throughout our married life, even toward the end, when she was making awful gurgling noises—the "death rattle." I was so physically and emotionally exhausted that I fell asleep in a minute or two, despite the noise that ordinarily would have kept me awake. Each morning as soon as I awoke I would look at her, checking to see if she was still breathing. Her heart continued to beat.

Beginning Saturday, April 3, Barbara's heart began racing wildly, making one last effort to stay alive, and then we knew that the end was near. Throughout Saturday and Sunday her heart continued to beat frantically, but on Monday it began to slow down. By the afternoon, her pulse could barely be detected. I sat in my office, a few feet from our bedroom, talking with the hospice chaplain, who had just finished singing to her. Jillian went in for Barbara's 3:00 PM liquid morphine, and she noticed bleeding from her mother's nose, which had never happened before. Jillian rushed into my office with the news, and we all remembered that the hospice nurse had told us recently that this occasionally happens. Arielle, Jillian, Karen, the chaplain, and I gathered around the bed. For days all of us had stroked Barbara's body, telling her how much we loved her and that we were ready for her to die, but now we were silent, looking at her and then at each other, not quite believing that death had finally, imperceptibly, arrived. I placed my hand on Barbara's mouth, trying to detect breath. I couldn't feel air escaping from her mouth or nose. Her face looked peaceful, and her eyes were closed. I had long become accustomed to her sunken eyes, so different from the radiant expression on her face when she was healthy, but now, for the first time in months, she looked at rest.

Many times Barbara looked dead when she was asleep; in death she looked asleep. George Eliot's observation about the drowned Maggie Tulliver in *The Mill on the Floss* describes the peacefulness of Barbara's death: "In the first moments Maggie felt nothing, thought of nothing, but that she had suddenly passed away from that life which she had been dreading: it was the transition of death, without its agony" (455). So, too, does Elisabeth Kübler-Ross evoke the "silence that goes beyond words": "Watching a peaceful death of a human being reminds us of a falling star; one of the million lights in a vast sky that flares up for a brief moment only to disappear into the endless night forever" (276).

I had never seen a dead person before, except for my grandmother and father, but there was nothing scary about Barbara's appearance, nothing that seemed cold and inanimate, like a marble statue. Despite wasting away, she still looked like Barbara. The chaplain, more experienced than I, felt for her pulse but could find none. Months after Barbara's death I read Barney Glaser and Anselm Strauss's book *Time for Dying* in which they discuss a relative's need for a "last touch": "Touching the body is part of [the] relatives' effort to help close the mystic gap between life and death" (217). Perhaps this explains why I kissed Barbara after she died, a kiss in death that was also a kiss of life. I had not thought about doing this in advance, but I cut a lock of her hair and placed it in a sealed envelope, as I had done with the locks of our daughters' hair when they were born. The chaplain, Joel Janzow, promptly called Alice Baker, the hospice case manager, who arrived within fifteen minutes. For several minutes Alice tried to detect a pulse, as she was required to do by law, and then she finally pronounced her dead. Within the hour men came from the funeral home and placed the body in a bag, which they then carried out of the house into a van. I felt nothing but relief: no sadness, loneliness, or grief. These emotions came later.

None of us engaged in the *conclamatio mortis*, the death shout that occurs in some cultures. There was no weeping or wailing, tearing of hair, rending of clothes, scratching of flesh, singing of dirges, or seeking isolation in darkened rooms. Nor did we cover the mirrors or partake of a "meal of consolation." These death rituals were for other mourners in different cultures. Nor did we inquire into the details of how the undertaker would prepare the body for interment. There are elaborate purification rites in Jewish burials, including the ritualized washing of the body and its wrapping in a pure white linen shroud. Among Orthodox and Conservative Jews a person watches the body from death to interment, protecting the soul. According to ancient belief, the soul is imprisoned in the body and is capable of being stolen by evil spirits until burial. None of these details were important to us.

I don't know when Barbara uttered her last words or what they were. After her death, I read Ray Robinson's compilation *Famous Last Words* in which he suggests that the "beauty of some of these last words is that they may open a window through which we feel we can catch a glimpse, if only for a moment, of the entire life that preceded it" (ix). The exit lines that I like the best, and that Barbara would have also liked, are those that affirm love, intimacy, and devotion. My favorite was expressed by Ida Straus, who refused a lifeboat offered to her and instead chose to die with her husband on the sinking *Titanic*: "We have been together for 40 years, and we will not separate now" (32). Barbara would have also liked Alice James's last words to her brother William: "Tenderest love to all. Farewell, am going soon" (43). Both Barbara and her mother would have been moved by Horace Mann's parting words: "Sing to me if you have the heart" (118). Caught in a violent snowstorm on Mount Everest, Rob Hall's dying words to his wife would have struck a chord within Barbara: "Sleep well, my sweetheart. Please don't worry too much" (135). And Barbara, practical to the end, would have smiled at hotel magnate Conrad Hilton's final words: "Leave the shower curtain on the inside of the tub" (170).

Barbara's death was not dramatic, as death often is when portrayed in literature and film. I think she would have agreed with Jane Kenyon's dying words, which appear in Donald Hall's moving poem "Last Days": "'Dying is simple,' she said. / 'What's worst is . . . the *separation*'" (42). Not for a moment did I ask Barbara to "rage, rage against the dying of the light," as Dylan Thomas urges in his villanelle "Do Not Go Gentle into That Good Night." I don't know whether she discovered, as does Ivan Ilych, a blinding revelation of the meaning of life and death. I don't know what her unverbalized thoughts and feelings were at the end. I don't know when she stopped hearing us. I don't know whether she truly accepted her death. I don't know when the essence of her life or spirit passed. But I do know that, with the exception of her aged parents, who were unable to travel, Barbara died in the presence of the most important people in her life, none of whom will remember her only as a statue.

"Marriage to a lover is fatal," Carolyn Heilbrun observes provocatively in *Writing a Woman's Life*; "lovers are not husbands. More important, husbands are not lovers. The compulsion to find a lover and husband in a single person has doomed more women to misery than any other illusion" (87). She quotes an equally provocative statement by John Bayley in *The Character of Love*: "A love affair brings human beings unnaturally together while marriage keeps them the right dignified distance apart" (229).

I was indeed fortunate that Barbara was my wife, lover, best friend, and soul mate. The vast majority of the fictional characters I teach do not enjoy a passionate marriage, if they are indeed married. Characters fall in and out of love—or lust—so quickly that it is more accurate to speak of their "love for love" rather than love for a specific person. This is true of nearly all the characters created by the authors whom I teach regularly: Thomas Hardy, D. H. Lawrence, Joseph Conrad, F. Scott Fitzgerald, and Ernest Hemingway. How few passionate, long-lasting relationships there are in literature—or in life. A friend told me after Barbara's death that ours was one of the few close marriages of which he knew. Heilbrun quotes admiringly an observation by Stanley Cavell in *Pursuits of Happiness* that the "mystery of marriage" has little to do with law or sexuality; "what provides legitimacy is the mutual willingness for remarriage, for a sort of continuous reaffirmation" (142). Adds Heilbrun, "The sign of a good marriage is that everything is debatable and challenged; nothing is turned into law or policy. The rules, if any, are known only to the two players, who seek no trophies" (95). I cannot imagine that I will find another Barbara, but I know that when we talked about this question, she said that after her death she wanted me to find a companion so that I wouldn't be lonely—and unlike Catherine Barkley, she did not impose conditions on future relationships.

One True Thing: "Please. Help Me. No More."

The title of Anna Quindlen's 1994 novel *One True Thing* is understated. There are many authentic aspects of this moving story, later made into a film directed by Carl Franklin and starring Meryl Streep as the dying mother, William Hurt as her remote, self-absorbed husband, and Renée Zellweger as the resentful grown daughter who is compelled to care for her mother, to whom she has never felt close. Despite a serious flaw at the end of the novel that weakens its medical credibility, *One True Thing* affected me in a way that no other novel or film has.

The prologue opens with the narrator, Ellen Gulden, reflecting on her brief experience in jail several years earlier. She recalls in vivid detail lying on a cot and thinking about her mother, who has just died of cancer. Closing her eyes, Ellen imagines her mother crying for help: "for a cup of tea, a glass of water, a sandwich, more morphine" (5). Gradually we learn that Ellen's family lives in Langhorne, a small college town, and that her father is the chairperson of the English Department of Langhorne College, "a fine but somewhat obscure small liberal arts college, a kind of poor relation of the Swarthmores and the Haverfords" (52). Ellen has just been charged with killing her mother, and she cannot understand why her father has not come to bail her out of jail. The prologue ends with Ellen declaring that she did not kill her mother though she wished she had—a statement that becomes clearer as we progress through the nearly four-hundred-page novel.

Much of the power of *One True Thing* arises from its ability to show how illness disrupts a caregiver's personal and professional life. Ellen is a twenty-four-year-old Harvard honors graduate when she learns from her father that her forty-six-year-old mother is stricken with ovarian cancer. "'Your mother procrastinated,' he said, as though she was somehow to blame. 'First she thought she had the flu. Then she imagined she was expecting. She didn't want to make a fuss. You know how she is'" (24). The statement reveals more about George Gulden than it does about Kate Gulden, particularly his need to blame someone for her illness, which he finds inconvenient. It is difficult to sympathize with a person who appears to love his wife for better but not for worse, who refuses to take responsibility for his actions, and who is condescending and self-absorbed. Ellen has always been distant from her nonintellectual mother, with whom she counteridentifies, and close to her academic father, who is witty, ironic, and courtly. George Gulden looks better from afar—especially to his adoring female students, who are willing to engage in clandestine extracurricular activities with this professor of desire.

George Gulden assumes that his intellectually accomplished and ferociously ambitious daughter, an editorial assistant and rising reporter for a major New York magazine, will put her career on hold in order to nurse her dying

mother so that he can continue to teach and, as he says by way of rationaliza-
tion, pay the medical bills. When Ellen resists and instead recommends that
he hire a nurse or apply for a sabbatical, he responds angrily, "you have no
heart" (30). The father knows how to play upon his daughter's guilt, especially
when he tells her that "another woman is what's wanted here" (33). The relationship between father and daughter is not precisely like that of Miss Havisham to Estella in Dickens's *Great Expectations*, but there is some of the
coldness, self-centeredness, and manipulation. Professor Gulden has an apt
pupil in his daughter, who has internalized his values and judgments, and when
he tells her that she must display empathy toward her mother, she retorts,
reminiscent of Estella's response to Miss Havisham, "Empathy is the one thing
I never really learned. . . . You never taught me empathy" (142). Unlike Miss
Havisham, George Gulden has never been jilted in love, and so there is no explanation for why he is so unempathic throughout the novel, so unable or
unwilling to care for the woman who has unselfishly dedicated her life to her
husband and children.

Kate remains the moral center of the story, the character who doesn't
allow suffering to blind her to others' needs. She reminds me, in so many ways,
of Barbara. Like Barbara, she is attentive to others, grateful to the nurses in
the hospital who give her chemotherapy. "Within weeks," Ellen observes in admiration, "she knew the names of all the nurses, their family backgrounds, the
ages of their children. As she waited they would smile and say her name: Good
morning, Kate, how are you?" (80). She not only brings out the best in people
but also knows how to make others feel comfortable in her presence. Thus she
tries to hide the disintegration of her body from her daughter, tries not to complain about the unbearable suffering, tries to pretend that she is not dying, not
because she is in denial but because she does not want to burden her family.

There are differences, however, between Kate and Barbara. As the disease spreads, Kate is confined to a wheelchair, and she begins to rage against
relatives and friends. "The outbursts seemed so different from her usual self
that I sometimes felt as though the cancer itself had a voice, and I was hearing it. Or it was the voice of the morphine" (110). Only once did Barbara exhibit such an outburst, when I was teaching and our children were taking care
of her. Like Kate, Barbara felt that she was being held captive, being imprisoned
by her loved ones, and we had to give her antipsychotic medication until she
lapsed into a coma a few weeks later. No longer able to care for herself, Kate
feels humiliated to be so dependent on others, and, in what is her most hurtful remark of the novel, shouts at her daughter, "You want me to be dead. You
want me to die so you and your father can get on with your lives" (110). The
accusation is unfair, but Ellen finds herself tearfully telling her lawyer-friend
Jonathan that "if I had any guts at all I would hold a pillow over her face" (111),
a statement that comes back to haunt her.

Nowhere is *One True Thing* more authentic than in depicting the harrowing pain of metastatic cancer. Pain management becomes the overriding and all-consuming issue, and the need for ever-increasing doses of morphine for "breakthrough" pain recalls our experience caring for Barbara. Quindlen captures the brutality of suffering and the way it enfeebles a patient, no matter how strong she may have been in health. "'I need a pill, Ellen,' she said, the trace of a whine in the ebb and flow of her inflection" (151). Increasing the morphine also increases the length of time the dying person sleeps, accelerating the transition to death. Like Barbara, Kate experiences hallucinations as a result of the morphine and gradually loses the will to live. George's statement that he cannot imagine life without his wife parallels many of my own statements. Sometimes I found myself identifying with him more than with the daughter, as when he says, "I can't imagine the light going out," to which she responds unempathically, "You're talking about her as if she was already dead" (145), a reply that fails to understand the depth of anticipatory grief. I identified even with his self-pitying statements, for they, too, are common in a time of grief.

As the life ebbs from her mother, Ellen feels like dying with her, breaking down, giving up, and she finds herself increasingly sobbing, losing control. Unlike me, at first she refuses to allow a nurse to make home visits, telling Teresa Guerrero, "Having a stranger in the house is too upsetting. I cannot afford to fall apart," to which Teresa replies, "Falling apart is curling up into a fetal position and staying in bed for a week. . . . What you were doing is having the emotional response an individual has to the loss of someone they love. We cry to give voice to our pain" (161). Quindlen knows how unbearable it is for caregivers to witness their loved ones dying, how even when caregivers believe they cannot go on, they are able to call upon resources they didn't know existed. Ellen is comforted by Teresa's experiences with other terminally ill patients, including a woman with pancreatic cancer who died in her husband's arms in bed. "[Teresa] told me about other people's troubles in a way that was strangely soothing, that made me feel part of a great sorority of pain and suffering" (207).

Teresa makes another important observation to Ellen, reminding her that "illness brings out different qualities in different people. Some are enriched by it—yes, I know, you do not want to consider the possibility, but it is true, and I have seen it. Some people have a talent for it and rise to the occasion. And some are diminished by their fear. They often deny or withdraw" (209–10). Quindlen ends this discussion perfectly, with Teresa maintaining that "suffering transforms," Ellen responding, "Suffering sucks," and Teresa having the final word: "I agree. With both conclusions, actually" (210). Illness becomes in *One True Thing* a test of character, as it does in *Wit*, but it is a test that bears no relationship to academic success.

Being Tested

I too felt like I was on trial as a caregiver. Of all the statements I received from relatives, friends, and acquaintances, the one that I thought about the most, and that both angered and inspired me the most, was expressed by a retired colleague, who said to me, upon hearing of Barbara's illness, "You will be tested." The statement haunted me night and day. Why was I being tested? Who was testing me? When would the test end? How would I know whether I passed or failed the test? These questions continue to this day. After Barbara's death I told my colleague how much his statement affected me, and he seemed surprised, for he not only failed to remember saying these words to me but also didn't understand why I placed so much importance on them. A deeply religious man, he believes, as I do, that life tests all of us and that we rise to the challenge as best we can.

Joseph Conrad also believed in the "test," and that's why his stories have been so important to me. His characters struggle, with varying degrees of success, to redeem themselves after betraying, however involuntarily, their own ideals of courage, loyalty, and heroism. Many of these characters commit suicide after failing the test, such as Martin Decoud in *Nostromo* and Axel Heyst in the ironically named novel *Victory*. Others initiate a series of actions that culminate predictably in self-destruction, such as the eponymous hero of *Lord Jim* and Razumov in *Under Western Eyes*. Still others surrender to the dark forces of greed, lust, or egotism and die mysteriously, such as Kurtz in *Heart of Darkness*. Many characters who remain alive at the end brood incessantly over whether they were a good-enough friend to the "nightmare of their choice," such as Marlow in *Heart of Darkness*. At least one character, Brierly in *Lord Jim*, commits suicide not because he has made a mistake—indeed, his illustrious career as a captain has been perfect—but because he is forced to consider his own potential weakness when imagining Jim's disgrace, a recognition of the "legitimate terrors of life" with which he finally cannot live.

I too struggled to pass the test, to prove that I am a good (or good-enough) son, husband, father, friend, teacher, and scholar. Taking care of Barbara became the most important test of my life, and I was always conscious of the need to do my best from the beginning to the end of her ordeal. Doing my best meant driving her to the hospital and sitting by her side during her chemotherapy treatments and pancreatic cancer vaccinations. It meant being with her when she received the results of seemingly endless medical tests. I did my best to lessen her pain, shore up her failing spirit, and remain with her to the end. She would have done the same for me. I am not implying that taking care of Barbara can be reduced to the need to pass the test. I took care of her because I loved and was devoted to her, but at the same time I was aware that I was being judged, or perhaps, more accurately, that I was judging myself. I did not want to fall short.

I was far from a perfect caregiver, however, and I recall making two statements that hurt Barbara deeply. As the disease began to spread, she would often tell me, when no one else was around, that she was "being tortured." I would usually listen without speaking, and then I would ask her if I could bring her something—more pain medication, another blanket or pillow, a cup of herbal tea, petroleum jelly for her cracked lips, anything—but on one occasion I said to her, "You're torturing *me*," a comment that was bound to upset her, as it did. I knew that I could have said, "I'm being tortured too," which would have been less hurtful—and less hateful—but I wanted her to know that I too felt like I was dying, that without a moment's hesitation I would have traded places with her, that what was happening was unspeakable, and that there were times when I couldn't endure the situation. We both cried after I made that statement.

The other time my words hurt her was when we arrived home one evening from a movie and discovered that our younger dog, Sabrina, had chewed a large hole in the family room love seat. Both Sabrina and our seven-year-old Belgian, Caleb, knew that their mistress was ill: she walked them every morning when she was healthy and would always play with them, but gradually she paid less and less attention to them, and they responded by leaving "unwelcome gifts" throughout the house, which I had to clean up. I became so angry at Sabrina when I saw the damage to the furniture that I turned around at Barbara and screamed, "When you die, I'm getting rid of these dogs." Like the other comment, this one hurt her deeply and caused both of us to cry. Only a dog-lover, which I was not, could understand Barbara's closeness to the dogs. She never made me promise to take care of them after her death, but I vowed that I would try my best. The dogs were inconsolable after Barbara's death, and, following the suggestion of a hospice nurse, we allowed them to sniff her body so that they could express their own sad farewell. Afterward, our vet prescribed an antidepressant to help them deal with Barbara's death, the same antidepressant, ironically, that I am taking.

My experience during Barbara's illness heightened my appreciation for *One True Thing*, which is unsurpassed in its compassion and insight into the caregiver's point of view. Quindlen describes Ellen's horror when helping her mother, now broken in body and spirit, into the bathroom. The heartbreaking descriptions of her mother's wasted body, and the shame each feels over the degradation of life, are unforgettable. It was impossible for me to read the novel without weeping, even months after Barbara's death. Kate's situation was not identical to Barbara's: there were as many differences as similarities. We were fortunate that our family was not wracked by the tensions that destroy

Ellen's family. Both Barbara and I were grateful to our daughters, whose love and devotion remained constant, and to our sons-in-law, no less loving and devoted. We did not have to worry about father-daughter or mother-daughter estrangement, as Ellen did. Kate was more fortunate, however, in that she did not exhibit, until the very end, the anxiety, depression, and panic that afflicted Barbara throughout her illness. And as Ellen concedes, her mother was "in every way a typical patient except that she died more quickly than many with her kind of cancer" (373).

Like Catherine in *A Farewell to Arms*, only to a greater degree, Kate finds life no longer bearable, and her last words to Ellen are a cry for help that her daughter cannot heed. "'Help me, Ellen,' she whispered. 'I don't want to live like this anymore.'" They stare at each other, each wanting something the other cannot give. "'Please,' she said. 'You must know what to do. Please. Help me. No more.'" Ellen tries to be helpful by telling her that she will feel better in the morning, but Kate cannot be distracted. "'No,' she said, and groaned again. 'It will not, It will not.' She sounded like a tired and irritable child." The repetition of the dialogue emphasizes the desperation of the pleas. "'Help me,' she whispered. 'You're so smart. You'll know what to do.' Then her eyes closed completely. 'Please,' she whispered once more" (229). Days later, Ellen sees her father feeding Kate, slowly lifting a spoon of rice pudding into her mouth, hears them talking softly, and then he walks into his daughter's bedroom and, sounding like his wife, repeats to her twice, "No one should have to live like that. No one." Rubbing his eyes, he says, "'She wants me to sleep with her in there,'" he added. 'I can't. I can't. Not tonight. I'm going upstairs'" (245). Ellen then goes into her mother's bedroom and witnesses her final gasps. "There was a sound like that a car makes when it won't start on a cold morning, an *eh eh eh eh* deep in my mother's throat, and I held tight to her hand as though I would crush it in my own long strong fingers. A shudder shook her body, and then the sound once more: *eh eh eh*, and one last long inhalation of breath" (246).

Two weeks after her mother's death, Ellen is informed that a pathologist "found something wrong during the autopsy" (256), and thus begins another nightmare for her, almost as excruciating as watching her mother suffer. The cause of death is not cancer but an overdose of morphine. Suddenly Ellen is the only suspect in what appears to be an act of euthanasia—the word means "easy death" in Greek. Events conspire against her. The media publicize her prize-winning high school essay advocating euthanasia, and her statements sound incriminating, as when she exclaims to her mother's oncologist Dr. Cohn, who ordered the autopsy and then dutifully conveys the results to the district attorney, "Who cares how she died? She should have been put out of her misery weeks ago. If she had been a dog they would have" (257). Ellen fails to take seriously the charge against her, which only increases public support for her prosecution. The district attorney asks for help from a famous pathologist in

Florida, and the school board considers disciplinary action against Mrs. Forburg, who befriends Ellen. Meanwhile, community opposition to her is fueled by a Kevorkian-like "doctor death" who hooks patients up to IV drips elsewhere in the country. She receives crank calls from both opponents and proponents of euthanasia, despite the fact that she keeps saying, "I didn't do it." Most of the residents of Langhorne assume that Ellen killed her mother, but they believe that she has done it out of kindness, not malice, as some people claim. Her boyfriend, with whom she has broken off relations, vindictively provides evidence against her, and her father, whom she suspects gave her mother the fatal overdose, refuses to support her. Ellen remains silent about her suspicions, vowing to protect him one final time. Her estrangement from him is now complete. She never forgets his final accusation that she is heartless.

How does Ellen feel about euthanasia? She acknowledges to her lawyer that she had invented some of the details in her high school essay, such as the incident in which she describes a fifteen-year-old dog being euthanized. "'What can I say?' I asked, shrugging. 'I was seventeen years old and I knew nothing about the subject. It's glib, it's self-righteous, and it's badly written'" (301). She also recognizes the world of difference between the theory and practice of euthanasia. "I still believe that people are kept alive long past the time when life is of any use to them. But when I wrote that essay, I knew nothing about the subject firsthand" (344). When her attorney asks her whether she discussed the essay with her parents, Ellen recalls vaguely that her mother thought euthanasia was a "horrible subject" and that her father was "livid" because the essay contained a grammatical mistake near the end: "A 'that' where a 'which' should be" (301). Ellen cannot bring herself to carry out her mother's request, but she admires her father for apparently doing so. "Perhaps she had asked of him, that last night when I heard them talking, what she had asked of me and he had had the courage and the love to do what I had not. For that possibility alone I believed he deserved my protection. At least that is how I think I felt when the woman I am today analyzes the one I was then" (267).

During the grand jury proceedings, the prosecutor, Ed Best, asks Ellen whether she believes that her mother's life in her final days "was worth living?" Ellen objects to his wording and offers the same language that I would use to describe Barbara's final weeks alive. "I think my mother had lost her dignity, her place, all the things that made her life happy. She was wearing diapers. She was sleeping almost constantly. And for a woman like her, who'd always been so capable, so full of life, so lively—it was a terrible thing. It was terrible for her and it was terrible for me" (345). The prosecutor then asks her if she believes "there are times when someone's quality of life is so compromised that death, whether natural or assisted, would be preferable," to which she answers in the affirmative. She responds in the same way when asked whether she believes that her mother's quality of life was "horribly impaired at the end of her life" (347). But she denies that she gave her mother a fatal overdose and then offers a powerful and moving statement about why she wrote an essay supporting euthanasia but could not act on her beliefs:

> In theory, I meant these things. But when it's real, when it's a real person—it's different. I was so busy keeping her clean and making her food and making sure she had her medicine, I never stopped to think about anything bigger than how we were going to get through the next hour. Maybe it was like having a baby in that respect. Everyone talks about how wonderful it is, how fulfilling, but I've always thought it seems like one little piece of drudgery after another, a feeding, a changing, a bath, and maybe it's only afterward that it seems wonderful. I didn't have time to think about anything more than all those little things, taking care of my mother. It's so much easier to know just how you feel about things, what you believe, when you're writing it on paper than when you really have to do anything about it or live with it." (348)

The grand jury decides not to indict Ellen for the death of her mother, and the news makes the AP wire. In the prologue, written eight years after the story's events, Ellen relates how supporters of euthanasia and physician-assisted suicide sought to enlist her for their cause, despite the fact that there was no evidence she had done what they advocate. "One doctor devoted to helping people with multiple sclerosis die by hooking a hose to a car's exhaust pipe came in person to my apartment, hose in hand. I closed one of his fingers in the door" (368).

After her mother's death, Ellen changes careers, rejecting the life of a writer for that of a psychiatrist. It is never entirely clear why she has gone into psychiatry. Perhaps she believes that it is more important to help people deal in depth with psychological problems than to write articles and books about issues that have little to do with real life. Perhaps her psychiatric training has allowed her to work through her grief over her mother's death. Only once does Ellen refer to being in therapy after her mother's death, but the reference is significant. "'As her daughter, would you have behaved differently?' my therapist asked once, with an unaccustomed gleam in her eye. And the answer is that, knowing then what I know now, I would have. I would have given her more opportunities to talk, to complain, to fantasize, to weep, to speak. But that is what I am in the business of doing now, and it sounds easier in retrospect" (373–74). Or perhaps the career of a writer is too close to her father's career. For whatever reason, she is now a mental health professional. She still supports euthanasia in theory if not in practice.

Ellen's father remains dead to her at the end of the story, while her mother's absent presence is alive and real. She remains bitter about the legal proceedings against her, but far worse than the bitterness is her inability to exorcise the memory of her mother's horrific death. "Death is so strange, so mysterious, so sad, that we want to blame someone for it. And it was easy to blame me. Besides, when people wonder how I survived being accused of killing my mother, none of them realizes that watching her die was many, many times worse. And knowing I could have killed her was nothing compared to knowing I could not save her. And knowing I'd almost missed knowing her was far more frightening than Ed Best and his little army of shrunken suits" (370).

Ellen has one more encounter with her father, a serendipitous meeting that proves epiphanic to her though not to him. One day she attends a play in Manhattan, and during the intermission, while waiting to telephone a patient, she sees him standing outside the theater. They begin their conversation in the old bantering way, and when she tells him that she has become a psychiatrist, working with depressed and suicidal adolescents, he responds glibly—and in character: "the stuff of fiction." Their conversation turns serious when he tells her that he doesn't criticize her for having given Kate a fatal overdose: "I never, ever blamed you. I would have done what you did in your position. Perhaps I should have." As Ellen stares in shock and disbelief, he adds, "It was the right thing to do. It took a good deal of courage. Real courage. Valor. I couldn't say that at the time because of the circumstances" (381).

"Two brilliant fools," Ellen thinks as she realizes suddenly the unthinkable: Kate had deliberately taken the overdose of morphine. Ellen's reconstruction is speculative, but there is no doubt in her mind that her mother had committed suicide, unwilling to endure more senseless pain and burden the family with unnecessary suffering. With the novelist's approval, for there is no ironic distance separating Quindlen from her narrator at the end, as there has been until this moment, Ellen concludes that she didn't believe that her mother "had it in her," implying that the suicide was an act of desperate courage and strength. Ellen decides to withhold the truth from her father, who had also underestimated Kate. "I suppose in some strange way he honored me with his assumption and I was damned if I would tell him otherwise. Let him think of me as a heroine from some little story" (383). Wondering how she could have so misread her mother, Ellen wonders how she could have so misread herself. Her final realization is that "it was possible to love and care for a man and still have at your core a strength so great that you never even needed to put it on display" (386)—a statement that applies as much to Ellen as to her mother.

The Double Effect

Kate's fatal overdose is the fatal flaw of *One True Thing*, the one thing, ironically, that is not true. Few if any oncologists would order an autopsy to determine if a terminally ill patient, whose body was wasted from disease, died of an over-dose of morphine. As Ira Byock states, "With severe pain, there is no maximum dose of pain medication; the right dose is the one that works" (206). In Kate's situation, oncologists would have prescribed as much morphine as necessary to diminish the pain. Doctors are very careful about dispensing narcotics and other prescription drugs, and after Barbara's death the hospice case manager made sure that I returned the unused supply of morphine to her, but there is no hesitation to increase a dying person's pain medication when necessary. And though I didn't know it at the time of Barbara's death, many oncologists would have ordered—with the dying person's or family's permission—sufficient morphine to alleviate the pain even if such a dose would be fatal. This prin-ciple, called by the Roman Catholic Church the "double effect," implies, as bioethicist Margaret Pabst Battin states in her book *The Least Worst Death*, that "one may perform an action with a bad effect—for instance, the death of a person—provided one foresees but does not intend that bad effect; one must be doing the act to achieve a different good effect (hence the name, 'double' effect)" (17). Four conditions must be met to justify the double effect: "the ac-tion must not be intrinsically wrong"; "the agent must intend only the good effect, not the bad one"; "the bad effect must not be the means of achieving the good effect"; and "the good effect must be 'proportional' to the bad one, that is, outweigh it" (17). Battin cites the example commonly used in Catholic moral theology: "a surgeon may remove a cancerous uterus in order to save the life of the mother, though this will also bring about the death of a fetus develop-ing there, provided the surgeon's intention is to save the mother: the surgeon foresees, but does not intend, that the procedure will also kill the fetus" (17). An even more common example is a physician prescribing a massive dose of morphine to allay a terminally ill patient's unendurable pain, knowing that it will lead to death.

Kate's situation meets all four criteria of the double principle, and for this reason no autopsy would have been ordered. Nor would there have been a suspicion of foul play, regardless of a caregiver's stated position on euthanasia. Ellen's legal problem may heighten the plot interest of the novel, but it is not medically realistic. Ironically, given the novel's flawed assumption that a fatal overdose of morphine to a terminally ill patient is illegal, it is surprising that Ellen does not feel resentment toward her mother for potentially implicating the family in a crime. And it is unlikely that a lucid Kate would have taken a fatal overdose had she realized that her actions might lead to her daughter's or husband's arrest, conviction, and imprisonment.

What *is* realistic is Ellen's psychological conflict over euthanasia. Since neither the doctors nor the nurses informed her about the possibility of pre-scribing a massive dose of morphine that would end Kate's suffering and life, Ellen cannot avail herself of this option. Nor is it an option that is often publicly

discussed. As Ian Dowbiggin indicates in *A Merciful End*, a study of the euthanasia movement in the United States, there is often a sharp difference
between what physicians do and say regarding end-of-life care. Dowbiggin's
observation about the 1960s is no less true of the present. "Privately, doctors
often withheld treatment from dying patients or eased them out of their misery. Publicly, however, they tended to dodge the issue and stand behind their
profession's position that the doctor's goal was to try to keep patients alive, not
hasten their departure from this world" (78).

Ambiguities inhere in the double effect. As Bonnie Steinbock observes
in the introduction to her edited volume *Killing and Letting Die*, doctors may
perform a hysterectomy on a pregnant woman if she has cancer of the uterus,
but, by contrast, "a woman whose life is endangered by a pregnancy because
of a heart condition, kidney disease, or tuberculosis may not abort, according
to Catholic law" (13). Dan Brock points out that there is "controversy in the
anesthesia literature about whether heavily sedated persons are actually free
of suffering or are simply unable to report or remember it. Although such patients are probably not conscious of their condition once sedated, their death
is unlikely to be dignified or remembered as peaceful by their families" (133).
The double effect has generated controversy over "how to distinguish direct
and indirect intention, between effects that are intended and effects that are
foreseen but not intended" (17).

Many authors of books on dying and death, such as Sherwin Nuland,
do not mention the double effect, even when they discuss euthanasia and
physician-assisted suicide; those who do discuss the double effect are often
philosophers and bioethicists. Ira Byock does not use the term in his book *Dying Well*, but it is clear from his discussion of a patient named Terry, who is in
horrific pain despite taking "megadoses of morphine," that the decision to give
her an infusion of the drug thiopental will produce a deep sleep from which
she will probably not awake. Both she and her family agree to this, and she
never regains consciousness. Byock concludes his discussion by noting that
the "story of Terry and her family explores the fine line between sedation for
the treatment of extreme terminal pain and euthanasia. . . . People unfamiliar
with the purposes of palliative care may see little difference between sedation
to control persistent physical distress and euthanasia. What may appear philo-
sophically to be a fine line is, in practice, a chasm" (216).

There are also ambiguities about the effectiveness of pain medication.
The oncologist Alan Astrow concedes that "the line between relief of suffering and end of life is often blurred" (45). Despite treating many patients whose
uncontrolled tumors have produced "intractable pain," he nevertheless opposes
physician-assisted suicide, maintaining that in "most instances . . . a with-
drawal of active medical treatment combined with unstinting use of analgesics
and sedatives to control symptoms allows the patient to die comfortably and

peacefully" (45). Astrow doesn't indicate whether "most instances" is closer to 51 percent, 99 percent, or somewhere in the middle. One physician, Ira Byock, *guarantees* that his patients will not suffer physically. "Eighteen years of clinical hospice experience has taught me . . . that physical distress among the dying can *always* be alleviated. The word 'always' in this context may sound facile, but I use it deliberately. Medical care for the dying stops working only when we give up. . . . Pain and other physical symptoms caused by advanced disease usually yield to relatively simple treatment" (215; emphasis in original).

Battin is more guarded, however: "Even a patient receiving the most advanced and sympathetic medical attention may still experience episodes of pain, perhaps alternating with unconsciousness, as his or her condition deteriorates and the physician attempts to adjust schedules and dosages of pain medication. Many dying patients, including half of all terminal cancer patients, have little or no pain, but there are still cases in which pain management is difficult and erratic" (105). Alan Mermann concludes on the basis of his research that 10 percent of terminally ill patients "have the most severe category of pain (severe pain, most of the time) in all categories (except coma)" (96), yet he also asserts, without equivocation, that he can "promise patients that they need not ever feel pain" (99). I have looked through many books and articles on pain management, and only Mermann and Byock seem to make this promise.

Timothy Quill and Margaret Battin cite more disturbing figures at the conclusion of their edited volume *Physician-Assisted Dying*: "Most experts in pain management believe that 95 to 98 percent of pain among those who are terminally ill can be adequately relieved using modern pain management, which is a remarkable track record—unless you are unfortunate enough to be in the 2 to 5 percent for whom it is unsuccessful. However, among hospice patients who were asked about their pain level one week before their death, 5 to 35 percent rated their pain as 'severe' or 'unbearable.' An additional 25 percent reported their shortness of breath to be 'unbearable' one week before death. This says nothing of the physical symptoms that are harder to relieve, such as nausea, vomiting, confusion, and open wounds, including pressure sores, which many patients experience" (323).

Without the promise of effective pain medication and the option of physician-assisted suicide, Ellen feels double guilt: guilt that she wants her mother to die, though for an altruistic reason, and guilt that she cannot act on her beliefs and honor her mother's final request. Nor is the guilt lessened by the fact that, without a fatal overdose, Kate probably would have died within a few days or weeks—Battin reports, for instance, that the estimated life expectancy for patients receiving euthanasia in the Netherlands is usually one or two weeks (*The Least Worst Death* 134). Unable to speak to the doctors, nurses, or her family about her mother's request, Ellen finds herself brooding over it, torturing herself. This alone would be emotionally stressful, quite apart from her exhausting caregiving tasks. In short, watching one's beloved die without being able to help her, without being able to honor her request to die, and without being able to unburden herself by speaking to a friend or therapist, is Ellen's worst torment. Mine too.

"Can You Give Me All the Medication?"

And now I must acknowledge the most distressing moment of Barbara's illness for me, a detail that haunted me for months after her death and that grieves me to this day. Not long before she lapsed into a semicoma, Barbara asked: "Can you give me all the medication?" She asked the question in a weak, barely audible voice, and I had to strain to hear her. Troubled by the question, and not exactly sure what she meant by it, I told her that I couldn't do that. She seemed to accept my answer, to which she offered no response, but a day or two later she made the same request to our children over the telephone, who responded in the same way that I did. Arielle then asked me if I should hide the morphine pills from her mother. The question compelled me, almost against my will, to ask Barbara what she meant by it. "Did you mean that you wanted me to give you a fatal overdose of morphine?" I asked, chilled by my own words, to which she responded, in a whispering voice, "yes." "I can't do that, sweetie; it would be too upsetting to me." After a pause, I added, "Do I need to hide the morphine from you?" "No," she responded, faintly, and we never discussed the subject again.

I'll never know whether Barbara was "in her right mind" when she asked for all her medication, nor what she would have wanted me to do if I had agreed to her request. She was taking so much morphine in the months preceding her death that she was often confused and disoriented. Sometimes her speech was wildly incoherent, and these were the times when she was "not Barbara." In addition, the relentless spread of the disease, and the fact that she was eating and drinking virtually nothing when she made the request to our children and me, suggests, at the least, that she was not thinking clearly. She was never suicidal before her illness, never mentioned suicide in her daily diary entries, and until the end made every effort to conquer the disease. Our friend Len's death was as devastating to her as it was to me, and she knew as well as I did the dark aftermath of suicide. She would not have wanted anyone in the family to do anything illegal, unethical, or morally questionable.

I can only speculate on the reasons for Barbara's question. Perhaps she felt that, like Kate, she could not endure more pain. She may have wished to end our suffering as well as her own. Perhaps she needed the assurance that, should the pain worsen, we would be willing to end it, even if it meant ending her life. Perhaps all these reasons are true. Robert Pearlman and Helene Sparks suggest that "the factors that motivate an interest in assisted death are similar to those that prompt people to complete advance directives and forgo life-sustaining treatment: the desire to control the timing and circumstance of one's death" (98). Such requests, I discovered later, are not uncommon, as Ira Byock explains: "It is a rare person dying of a terminal illness who does not think about suicide. Most often, I have found, persistent thoughts of suicide are really a response to unbearable pain" (44). Eric Cassell makes a similar observation: "Sometimes patients with terminal illness will ask for help in dying. It is important to understand that such requests do not arise because someone wants to die. Rather, the patients would rather die than live as they are" (289). Cassell concedes that "not all suffering can be relieved, no matter how good the care. But most end-of-life care is not good, and with even the very best treatment, the suffering of some patients is terrible and unremitting" (289).

I will always remember the pathos of Barbara's question and the horror that it evoked in me, but it is impossible to know what she was thinking at the time—whether, indeed, she was thinking of anything as she transitioned from life to death. In my efforts to recall precisely the time between her question and lapsing into coma, I confront the mystery of death. Ellen's observation about her mother's situation recalls Barbara's as well: "It had become difficult to tell whether she was awake or asleep under the thin blanket of consciousness, or simply lying with her eyes closed, thinking the unimaginable thoughts that anyone must feel when they are standing on the bluff overlooking the abyss" (Quindlen, 234).

The less Barbara said, the more was left unsaid, and we had come to the end of her speaking days. If, as I suggest to my students, death is the most difficult subject in the world to interpret, silence is the next-to-most difficult. I could not interpret Barbara's silence at the end, a silence that was soon followed by death. Hereafter it was impossible to know what, if anything, she was thinking. We still spoke to her, telling her how much we loved her and that we were ready for her to leave us. We knew that hearing is the last sense to disappear, and so we spoke to her as often as possible. But she could not respond, could not give us a signal that she heard us, could not tell us whether talking to her was welcome or unwelcome. As her body shut down, she withdrew into herself, into the forever unknowable mystery. We were freshmen in Len's English class when I first saw her: she was the beautiful, alluring person who never spoke, whose thoughts remained veiled, whose silence intrigued me. Silence marked the beginning of our relationship; now it marked the end.

Calling Up Ghosts

Like Ellen, I felt so helpless when I was unable to honor a dying person's final request, and I tried to put the question out of my mind. While Barbara was still alive, I do not recall discussing the request for a fatal overdose of morphine with our friends, doctors, nurses, or psychotherapist. Only after Barbara died did I permit myself to discuss this question—and then, paradoxically, I could not stop talking about it. Her suffering was so severe that I felt only relief, not sadness, on the day she died. Afterward came the crushing sorrow and loneliness, which I expected, along with feelings of self-blame, which I did not expect. This self-blame began to lessen only when I realized, as I had not at the time of her request, that I was once again thrust into the same Catch-22 situation produced by Len's telephone call thirty-six years earlier, when he told me he was in the process of committing suicide. In both situations I felt powerless, guilty, and confused. The term "survivor guilt" does not adequately convey the horror of remaining alive when a loved one is dying or dead. Len and Barbara are forever linked for me, both ending their existence with a plea for death.

There were, admittedly, many more differences than similarities between the two situations. Unlike Len's suicide, which was the result (though he denied it) of prolonged depression, Barbara's question about ending her life was rational in the sense that she was terminally ill and wracked by pain. There would have been a legal mechanism for physician-assisted suicide if we were living in Oregon or in Holland. No such mechanism exists in New York State, and as unbearable as it was to watch my beloved wife suffer, it would have been more unbearable to be the agent of her death. I'm not sure I would have been able to give her a fatal overdose even if I was convinced that this was what she wanted me to do.

And yet was it mainly for my own sake that I chose not to give Barbara a fatal overdose? I told her, after all, that it would be too upsetting for *me*: did that mean that I was thinking more about my own needs than about hers? After Barbara's death, I broke down in tears when I told Glenn about my feelings of guilt over her question, and he reminded me that I had taken excellent care of her throughout the long ordeal. When he asked me why I was blaming myself for a situation over which I had no control, blaming myself for simply being human, I realized that I wanted to be not human but God, able to save the person whom I loved more than life itself. As Ellen says in *One True Thing*, "And knowing I could have killed her was nothing compared to knowing I could not save her" (370).

Barbara and I were so close, so devoted to each other, so attuned to each other's feelings, that I rarely felt a conflict between her needs and my own.

Helping her was helping myself. I wanted her suffering to end, as well as our family's suffering, but I could not give her a fatal overdose. Not only would such an action be illegal, but I could never be sure that she was medically competent to make the decision. Moreover, telling Arielle and Jillian that I planned to give their mother an overdose would have made them accomplices. At no time did I discuss with Barbara's doctors and nurses the possibility of a fatal dose of morphine, and I knew nothing at the time about the "double effect."

Was there, then, no way to diminish Barbara's suffering? A week or so after making the request for all of her medication, she lapsed into a semicoma. It was never clear when exactly this happened: the hospice nurses said that it is difficult to tell when this occurs. She lost the ability to swallow about two weeks before her death, and we then had to switch to a new pain management system, a transdermal (across the skin) patch consisting of the narcotic fentanyl, supplemented with liquid morphine, Roxanol, which we gave her every two hours, round the clock, and then, when the pain continued, every hour. The liquid morphine left a bitter taste in her mouth, and she made a gurgling sound whenever we squirted it into her mouth with an eyedropper. Her face would grimace, and her eyes would roll back in her head, giving her a grotesque, almost Frankenstein's monster look. This was the only time that she didn't "look" like Barbara. In the beginning, we would give her a few drops of water to wash away the bitter taste, but when the hospice nurses told us that the water might prolong her life, and therefore her suffering, we decided to withhold that from her in an effort to hasten her death.

We were told that, as a rule, most people can live six minutes without oxygen, six days without water, and six weeks without food. From then on, we began counting the days without water. As we approached the sixth day, we were certain that she would die, but day six came and went, as did days seven, eight, nine, and ten. Since she was unable to ask for water, I never felt that we were acting cruelly. In fact, according to one of the booklets we were given, "A Patient and Family Guide to Hospice Care," the lack of water stimulates painfighting endorphins in terminally ill patients. "Dehydration often happens as a natural part of dying and is not painful. Research shows that the body makes its own natural painkillers when the body begins to dehydrate. This means that dehydration is helpful and eases suffering making dying easier. To force fluids at this time may make the body's heart, lungs and kidneys work too hard. It may also increase swelling, vomiting and lung congestion." I came across a more detailed confirmation of this in Virginia Morris's book *Talking about Death Won't Kill You*. "Studies suggest that when nutrition and hydration intake is reduced, the body releases larger quantities of endorphins, natural pain-relieving and comfort-inducing chemicals. Dehydration, which causes the patient to lapse into a coma and die peacefully, has even been called 'nature's anesthetic'" (135). I felt no guilt about withholding water from her, just as I suspect I would have felt little or no guilt if we had lived in a state that permitted physician-assisted suicide. Only on day eleven did Barbara die; her heart finally stopped beating. A lifetime of excellent health, and a passion for life, ironically worked against her, denying her a faster, more merciful death.

Physician-Assisted Suicide

For years I have been opposed to physician-assisted suicide, believing that "rational" suicide was inherently irrational, but I began to rethink my opposition when I attended a lecture at Union College on October 25, 2004. Gerrit Kimsma, a Dutch general practitioner and a professor of medical ethics at the Free University of Amsterdam, spoke on "euthanasia and end-of-life care in the Netherlands." He began his lecture by observing that he was "perplexed by the heavy emotions" surrounding the controversy. He listed three main categories of end-of-life care: euthanasia, "ending someone's life at a request"; physician-assisted suicide, "helping someone end life at a request"; and alleviating pain and suffering, which he defined as "death in the course of pain treatment." Of the three, he focused almost entirely on physician-assisted suicide, noting that although end-of-life care was still technically illegal in the Netherlands, legislation has granted it a special category, so that physicians will not be prosecuted for assisting terminally ill patients to die provided that strict requirements are met. To qualify, patients must be terminally ill and suffering from unbearable pain, which cannot be relieved in any way. About 85 percent of patients who receive approval for physician-assisted death suffer from cancer, and about one in three requests are honored.

Kimsma discussed the motivation behind physician-assisted death: preventing unbearable suffering, preventing loss of dignity, preventing fatigue without hope, preventing suffocation, and preventing becoming a burden to others. During the question-and-answer period following the talk, I asked him a "slippery slope" question: whether, in his judgment, terminally ill patients are pressured into agreeing to death by their family, who may feel financially and emotionally burdened. "That's an interesting question," he responded, but he thought this was not a problem, partly because terminally ill patients in the Netherlands, unlike those in the United States, qualify for free medical treatment in their homes. Kimsma never fully addressed the possibility that some caregivers might pressure the terminally ill to die for emotional and financial reasons, but he said that the opposite pressure is far more common: caregivers are unable to let their loved ones die, contrary to the latter's wishes. He reported that 90 percent of the Dutch public favor end-of-life care, and that there is the same high support from the medical and nursing professions—unlike their American counterparts, who remain opposed. He observed that there was no

proof of age discrimination—the elderly being pressured into opting for death—
nor was there discrimination against the handicapped or minorities. End-of-
life care treatment, he added, has resulted in increased attention to palliative
care.

One of the most persuasive aspects of Kimsma's presentation was his
moral justification: beneficence, nonmaleficence, respect for the patient's autonomy and dignity (in certain situations, he said, we can be autonomous only
if others help us to be autonomous), and nonabandonment (the physician remains with the patient until death). Sherwin Nuland also offers a sympathetic
discussion of the Dutch approach to end-of-life care. "*Involvement* is the essence
of the thing. Family physicians who make house calls are the primary providers
of medical care in the Netherlands. When a terminally ill person requests euthanasia or assistance with suicide, it is not a specialist to whom he is likely to
go for counsel, or a death expert. The probability is that doctor and patient will
have known each other for years" (156; emphasis in original). Kimsma indicated,
contrary to what I had thought, that physician-assisted suicide aids in the
caregivers' recovery and lessens their own fear of death. In a chapter appearing in *Physician-Assisted Dying*, Kimsma and Evert van Leeuwen state that
their in-depth interviews of terminally ill patients and their families reveal that
physician-assisted death is a positive experience. "The accumulated data suggest that assisted death gives patients and families a greater chance to bring
closure to relationships, more time to prepare for the death of a loved one, and
more interaction with medical and nursing staff, all of which may derive from
greater opportunity to talk openly about death and dying" (235).

Throughout his presentation and the question-and-answer period,
Kimsma struck me as thoughtful and compassionate, and he never engaged in
the "heavy emotions" associated with the controversy. I felt strangely calm and
reassured throughout his talk—not for a moment did I fear being emotionally
overwhelmed, as I often was in the months following Barbara's death. I never
told Barbara's father about her request for all her pain medication toward the
end of her life, but he intimated that he might choose that option for himself
were it legal: "they shouldn't have jailed Dr. Kevorkian," he told me during a
telephone conversation. Kimsma also brought up Kevorkian's name, but not
in a complimentary context: there were no Kevorkians in the Netherlands, he
said, and 85 percent of physician-assisted suicides are done by family physicians. Most bioethicists believe that the sensationalistic Kevorkian has set
back the assisted-death movement by years if not decades. As I was driving
home, I realized that the talk had convinced me that, unlike in the United States,
the Netherlands has succeeded in maintaining a delicate balance between the
duty to protect life and the need for compassion in dying. Regardless of how
one feels about euthanasia and physician-assisted suicide, Sherwin Nuland's
conclusion strikes me as incontrovertible: "As with all issues that deal with hu-

man life, there is no universal answer, but there should be a universal attitude of tolerance and inquiry" (157).

Writing in 1994, Margaret Pabst Battin predicted that the "right-to-die issue, including . . . withholding and withdrawing treatment, assisted suicide, and active euthanasia, will become *the* major social issue of the next decade— that is, the focus of the most volatile public controversy—replacing abortion in that role" (8–9; emphasis in original). That prediction has not come true. In an article published in the *New York Times* on the day when Congress attempted to reverse a federal judge's order to remove a feeding tube from Terri Schiavo, a severely brain-damaged Florida woman who had been in a "persistent vegetative state" for fifteen years, John Schwartz noted that acceptance for physician-assisted suicide appears to be increasing. "Surveys suggest that more than half of Americans find physician-assisted suicide morally acceptable. In a 2004 Gallop survey, 65 percent agreed that a doctor should be allowed to assist a suicide 'when a person has a disease that cannot be cured and is living in pain,' up from 52 percent in 1966" (March 21, 2005). And yet opinion polls in the United States are deceptive, indicating uncertainty. As Ian Dowbiggin states, "Americans endorse a generalized and abstract right to die, but when pollsters ask questions relating to specific medical situations, public support declines" (175). Nor is it easy to craft laws legalizing physician-assisted suicide that will attract large-scale support. Physicians prefer the ambiguities of terminal sedation to the complexities of physician-assisted suicide.

Nevertheless, if the right-to-die movement has not replaced abortion as the single most explosive social issue of the twenty-first century, it remains one of the most controversial medical, legal, moral, and theological questions in the United States. "The 1997 U.S. Supreme Court decision in *Vacco v. Quill* and *Washington v. Glucksberg* gave strong support to terminal sedation, saying that pain in terminally ill patients should be treated even to the point of rendering the patient unconscious or hastening death. Terminal sedation is already openly practiced by some palliative care and hospice groups in cases of unrelieved suffering, with a reported frequency from 0 to 44 percent of cases" (Brock, 132–33). Oregon passed the Death with Dignity Act in 1994 by a margin of 51 percent to 49 percent, and the law was reaffirmed by a higher margin in 1997, but the conservative agenda of President George W. Bush is opposed to physician-assisted suicide, and the executive branch of the federal government immediately challenged Oregon's right to enact the law. As Linda Ganzini's summary of the history of Oregon's Death with Dignity Act makes clear, the issue pits federal rights against states' rights:

In November 2001 U.S. Attorney General John Ashcroft reinterpreted the Controlled Substances Act as prohibiting physicians from prescribing barbiturates with the intent to hasten death. (To date, all deaths by physician-assisted suicide in Oregon have been from barbiturates.) Judge Robert Jones of the U.S. District Court for Oregon issued a restraining order preventing implementation of the reinterpretation. In September 2002 Ashcroft appealed this decision to the U.S. Court of Appeals for the Ninth Circuit, but in May 2004 this appeal was denied. A further appeal to the U.S. Supreme Court seems likely. If the Department of Justice eventually prevails, the physicians who prescribed barbiturates, the only medically prescribed substances that could reliably cause a safe and peaceful death, would run a substantial risk of losing their Drug Enforcement Agency licenses despite the fact that physician-assisted suicide would remain legally permissible under the state's Death with Dignity Act. (166)

Based on Barbara's experience, I now find myself more sympathetic to physician-assisted suicide. If our family had had that option, and if we had been convinced that Barbara was rational when she made her request, she would have been spared days or weeks of unnecessary suffering.

Nine months after Barbara's death, I received a telephone call from her home hospice nurse, Geraldine Breitenstein, who told me that she had been thinking about our family and wondered if she could visit me. I was delighted to hear from Gerry, who was as important to our family as Teresa Guerrero was to Ellen's family in *One True Thing*. I made lunch for Gerry, and we talked for nearly two hours. She told me that Barbara was a special person to her—special in her love for life, her radiant beauty, her devotion to her family, and her many talents—and here Gerry looked up, at the stunning Tiffany-style chandelier that Barbara made, which hangs over the kitchen table where we were sitting. Gerry told me how, shortly before lapsing into a coma, Barbara asked for assistance to walk into the children's bathroom, where she lifted the top of the toilet tank and jiggled the lift chain attached to the top of the rubber flapper, which had become stuck, resulting in the water continually flowing. For years Barbara had worked on that and the other two toilets, using fishing line to connect the bowl refill tube with the flapper. "I'm afraid Jeff isn't too good at fixing these things," she said smilingly to Gerry, who was amazed that a terminally ill patient could be so focused on the practical details of life. Ironically, a day before Gerry's visit I had hired a handyman to replace all three toilets, which were over thirty-five years old, and which all bore traces of Barbara's ingenious maintenance.

I was anxious to speak to Gerry about Barbara's suicide request because for months I had been feeling guilty that I had not shared this information with her. I was flabbergasted by her response. "Oh, yes, you told me about that. We talked about it." I looked at her in disbelief. How could my memory have been so faulty? Did I "forget" this detail—or "repress" it? Prior to Gerry's visit, I had been blaming myself for not telling hospice about Barbara's request when, in fact, I had. Ed Dick, with whom I had lunch two weeks after I saw Gerry, also confirmed that I had spoken about Barbara's suicide question to him. He said that after I had told him about the suicide request, he asked her about the question on the next-to-last time he visited her at our home, when she was still conscious, but he couldn't remember her response.

How could I recall in vivid detail countless incidents during Barbara's illness and have total amnesia about the most disturbing moment? I found myself in the position of an unreliable narrator, revealing one story to readers of *Dying to Teach* while inadvertently concealing another story. Ironically, the story I revealed was far darker and more self-accusatory than the truthful one I concealed. Forgetting that I had shared Barbara's suicide question with Gerry and Ed, I unconsciously made it into a terrible secret, one that caused me unspeakable guilt and self-blame. My only explanation is that the dark shadow of Len's suicide had cast itself over Barbara's suicide request, causing me to conflate the two events. For years neither Barbara nor I spoke about Len's suicide; now memory played a trick on me, forcing me to conclude that, contrary to reality, I withheld knowledge about Barbara's suicide question from the people who were helping us to take care of her.

"Traumatic events are extraordinary," writes Judith Herman in *Trauma and Recovery*, "not because they occur rarely, but rather because they overwhelm the ordinary human adaptations to life" (33). These traumatic events, continues Herman, may involve a "close personal encounter with violence and death." From my conversation with Gerry and Ed, I learned that memory is highly selective and capable of major alteration in a relatively brief period of time. "How victims remember trauma is the most divisive issue facing psychology today," asserts Richard McNally in the opening paragraph of his book *Remembering Trauma*. "Some experts believe that rape, combat, and other horrific experiences are engraved on the mind, never to be forgotten. Others believe that the mind protects itself by banishing traumatic memories from awareness, making it difficult for many people to remember their worst experiences until many years later" (1).

Until Barbara's diagnosis, Len's suicide was the most traumatic event in our lives, and the event had overwritten Barbara's suicide request, replacing my conversations with Gerry in late March 2004 (which I still cannot recall) with the story of Len's death, which I had not shared with anyone for years. Barbara's suicide request was for me a traumatic stressor, which is defined in the *Diagnostic and Statistical Manual of Mental Disorders*, published by the American Psychiatric Association, as involving "actual or threatened death or serious injury, or a threat to the physical integrity of self and others," producing "intense fear, helplessness, or horror" (427–28). McNally notes that terror is not the only traumatic stressor: "Stressors can traumatize by inciting guilt and shame, not just fear" (85). I did not experience the symptoms of post-traumatic stress disorder—intrusive recollections, nightmares, flashbacks, or psycho-physiological reactivity to reminders of the event—but Barbara's suicide question awakened in me the same feelings of guilt, horror, and helplessness that I experienced during and following Len's suicide.

I don't know whether it was weeks or months following Barbara's death that I began misremembering a crucial detail of the story, nor when I began to experience the intense feelings of guilt that I did not feel on the day of her death. But now I know how treacherous memory can be, how, in McNally's words, "postevent misinformation may alter, overwrite, or replace the original memory of the witnessed event" (69). As Laurence Kirmayer suggests, in a striking metaphor, memory is "anything but a photographic record of experience; it is a roadway full of potholes, badly in need of repair, worked on day and night by revisionist crews. What is registered is highly selective and thoroughly transformed by interpretation and semantic coding at the moment of experience" (176).

Gerry also told me, when I asked her if she knew about the double effect, that Barbara was taking enough morphine tablets when she was still able to swallow, and enough Roxanol when she was unable to swallow, to terminate the lives of most patients. Barbara simply did not want to die, Gerry said, no matter how much morphine she was given. In Gerry's view, Barbara was so attached to life that she could not let go. She stated that Barbara's death was one of the most difficult, drawn out deaths she has witnessed—so wrenching, she said, that she would be unable to continue working for hospice if many deaths were like Barbara's.

Gerry helped us to cope with death. Barbara found it easier to talk to Gerry than to me about death—partly because Barbara knew how painful her death would be to me. She also knew that, unlike me, Gerry was experienced with death, seeing it every day in her work. Gerry was not afraid of death. Barbara often asked her whether she thought the end was near, and Gerry would answer, "I don't think so. You're still walking and talking. You're not ready yet," to which Barbara responded, "how will I know when it's time?" "You'll know," Gerry responded reassuringly. Gerry is a gentle, compassionate, and insightful nurse, and while having lunch with her, I was struck by her calmness and serenity, which never failed to help all of us during the long ordeal. We could not have asked for a better nurse, guide, and teacher.

So, too, is Teresa Guerrero a trusted nurse, guide, and teacher to the Guldens. Ellen's statement that she did not kill her mother, though she wished her dead, reminds us that literature allows us to explore feelings and thoughts that may be too dangerous or painful to acknowledge in real life. A play like *Wit* or a novel like *A Farewell to Arms* or *One True Thing* enables us to talk about topics about which we may be reluctant to speak, in the process arriving at a deeper, more truthful investigation of life-and-death issues. Literature heightens our awareness not only of the luminescence of life but also of the darkness into which we inevitably fade. George Gulden is correct when he states that "all fiction takes as its greatest central mystery death, mortality" (145). Had he had been a more perceptive student of literature, he might have realized that literature and life are mutually interdependent and mutually reinforcing. Both can help us to prepare for death.

"Caring for a dying loved one," writes Ira Byock, a former president of the American Academy of Hospice and Palliative Medicine, "is a powerful way to express love, devotion, and reverence. Allowing a spouse or grown child to care for one becomes a final gift from the person dying. The physical acts of caring can help family members in their own grief" (160). Just as Ellen receives this gift from her mother, so did we receive this gift from Barbara. That this gift is fraught with so much pain and sadness does not make it less valuable. Many dying patients fear becoming burdens on their families, as did Kate and Barbara, but Byock is right when he observes that terminal illness makes possible the expression of caregivers' love, devotion, and reverence—a legacy that our family will never forget.

Barbara's death scene may not have been as dramatic as those in *Wit*, *A Farewell to Arms*, or *One True Thing*, but her ending revealed a serenity that was absent from these literary works. Professor Bearing dies without any of her relatives, friends, or students in attendance; Catherine dies and immediately becomes a statue to her frozen-hearted lover; and Kate dies without healing the wounds between her husband and daughter. It is true that Kate's illness serves as a gift to her daughter, who learns how much there is to admire about her mother, but neither her dying nor her death is a gift to her husband, who has been emotionally absent throughout the ordeal. But Barbara's death scene was not only a gift to us but also a profound learning experience. It would be facile to say that she was dying to teach us about the fleeting beauty of life, which must be appreciated precisely because it is so short lived: there is no good explanation for why she had to die from this dreaded disease. Nevertheless, throughout her illness as well as her life she was determined to teach us everything we needed to know to survive without her. There was no dignity in her physically wasting away in front of us, but her spirit did not waste away, nor did love for her family disappear. I hope that when I am lying on my deathbed, I will have learned everything that she was dying to teach.

3
MY EULOGY FOR BARBARA

I decided to write my eulogy in January 2004, when Barbara's doctors told us that she was close to the end. I could have waited until her actual death, but I didn't know whether I could write a eulogy in two or three days, the time interval, according to Jewish custom, between death and burial. Besides, I wanted as much time as possible to write what would surely be the most important speech of my life. And so I wrote a first draft that I continued to revise until her funeral three months later. I wanted to memorialize the woman who had been the center of my universe for four decades. She was not only my wife but also my best friend and soul mate, the person who had transformed my life from the moment we began dating. I had never before written about her— I never had to since we rarely spent a day apart from each other. I also wanted to describe her to those who had not been fortunate enough to know her. Writing was a way to mourn her loss and grieve her death, allowing me to re-create her in heartfelt language, to which I can return again and again whenever I want to be reminded of her beautiful life, a life that will never end for those who knew her.

A Eulogy for Barbara

Barbara and I met in the fall of 1963 in our freshman English class at the University of Buffalo. She was not yet seventeen years old. For me, though not for her, it was love at first sight: I couldn't take my eyes off her long flowing hair, green eyes, high cheek bones, olive complexion, and delicate nose. She had a natural, unself-conscious beauty that never faded, not even after her illness. Two of the black-and-white photos I took of her in 1967 now hang on my office wall at the university; students who walk into my office invariably comment on her exotic features. Barbara and I could not have been more different in class: I spoke incessantly, enraptured by my own words, while she remained silent like the sphinx, which only increased her mystery to me. I was annoyed that she received higher grades on her essays than I did. Early in the semester I told our English teacher, Len Port, how much I liked her, and not long afterward he summoned us to his office. I didn't realize it at the time, but he was a matchmaker: he deliberately failed to appear, and she and I were forced to speak to each other for the first time while waiting for him.

Our relationship began inauspiciously. Our first date was November 22, 1963, a day that no one of our generation will ever forget. After classes were canceled because of President Kennedy's assassination, we decided to see a movie; we were among a handful of people in the theater as we watched Laurence Olivier play Heathcliff in Emily Brontë's *Wuthering Heights*. On our third date I walked her back to the dormitory and asked if I could kiss her goodnight. "No" was her immediate reply. I turned around and left, vowing never to ask her out again. A few months later I broke that promise, and we began seeing each other. When I later told her how hurt I was by her rejection, she replied, "It was a stupid question: you should have just kissed me."

We dated throughout college and were married in August 1968. Barbara's only precondition for marriage was to have a dog. I had been bitten by a German shepherd when I was a child and therefore agreed reluctantly, hoping she would forget my promise. Barbara never forgot anything in her life, and within a few months we acquired the first of five Belgian sheepdogs. I remember little about our wedding except that I didn't want to be there: I wanted to be married but did not believe in marriage rituals. I should add that this was during my adolescent rebellion stage, a stage that continues to this day. I enjoyed our daughters' weddings far more than our own, and I still have not looked at our wedding photos. The one detail that I remember about our wedding is that I asked the bandleader to play the Barbra Streisand song "Never Will I Marry" for our first dance, but he ignored my request, perhaps because he did not appreciate my wry irony.

Two weeks after our wedding I received a phone call from Len, telling me that he was in the process of committing suicide; Barbara and I were devastated by his death. A month later we were in Cornell's graduate library, where I spent most of my time studying. Though she rarely read the *New York Times*, and never the obituary page, a premonition compelled Barbara to do so, and she saw the obituary of Len's wife, Phyllis, who had died, perhaps by her own hand, on his birthday. This was the first but not the only time that Barbara felt the existence of a supernatural force shaping her life.

Barbara began her career as a first grade teacher, but she never liked teaching, and she resigned after receiving tenure. She felt that if she continued teaching, she would never want any children of her own. She believed at the time that she could never love a child as much as she loved our dog Cybele. The night before she gave birth to Arielle in 1973, she started crying, fearing that she had made a great mistake by becoming pregnant. As soon as Arielle was born, however, Barbara felt an immediate and intense maternal bond, which only increased over time. Her devotion to her children and her dogs never wavered. I soon realized that if I were foolish enough to give her an ultimatum between choosing her husband or dog, I would be the one sleeping in the doghouse. She would have loved to be reincarnated as a dog and cared for by a person like herself.

Unlike me, Barbara could do almost everything well, and she had a multitude of talents, interests, and hobbies. Not only did she excel at her professional work, first as a teacher and then as a computer analyst, but she loved arts and crafts. She created a magnificent stained glass chandelier that would have delighted Tiffany, and no one was better at crocheting blankets or knitting sweaters. She made Arielle's exquisite wedding gown, and after finishing it, she sewed into the back of the dress a label with the following words: "For Arielle on her wedding to David Albert, October 7, 2000. Every stitch sewn with love by her mother Barbara Berman, with support from her mother, Jean Lederman Kozinn, and with spiritual guidance from her mother, Sarah Seliznick Lederman." In her diary she wrote: "I think it was a spiritual experience sitting on the bedspread that my grandmother spent two years hand crocheting for me thirty-five years ago and working on Arielle's gown and veil. She would have been proud. So many memories of my grandmother were involved with sewing and making things. I can hear her needle piercing the hatforms as she was working on her millinery. They were works of art."

Everything Barbara made was a work of art, and she was meticulous to a fault. Her eye invariably spotted misweaves and imperfections, and she demanded of others what she expected of herself, which was nothing short of perfection. Once she became upset with a stone mason because he repaired our garage wall without lining up the mortar pattern of the bricks. No one but Barbara could see the difference, but that did not stop her from taking him to small claims court. To support her argument, she took photographs of the other houses on the block, demonstrating that all their mortar patterns lined up perfectly. She won the case. Later she said that she regretted not becoming a lawyer, an ambition our younger daughter, Jillian, has fulfilled. It is not easy living with a person whose standards are so high; she was as mechanically inclined as I am mechanically declined, and I became dependent upon her ability to fix anything. She could repair faulty wiring, broken toilets, temperamental boilers, cracked floor tile, and leaky faucets. By contrast, I was hopeless. Her favorite story about me was the time I spent two hours replacing a head light in our car, only to discover that I had replaced the wrong light. Once in exasperation I said to her, "You're such a perfectionist that I don't understand why you married me." Without hesitation she replied, "I didn't think about it very much." Lucky for me that she didn't.

Barbara was a good person. She befriended nearly everyone with whom she came into contact, and she never forgot to wish a relative or friend happy birthday. Mentioning Barbara's name would invariably bring a smile. If you were Barbara's friend, you were a friend for life, and several credit her for turning around their lives by encouraging them to end abusive relationships or by finding employment for them when they lost their jobs. She was never too busy to bake cookies for friends who were ill or send cards to cheer them up.

Barbara saved everything she received, regardless of whether it had intrinsic value; each object was a treasure that reminded her of a person or an experience. Many married couples argue about money; we argued about whether I was allowed to throw out what I considered junk but what she cherished as family heirlooms: a desk that she had used in elementary school, an unused tire for a car that was now rusting in a junkyard, or a broken typewriter or adding machine that her father had used forty years earlier. She saved all her report cards from elementary school; marbles from her childhood; the letters her parents sent to her when she was in college; old AAA tour books; maps and globes that are now out of date; rocks and seashells from our trips; and even a bath towel, now filled with holes, which her parents gave us when we became engaged. As our children were cleaning out her closets, they noticed bags of dog hair that Barbara intended to weave into a sweater. She was thrifty and self-sacrificing to a fault and preferred to buy gifts for relatives or friends than for herself.

Barbara's worst quality was that she was a worrier, and here we were unfortunately similar. For decades she worried about the health of her mother and father, who are now eighty-nine and ninety, respectively. She worried about events that happened and those that did not. She was grief-stricken when we had to put a dog to sleep, and one of her dying wishes was to have the cremated ashes of her beloved dog Ebony placed in her burial casket. In therapy I learned a new word—catastrophizer—and it immediately resonated within me. Perhaps we were catastrophizers because of our parents, who had difficult lives during the Depression; perhaps we were catastrophizers because we are Jewish and therefore keenly aware of persecution and suffering. For whatever reason, we spent too much time fearing the worst. Both of us were blessed in so many ways—with our children, relatives, friends, work, and with each other.

Catastrophe finally struck on August 12, 2002, one day after our thirty-fourth anniversary, when Barbara was diagnosed with metastatic cancer. No one can explain why Barbara, who could have been a poster child for living a healthy life, and who comes from a long-lived family without any history of cancer, was stricken by such a virulent disease. We were fortunate to have the best medical treatment. No one could ask for a more devoted oncologist than Dr. Fred Shapiro; and we were equally fortunate to have the loving help of my cousin Dr. Glenn Dranoff, through whose influence Barbara was accepted into a clinical trial for an experimental pancreatic cancer vaccine, which almost certainly prolonged the quality of her life by several months.

Shortly after Barbara's diagnosis I received a letter from my dear friend Randy Craig's brother, David, whose wife had died recently after a long battle with breast cancer. David wrote that the last months of their marriage were the happiest of their life, the time when they felt the greatest understanding, contentment, and intimacy. I think that Barbara would agree with me that as close as we were before her diagnosis, we became even closer afterward. Scarcely a day went by without declarations of our love for and devotion to each other. We had always been close with our children, who have also been our best friends, but we became even closer, and our admiration for their husbands became even greater. For the first time in our lives, our children began to parent us. Arielle and Jillian took turns coming home every weekend, as did their husbands, Dave and Alex, and all four unselfishly put their lives on hold in order to prolong Barbara's life. No parents have been prouder of their children than we are of ours.

In one of the most quoted lines of twentieth-century poetry, Sylvia Plath observed in "Lady Lazarus" that "Dying / Is an art, like everything else. / I do it exceptionally well." It is impossible to take comfort in a loved one's suicide: the legacy—or illegacy—of suicide is lifelong anger, guilt, confusion, and sorrow in family and friends. By contrast, dying with courage, strength, and dignity, as Barbara did, makes it easier for loved ones to grieve their loss. Barbara's acceptance of death was her final gift to her family, allowing us to take comfort in a life that was extraordinary to the end. She remained fiercely protective of her children; she would often tell me that she was being tortured by physical pain, but she never expressed this to Arielle and Jillian. She wished to spare everyone from the grief arising from suffering and death. She always had a grateful smile for the nurses in the chemotherapy room, who came to feel a special affection for her. She would bring photographs of our new grandson to show the nurses, and equally important, she would admire the nurses' photographs of their own grandchildren. She always appreciated the help I provided and told me repeatedly that it is more difficult for the caregiver than for the dying person. She never gave up on life, even when life gave up on her.

Barbara and I did not spend much time talking about the unfairness of her illness. We had no regrets about anything except that we did not have more time together. She felt little anger and no bitterness. She died during what would have been the best time in her life, when her children were grown up, happily married to wonderful men, successful in their careers, and beginning families of their own. She delighted in our new grandson, Nate the Great, who filled her heart with joy.

Premature death always raises the most fundamental religious and existential questions, and each person will answer these questions differently. Amid tragedy, those with strong religious faith may have emotional resources lacking in those without religious faith. I wish I could believe that Barbara is now in a better world, that there is a reason for her death, and that one day I will be reunited with her. What I do believe is that she will always be alive to those of us who were privileged to know her. I want to end by quoting a passage from Charles Dickens's novel *Nicholas Nickleby*: "In every life, no matter how full or empty one's purse, there is tragedy. It is the one promise life always fulfills. Happiness is a gift and the trick is not to expect it, but to delight in it when it comes and to add to other people's store of it." Barbara was one of those rare people who increased the store of happiness in the world.

How would Barbara feel if she read my eulogy? I have often wondered about this question. On three separate occasions I asked her if she wanted to read it, and each time tears welled up in her eyes. When I asked her if she thought reading the eulogy would make her sad, she nodded. Perhaps she sensed that I was retreating from her by eulogizing her, preparing for a future in which she would become only a memory, no longer a living character. There may have been other reasons she did not want to read my eulogy of her. John Bayley observes in *The Character of Love* that "when the dying Balzac asked for Dr. Bianchon, one of his own characters, he was putting himself as he slipped out of life in the position of one of his own readers" (237). The opposite may have been true for Barbara. Perhaps she did not want to see herself as a character, a linguistic construction, who would outlive the dying woman on whom the character was based. Perhaps she did not want to see herself as a reader who would be witnessing her own extinction. Perhaps she did not want to be reminded of her impending death. I wanted to immortalize her through my words, but she may have felt too depressed to appreciate the consolations of art. In a different context, Nabokov's Humbert implores readers in *Lolita*: "Imagine me; I shall not exist if you do not try to imagine me" (128). Perhaps

Barbara would have derived a degree of comfort had she been able to imagine her existence in a book.

I had never written a eulogy before, and I had attended few funerals in which the deceased was eulogized. The eulogy is a prose counterpart to its literary cousin, the elegy, a form of lyrical poetry that laments and praises the dead. As Sandra Gilbert observes in *Inventions of Farewell: A Book of Elegies*, "Whether (with Dylan Thomas) counseling readers to 'Rage, rage against the dying of the light' or (with Walt Whitman) taking comfort in the serene arrival, 'sooner or later,' of 'delicate death,' most writers of verse have 'sooner or later' had to face bereavement. Aesthetic assumptions and poetic styles have altered over the centuries, yet the great and often terrifying themes of time, change, age, and death are timeless, even though cultural imaginings of them may differ radically" (25).

I recalled studying in graduate school many of the famous elegies in literature—John Milton's "Lycidas"; Percy Bysshe Shelley's "Adonais," his lament over John Keats's death; and Tennyson's ponderous *In Memoriam*, which was a great source of consolation for Queen Victoria after Prince Albert's death—but I knew little about the eulogy. Only several months after Barbara's death, when I started to research the eulogy, did I realize the extensive body of commentary. Surprisingly, not all eulogies are positive, as Phyllis Theroux notes in *The Book of Eulogies*. She cites several examples of eulogies that are "skillful demolitions" (17), verbal equivalents of homicide. Examples include the sketch of Queen Anne of England (1665–1714) by Sarah, Duchess of Marlboro, whose scathing eulogy would be grounds for a public beheading: "In a word, she had little zeal for the happiness of others . . . and at last preferred her own humor and passion before the safety and happiness of her own people and of all Europe, which she had either not sense enough to see or not goodness enough to regard" (182). Sometimes the deceased's own brutal words are quoted in a eulogy, as when William Herman Knickerbocker cites the poisonous literary pronouncements of Riley Grannan (1868–1908): "He penned the shortest and most lethal book review on record: 'The covers of this book are too far apart.' As well as the shortest and most savage obituary: 'Here lies Frank Pixley—as usual.' Evangelists were 'a he-harlotry of horribles,' and do-gooders were advised: 'If you find a man starving, the least you can do is loan him your umbrella'" (217).

But nearly always eulogies are positive. Indeed, the eulogy is often called "funeral praise," and it is, according to Theroux, the "oldest and, in some ways, least valued of our literary forms. It is practiced by amateurs. When someone dies, it is customary for a member of the family or a friend to 'say a few words,' composed under great duress, about the deceased. Mourners are not literary critics; we will accept any words at all, as long as they are not mean-spirited, or self-serving, and if a particularly moving or graceful tribute is delivered, we are grateful for the balm" (13).

I was indeed an amateur at writing a eulogy, but I was also a literature teacher and scholar, sensitive to language, and therefore I sought to make every word count. I had a limited amount of time to describe Barbara to those who did not know her, and I intended to celebrate her life rather than dwell on the painful details of her death. I wanted to bring smiles to the mourners, but I knew that my words would inevitably bring tears to their eyes: striking the right tonal balance would be a challenge. And so I decided to begin with light reminiscences, which would allow me to maintain my composure, and then I would move slowly toward the final months of Barbara's life, a subject that would make greater emotional demands on everyone in the funeral chapel. Above all, I wanted my eulogy to be as truthful as possible. Most of the funerals I have attended, including my father's, were impersonal and generic, revealing little about the deceased's life. I wanted Barbara's funeral to be different, so that those who attended, regardless of whether they were close friends or distant acquaintances, would learn about her life and what she has meant to our family.

The Work of Mourning

Only after Barbara's death did I read Jacques Derrida's *Work of Mourning*, a collection of essays written to memorialize colleagues and friends, including some of the most influential twentieth-century literary theorists and philosophers, such as Roland Barthes, Paul de Man, Michel Foucault, Louis Althusser, Emmanuel Levinas, and Jean-Francois Lyotard. Derrida died of pancreatic cancer in October 2004, at the age of seventy-four. In an obituary of the French philosopher that appeared in the *Jewish Week* on October 15, 2004, Liel Leibovitz notes that "Jacques Derrida would have been suspicious of this obituary"—largely because in "eulogizing him, one is compelled to explain his theories, and, attempting to do that, one often finds oneself staring at the abyss" (41).

Like many students of literature, I have tried, with varying degrees of success, to understand and appreciate the labyrinthine complexity and at times wilful obscurity of deconstructive criticism, which emphasizes the internal problems of language. For Derrida, these problems lead inevitably to aporia, contradiction, and irresolvable paradox, the point at which a text undermines its own fundamental presuppositions. In his effort to subvert the "metaphysics of presence," Derrida seeks to show that language is always unstable, indeterminate, and illusory: language can never refer to anything beyond itself because there are no ultimate referents or transcendental signifieds. As one of his critics notes, if, as Derrida claims, there is no way for language to escape its own internal contradictions, if there is no foundational reality, and if all texts eventually deconstruct themselves, this radical skepticism leads to an impossible situation: "having deconstructed Humpty-Dumpty, [Derrida's theoretical approach] cannot put Humpty-Dumpty together again" (Abrams 40).

Derrida's *Work of Mourning* is a cautionary tale, relentlessly warning of the dangers of bearing witness and memorializing the dead. In his tribute to Paul de Man, Derrida observes, in characteristically mystifying language, that "speaking is impossible, but so too would be silence or absence or a refusal to share one's sadness" (72). How can one acknowledge the loss of an admired friend without returning to one's own loss? One can't, as he concedes in his tribute to Louis Althusser: "Although I find a certain intolerable violence in this movement that consists in bemoaning one's own death upon the death of a friend, I have no desire to abstain completely from it" (115).

The Work of Mourning is valuable because it reminds us of the potential problems of the eulogy. One cannot entirely avoid these problems, but one can minimize the risks. "In all these essays of mourning," the editors remark, "Derrida is acutely aware of the dangers involved in speaking of the dead in the wake of their death, the dangers of using the dead, and perhaps despite one's own best intentions, for one's own ends or purposes" (6). The danger is especially great, Derrida states in his tribute to Lyotard, when speaking about one's friendship with the deceased, for one then runs the risk of appropriation. Such personal testimony "always risks giving in to an indecent way of saying 'we,' or worse, 'me'" (225). How, then, Derrida asks, can we allow the deceased to speak for themselves when they can no longer speak for themselves? "How to leave him alone without abandoning him? How, then, without further betrayal, to disavow the act of narcissistic remembrance, so full of memories to cry over or to make us cry?" (225). Derrida's answer, though he never uses such an unambiguous word, is to try to avoid exploiting the dead for our own selfish needs, to take responsibility for our words, to preserve the differences between self and other, to affirm the deceased's uniqueness, to resist the tendency to bemoan another's death mainly for self-pity, and to recognize that when we mourn for others, we are mourning for those who are "in us" but already beyond us.

I tried to follow this advice in my eulogy to Barbara. I attempted to tell the story of her life and death as accurately as possible, allowing her wherever possible to speak in her own words, and affirming her uniqueness. I tried not to bemoan unduly my own loss at the expense of her loss. Watching her suffer was the worst part of our family's ordeal, and now that she is gone, tears come to our eyes when we reflect on what she is missing. She is, as Derrida writes, "in us" but forever beyond us. And I tried to be faithful to the "ethics of mourning" about which R. Clifton Spargo writes, which involves remaining "truly dedicated to the memory of the other" (5). Mourning implies, according to Spargo, not only the difficulty posed to memory "by the lapsing significance of the dead," but also the "philosophical acceptance of injustice," thus giving it a "sense of impossibility" (8–9).

Religious Beliefs and Disbeliefs

My students often hear me say that every interpretation reveals something about the interpreter, and I was keenly aware that in speaking about Barbara's life I was also describing my own life, including my perceptions, values, beliefs, and assumptions. "Eulogies are always double portraits," Theroux observes, and "we are aware as much of the eulogist as the eulogized" (14). As I implied in the eulogy, my attitude toward Barbara's death changed but not my disbelief in an afterlife. Unlike the hospice nurses, staff, and volunteers, for whom I have great admiration, and who without exception used the euphemistic word "pass," I prefer the stark honesty of "die." So does Patricia O'Connor. "In situations where people need sincerity, what do they get? Denial. There's no shame in saying somebody died, but the vocabulary of mortality avoids it" (174). "Pass" also has spiritual implications that I do not share: I believe that our journey begins with birth and ends with death. I don't tell my students whether they should use "pass" or "die" in an essay, but I do point out to them the different connotations and implications of each word. Since language both reflects and shapes our belief—or disbelief—system, I used "dying" and "death" throughout Barbara's illness.

I am in a small minority, for most people avoid using the word "die." In his column "The Death Beat" published in the July 8, 2002, issue of the *New Yorker*, Mark Singer reports on the Fourth Great Obituary Writer's Conference, in which a federal judge offered examples of euphemisms for "die," including "ushered to the angels," "passed from this plane to a higher plane," "made his transition," "passed into life's great adventure," "received his final marching orders," "departed this life on his Harley-Davidson," "graduated to phase two of God's eternal plan," and "became a handmaiden of God." It is easy to laugh at some of these examples, but it is hard to avoid euphemisms entirely. For example, I now refer to Barbara as my "deceased" rather than "dead" wife.

Barbara's parents are both religious, and when she was growing up she went on Saturday mornings to a Conservative temple in Borough Park, Brooklyn, a neighborhood that was predominantly Jewish both then and now. (All but one of the families in her large apartment building were Jewish.) She developed a deep appreciation for the rituals, songs, and traditions of Judaism. Few girls were bat mitzvahed in the late 1950s, and had she been born a decade or two later, she would have almost certainly undertaken this rite of passage, as did our daughters. I was bar mitzvahed in Long Island, where I grew up, and I can vaguely recall my rabbi telling my parents at the time that he thought I should become a rabbi; but I quickly lost whatever religious faith I had, though not my identification as a secular Jew. In many ways I resemble a Talmudic scholar, poring over the meaning of an obscure literary text and arguing with other commentators. Jews are called "people of the book," a statement with which I strongly identify. Had Barbara been married to a more religious man, she might have observed the Jewish rituals and perhaps retained a stronger belief in God. She might have also had an easier time accepting death. As Barbara Younoszai observes, "Whether a very religious person believes in one of the world's great religions or another, less widely known faith, some studies suggest that he or she may be prepared to accept death with more equanimity" (70). In the last months of her life, I could hear Barbara tell her father on the telephone that one day they would all be together again, but I don't know if she believed that or was telling him what he wanted to hear.

I always took it for granted that Barbara was a disbeliever, like me, but she disagreed with me on one notable public occasion. In February 2003, her deteriorating health forced her to resign from work. Three months later, when she was feeling better, her colleagues made her a retirement party. Unable to speak above a whisper—she had a paralyzed vocal cord that was unrelated to her cancer—she asked me to give everyone an update on her condition and to express her gratitude for the many kindnesses she received from her supervisors and coworkers. Toward the end of my impromptu speech I stated that we were grateful for the many people who told us that they were praying for Barbara, although neither she nor I believed in God. "Speak for yourself," she remonstrated, which prompted everyone to laugh.

My cousin Glenn's religious views could not be more different from my own. Deeply religious and mystical, he believes that everything happens for a reason. He sees no contradiction between science and faith. I invariably ask him spiritual questions whenever I see him, from which he concludes that I must be spiritual too. If one can be spiritual without believing in God, perhaps I am. It was through Glenn's influence that I began rereading the Old Testament during Barbara's illness, but although I was moved deeply by the story of Job, I don't think it made it easier for me to accept her death. And yet like so many others struggling to understand the meaning of suffering, I find myself drawn again and again to the Book of Job, which, unlike the Christian Bible, does not justify pain as a preparation for the afterlife. "Teach me, and I will be silent," Job says to God, "make me understand how I have gone wrong" (6:24). Job is silenced at the end of the story, acknowledging that no human can understand God's ways. As oncologist Jerome Groopman states in *The Measure of Our Days*, "of all the issues wrestled with by the rabbis in the Talmud and later, the meaning of suffering was one that they concluded was unanswerable. It remained an enigma why suffering in this life had to be; it was not rationalized by an afterlife. Indeed, heaven and hell were not prominent in Jewish belief, and purgatory did not exist" (146).

Soon after Barbara's diagnosis I began reading books about dying and death. The most compelling—and disturbing—was Sherwin Nuland's *How We Die*, an eloquent study by a surgeon who has an encyclopedic knowledge about the subject. No novelist or poet could improve upon Nuland's personification of cancer:

> Cancer, far from being a clandestine foe, is in fact berserk with the malicious exuberance of killing. The disease pursues a continuous, uninhibited, circumferential, barn-burning expedition of destructiveness, in which it heeds no rules, follows no commands, and explodes all resistance in a homicidal riot of devastation. Its cells behave like the members of a barbarian horde run amok—leaderless and undirected, but with a single-minded purpose: to plunder everything within reach. This is what medical scientists mean when they use the word *autonomy*. The form and rate of multiplication of the murderous cells violate every rule of decorum within the living animal whose vital nutrients nourish it only to be destroyed by this enlarging atrocity that has sprung newborn from its own protoplasm. In this sense, cancer is not a parasite. Galen was wrong to call it *praeter naturam*, "outside of nature." Its first cells are the bastard offspring of unsuspecting parents who ultimately reject them because they are ugly, deformed, and unruly. In the community of living tissues, the uncontrolled mob of misfits that is cancer behaves like a gang of perpetually wilding adolescents. They are the juvenile delinquents of cellular society. (207–8)

Nuland's book was almost too painful on the first reading. I found his descriptions of dying frighteningly graphic, and I did not want to accept his thesis that death with dignity seldom occurs: "The belief in the probability of death with dignity is our, and society's, attempt to deal with the reality of what is all too frequently a series of destructive events that involve by their very nature the disintegration of the dying person's humanity. I have not often seen much dignity in the process by which we die" (xvii). I raced through *How We Die*, partly because I did not want to absorb its chilling observations and conclusions, and also partly because I did not want Barbara to see me reading a book whose blunt title, appearing in bold letters, looked like a bludgeon. I reread Nuland's book shortly after her death and found myself agreeing not only with his descriptions of the final state of terminal cancer but also with his many wise statements about how we can prepare for death, including learning as much as possible: "Better to know what dying is like, and better to make choices that are most likely to avert the worst of it. What cannot be averted can usually at least be mitigated" (143). Nuland argues, on the one hand, that patients and their caregivers should pursue every opportunity for cure or effective treatment—"It behooves every patient to study his or her own disease" (260)—and, on the other hand, that "heroic" measures for cure may interfere with a patient's wish to die. I began to understand and accept his paradoxical statement that "hope can still exist even when rescue is impossible" (241). Most of all, I agree with his conclusion that dignity arises not from the process of death but from the way in which we have lived. "The greatest dignity to be found in death is the dignity of the life that preceded it. This is a form of hope we can all achieve, and it is the most abiding of all. Hope resides in the meaning of what our lives have been" (242).

Writing as Healing

It was both hard and easy to write the eulogy—hard in that I didn't know how to summarize in a few words a lifetime spent with Barbara, and easy in that the words flowed as if they had a life of their own once I started. This flow was not like Sylvia Plath's striking metaphor of art as bloodletting: "The blood jet is poetry / There is no stopping it," she affirmed in her poem "Kindness" (270). Rather, as I was writing the eulogy, I was aware of my attempt to bring Barbara back to life even as her life was ending: perhaps every eulogy is an effort to immortalize a mortal being. If I could not prevent her from dying, then at least I could keep her memory alive to readers, including her children and grandchildren. I could also provide a degree of comfort to those who mourned Barbara's death. This is indeed one of the main purposes of the eulogy, as Jill Werman Harris states: "Eulogies are a consolatory art, offering the interpretation and emotional support that a profound crisis often requires. They comfort the bereaved and are enormously cathartic for the eulogist, providing an opportunity to release the powerful emotions brought on by the death of a loved one. As Longfellow wrote, 'The friends who leave us do not feel the sorrow of parting, as we feel it, who must stay, lamenting day by day.' By remembering the dead, that sorrow is somehow transformed, the anguish transcended if only momentarily" (xvii).

As Judith Harris notes in *Signifying Pain*, "Writing about painful experiences defends against world-dissolving powers that often accompany trauma, depression, and mourning" (1). Harris demonstrates eloquently that words "can serve to allay anxiety and dread; they can begin to lift the oppressive weight of dolorous moods and infirmity" (2). To accomplish this, the writer "must be opened to vulnerability, to innerness and permeability to grasp the edge of words, even when that edge is harrowing in its impermanence: hovering between death and life" (2). Malcolm's lines to Macduff in Shakespeare's *Macbeth*— "Give sorrow words. The grief that does not speak / Whispers the o'er-fraught heart, and bids it break" (4.3.208)—characterize one of the purposes of the eulogy: to speak the grief that might otherwise break the heart. Increasingly, writers from widely differing disciplines have penned memoirs in which they open up their vulnerability to readers: examples include William Styron's *Darkness Visible*, Kay Redfield Jamison's *An Unquiet Mind*, Andrew Solomon's *Noonday Demon*, and Sharon O'Brien's *Family Silver: A Memoir of Depression and Inheritance*. The belief in writing as a form of healing is shared by a growing number of creative writers, literary theorists, and clinical and experimental psychologists, including James Pennebaker, whose influential study *Opening Up: The Healing Power of Expressing Emotions* provides impressive documentation of the therapeutic value of writing. Two books entitled *The Writing Cure*, one written by the well-known Lacanian literary critic Mark Bracher, the other edited by experimental psychologists Stephen Lepore and Joshua Smyth, affirm the educational, psychological, and physiological benefits of writing. "All sorrows can be borne," writes Isak Dinesen, "if you put them into a story or tell a story about them" (qtd. in Arendt, *The Human Condition* 175).

It was easier to write my eulogy of Barbara than it was to read the words aloud, for each time I recited the speech in the privacy of my home office, I welled up in tears. I found my voice shaky even when reading the lighter moments of the eulogy, which I included to show her perfectionist side. I knew that I would be deeply disappointed if I could not read the eulogy at the funeral. I was so anxious that I thought about taping the eulogy in advance and then playing it at the funeral, but that struck me as staged. Reading the eulogy at the funeral took on the same importance to me as taking care of Barbara during her illness: I did not want to fail.

And so with Barbara's approval, I decided to read the eulogy to my writing class, both as a trial run and as a way to offer students my own example of risky writing. They had been sharing their personal writings with me throughout the semester, and I wanted to reciprocate. I have discovered in every personal writing class that self-disclosure begets self-disclosure. Moreover, I believe in the adage that authors write best from their own experience. Here was a real-life experience in which all of my students would find themselves one day: confronting the specter of death from the point of view of the dying person or the caregiver. Here was an opportunity to describe, to others and myself, how and why Barbara has meant the world to me, and how my world would be forever changed by her death. Here was an opportunity to put into practice the adage I give to my writing students every class: show instead of tell; use concrete details; avoid clichés; compress your language; revise until every sentence is grammatically correct and stylistically graceful; and make the reader *see* your story. Above all, I wanted to write truthfully, which means not only engaging the minds and hearts of readers but also describing my wife without distorting or idealizing her life. It is always problematic when writers are too close to their subjects, when they are so much "in love with" their characters that they cannot see their human failings. I was indeed in love with my subject, but the challenge was to allow my students to see Barbara as I have seen her, and to convey to them, as I would later convey to the mourners attending her funeral, her special qualities.

I have been teaching since the early 1970s, and I often discuss with students personal issues that bear upon a course's curriculum. To discuss a subject, one must first achieve distance from it: such distancing inevitably helps us to achieve perspective and find solutions to a problem. Students often identify with their teachers' personal stories in ways that are both educationally and psychologically useful. The best way to understand a story is to teach it; I learn from the process of teaching. Similarly, sometimes the best way to explore a personal issue is to find a way to connect it thematically with a class reading or writing assignment. Teaching, like reading and writing, can be a powerful form of problem solving.

I am not the only person who finds teaching indispensable to psychological health. An extreme example may be found in *Man's Search for Meaning*, Viktor Frankl's memoir of his life in a concentration camp. "It is a peculiarity of man that he can only live by looking to the future—*sub specie aeternitatis*. And this is his salvation in the most difficult moments of his existence, although he sometimes has to force his mind to the task" (72–73). During one of his bleakest moments, when he was almost in tears from pain and bitterly cold from limping from the concentration camp to a work site, Frankl kept thinking of the unbearable conditions of his existence and wondering how he would have the strength to continue. To survive, he forced himself to imagine a future in which he was no longer imprisoned in the death camp:

> Suddenly I saw myself standing on the platform of a well-lit, warm and pleasant lecture room. In front of me sat an attentive audience on comfortable upholstered seats. I was giving a lecture on the psychology of the concentration camp! All that oppressed me at that moment became objective, seen and described from the remote viewpoint of science. By this method I succeeded somehow in rising above the situation, above the sufferings of the moment, and I observed them as if they were already of the past. Both I and my troubles became the object of an interesting psychoscientific study undertaken by myself. What does Spinoza say in his *Ethics*?—"Affectus, qui passio est, desinit esse passio simulatque eius claram et distinctam formamus ideam." Emotion, which is suffering, ceases to be suffering as soon as we form a clear and precise picture of it. (73–74)

The Holocaust is an incomparable event in history, the horror of horrors, and I don't wish to equate Frankl's situation with my own. Nevertheless, as Parkes and Weiss state at the opening of their book, "Bereavement, the loss by death of someone loved, is the most severe psychological trauma most people will encounter in the course of their lives" (ix). Losing one's spouse, Bernie Siegel notes, places one's own health in jeopardy, heightening the risk of "cancer or other catastrophic illness in one or two years. Recent studies have confirmed that grieving spouses have depressed immune systems for over a year" (74). Lynn Caine reports a 1984 study indicating that the "mortality rate for widowed persons under age forty-five is seven times higher than for non-widowed persons" (20). An article in *Newsweek* states that "surviving spouses die at twice the normal rate during the first year of bereavement, as they become more isolated and less motivated to take care of themselves—and the risk of suicide increases 22-*fold* for people whose spouses take their own lives" (April 25, 2005; emphasis in original). Just as Frankl imagined a time when he would be lecturing on the Holocaust, so did I foresee a situation in which I would describe to my students my wife's life and our preparations for her death. One day my students would surely find themselves in similar situations, and my story about Barbara might help them understand and cope with their own experiences.

I am not the only English professor to talk about his deceased wife. Virginia Morris reports, though without providing documentation, that Richard Sewall, a distinguished Yale English professor and biographer of Emily Dickinson, spoke about his wife, who died of pancreatic cancer. "In his talk, Richard said that his wife's final year 'was the most educational year of my life, the high-water mark of my experience as a human being,' for it was during that year that he learned not to be embarrassed about talking about love or about death. And it was during that year that he learned that the ending, sad as it is, is what gives meaning to all that comes before. Borrowing lines from Emily Dickinson, he explained, 'There's something in the flight / That clarifies the sight'" (6).

It is not likely that Professor Sewall read his wife's eulogy to a writing class—I have never heard of a college teacher doing this. Nor are teachers advised to share their personal crises with students, as Elaine Showalter writes in her useful book *Teaching Literature*: "Dumping our woes on our students, whether the pain of an illness or an ongoing divorce, is never a good idea. Stoicism at these private moments is its own best reward" (134). After Barbara's death I discovered that although teachers share many aspects of their lives with students, death is not one of them. For example, in an article appearing in the March 18, 2005, issue of the *Chronicle of Higher Education*, Jonathan Silin, a member of the graduate faculty at the Bank Street College of Education in New York City, acknowledges that he has not revealed to his students the death two years earlier of his lifelong companion, despite the fact that for the past twenty years Silin's professional writings have combined intensely personal and highly theoretical components. "I worried that such a disclosure would place an undue burden on them—students whom I don't know well and many of whom are struggling to become adults. Would a perception of my vulnerability affect their ability to challenge me and test their own ideas against my own? I was not willing to risk becoming another person for whom they would need to care, nor did I trust my ability to handle the complex emotions that such an announcement might evoke in my students or me." At the end of the article, however, he admits that he has begun to question his "self-imposed silence in the classroom," particularly because of his commitment to "transparency as an essential way of prompting students to examine their assumptions about teaching and learning." Silin's silence is representative of teachers' reluctance to share their death experiences with students. Even psychologically oriented teachers and mental-health professionals adhere to this silence. On March 16, 2005, I sent a query to PSYART, the literature and psychoanalysis listserv moderated by Norman Holland of the University of Florida at Gainesville. Only three of the more than eleven hundred subscribers acknowledged speaking about relatives' or friends' death to students.

Lack of precedent did not seem a good reason to avoid reading the eulogy to my students. There was nothing in the eulogy that struck me as too private or personal for a public audience. There was, admittedly, a performative aspect of the eulogy in that I wrote it for an audience. But why shouldn't that audience include students as well as relatives and friends? In reading the eulogy to my writing class, I sought to create what Ken Bain calls a "natural critical learning environment" in which "people learn by confronting intriguing, beautiful, or important problems, authentic tasks that will challenge them to grapple with ideas, rethink their assumptions, and examine their mental models of reality" (18). Bain includes many exercises to stimulate students' personal and intellectual development, and he cites a medical school professor who encourages her students to "confront their own mortality and the frailties of the human condition, a reality in which people do die, and a profession that must care both for healing and for helping people and their families face the inevitable with dignity and peace" (90). One of my doctoral students, Cailin Brown, regularly gives her writing students an assignment that she herself received when she was a young journalist: writing one's own obituary. I have never asked my students to do this, or to write a self-eulogy, but I think there is value to both assignments.

Would a class of writing students regard hearing a teacher's eulogy as conducive to a natural critical learning environment? This is one of the many questions I had about the pedagogical experiment. No subject is more difficult to write about than death. In *Diaries to an English Professor* I wrote about my mentor's suicide, but now I was writing about a death in process, a much harder challenge. Should teachers share such personal writing with students? Would it be painful for them to hear the eulogy? *Too* painful? How would hearing the eulogy change the students' perception of their teacher and affect their future writings? To what extent would hearing the eulogy be an educational experience? Would it motivate students to write about their own experiences with death? The only way I could answer these questions was to read the eulogy to my students and then invite their responses.

4
AN OPTIONAL
WRITING ASSIGNMENT

Most of my colleagues, along with a few graduate and undergraduate students from previous courses, knew about Barbara's illness, but I hadn't informed anyone in the Expository Writing course I taught in the spring of 2004. I didn't feel the need to tell them about her illness, as if it were a professional or personal duty, which it clearly was not. Nevertheless, I knew that sooner or later they would find out about her death, and I wanted to tell them myself rather than have them learn about it from someone else. I decided to tell them in early March, when Barbara's doctors and hospice nurses told us that death was imminent. The students were writing essays that week on "The Dark Side of Diversity," the chapter in *Risky Writing* that explores undergraduates' ambivalence toward their own race, class, gender, or religion. I announced at the beginning of the class that I wanted to reserve the last twenty minutes of the hour for reading an essay that I had just written. The students seemed mildly puzzled, but no one said anything. The class proceeded as usual, and then my turn came. In a quiet, measured voice I revealed that my wife was terminally ill with cancer and close to death. I told them that I wanted to share with them the eulogy that I hoped I would be able to deliver at her funeral. Anyone who wished to leave class before hearing the eulogy could do so, I added. Finally I said that the class would be over when I finished reading the eulogy. And with that, I began.

During the reading I didn't lift my eyes from the copy of the eulogy on my desk. I didn't dare look up, fearful that I would be unable to continue reading if I saw anyone teary eyed. I could hear several students from different sides of the classroom fighting back sobs, but apart from that there was eerie silence, quite different from the ubiquitous white noise of the classroom. On three occasions I could hear my voice falter and break, but each time I paused, regained my composure, and resumed the reading. I thanked my students when I finished, and everyone quietly walked out of the classroom. On the way back to my office, I passed a colleague, who asked me how my class had been; "Okay," I responded neutrally, without elaboration.

It was difficult to read aloud the eulogy, but afterward I felt better, the way nearly all of my students feel after reading aloud their own emotionally charged essays. I felt exhausted and drained from the reading but also relieved, for no longer did I need to conceal Barbara's illness from my students. Finding the words to express my feelings, and then reading those words aloud, helped me to remain in control. My students' silence struck me as profoundly respectful, but I couldn't be sure how they felt unless I found a way to ask them. I knew from years of teaching experience that most students are reluctant to speak in class, even in self-disclosing courses. I wanted them to have the time to reflect on their feelings, which is why I ruled out an in-class essay, and I also wanted them to have the opportunity to remain anonymous so that they could be as truthful as possible. I did not want to require them to write about their feelings, and so I decided to make the assignment optional. I handed out to them the following assignment at the beginning of the next class:

> Last week I read to the class the eulogy I have written for my beloved wife, who is now close to death. It was wrenching for me to read it aloud, and I would like to know how you felt about the reading. If you would like to share your responses with me, you may do so in an optional essay. Please discuss any or all of the following questions. Did you think that it was appropriate for me to read the eulogy to you? How did you feel when you heard me read it? Was it painful to hear? *Too* painful? Did I disclose too much of my private life to you? Did the eulogy change your impression of me? Would your response to the eulogy have been different if you read it instead of hearing me read it? Do you think that my reading of the eulogy will change your feelings about the course? If so, how? To what extent did hearing the eulogy encourage you to reflect upon relatives' or friends' deaths?
>
> I would like your essays to be anonymous so that they will be as honest as possible. Here's the procedure I would like you to follow. If you decide to write the essay, it will count toward the required forty pages (you can receive up to three pages of credit for the essay), but it will not contribute toward your grade. Don't put your name on the essay. Please submit it to me no later than next Tuesday. I won't be handing these essays back to you, and I may decide to include some of the anonymous comments in a future essay on how my students responded to the eulogy.
>
> When you submit the folders containing all your writings at the end of the semester, simply indicate how long your optional essay was, and I will credit that toward the forty pages. In a week or two I'll summarize the class's response to the eulogy and my feelings about reading it to you.

Human Research

I wasn't certain that I would later write about my students' reactions to the eulogy, and therefore I did not consult the University Institutional Review Board (IRB), which must approve all human research. Only later did I seek and receive IRB approval. But I tried to be as sensitive to my students' well-being as possible, which is why I made the assignment both optional and anonymous. I told my students that they might consider changing the font of their printers so that their essays would not resemble their earlier or later writings.

For more than a decade I have encouraged my students to write about their lives, and I have tried to determine, as accurately as possible, how that writing has affected them. In conducting ethnographic research, I have written about my students' lives while safeguarding their privacy. IRB approval requires researchers to receive "informed consent" from their subjects, in this case, students taking an undergraduate writing course. The four basic principles of biomedical research, as defined by Tom Beauchamp and James Childress in their authoritative textbook, include "(1) *respect for autonomy* (a norm of respecting the decision-making capacities of autonomous persons), (2) *nonmaleficence* (a norm of avoiding the causation of harm), (3) *beneficence* (a group of norms for providing benefits and balancing benefits against risks and costs), and (4) *justice* (a group of norms for distributing benefits, risks, and costs fairly)" (12; emphasis in original). These principles inform my own work.

Yet no matter how careful investigators are, all ethnographic research involves potential risks. As G. Thomas Couser points out, the representation of vulnerable subjects in life writing is fraught with ethical difficulties, some of which remain even when writers receive informed consent from their subjects. Couser quotes Ruthellen Josselson's statement that "language can never contain a whole person, so every act of writing a person's life is inevitably a violation" (14). "Truth" is complex, elusive, and ambiguous; to convey the truth of students' responses to their teacher's emotionally charged eulogy inevitably involves a degree of oversimplification, both on their part and my own.

Teacher and student also risk increased vulnerability. "When you write vulnerably, others respond vulnerably," Ruth Behar observes, adding that the "practitioner of emotional writing," including herself, is "sometimes at a loss to say how much emotion is bearable within academic settings" (16–17). Many of Behar's questions in *The Vulnerable Observer* bear upon my own teaching and writing. "What is the writer's responsibility to those who are moved by her writing? . . . Should I feel good that my writing makes a reader break out crying? Does an emotional response lessen or enhance intellectual understanding? Emotion has only recently gotten a foot inside the academy and we still don't know whether we want to give it a seminar room, a lecture hall, or just a closet we can air out now and then" (16–17). These are difficult questions to answer, since they depend largely on the specific contexts in which they are asked. I hoped my students' responses would answer some of these questions.

"I Will View My Future Professors Differently"

Fifteen of the twenty-two students who heard me read the eulogy turned in essays. They were generally well written, containing fewer grammatical and stylistic errors than earlier writings. (As with the diaries and essays appearing in my other books, I have not edited my students' prose.) The disclosure of my wife's illness stunned all fifteen. They felt that the eulogy gave them insight into my personal life and that I was no longer simply a "teacher" to them. "The eulogy definitely changed my impression of you," one student wrote.

> I knew little about your life before you read it. My impression was that you were a man who just did his job every Tuesday and Thursday by teaching this class to us. I knew you had a wife, children, and a grandson. I figured you had a house too. I figured you spent much time with your family and had hobbies like reading, writing, and jogging. I had no idea Barbara was so ill. I had no idea that so much of your time was spent caring for her and spending with her the last days you will have with her here on this earth. This isn't something we students think about professors. Maybe I have had professors who have endured the same tragedy you are enduring now at the time they taught me, but they never let us know it. I think that after hearing the eulogy you wrote for Barbara, I will view my future professors differently.

I had assumed, before giving the optional assignment, that greater knowledge of a teacher's personal life would result in demystification and dei-dealization. English teachers, after all, are seldom idealized in novels and films. Many English professors who appear in plays and novels about dying and death come across as self-absorbed, vain, and unempathic, as in Margaret Edson's play *Wit* and Anna Quindlen's novel *One True Thing*. There are a few positive portrayals, such as the benevolent portrait of Mr. Chips and the pedagogue whom Tobias Wolff describes in his novel *Old School* (which resembles his 1989 memoir, *This Boy's Life*):

> How did they command such deference—English teachers? Compared to the men who taught physics or biology, what did they really know of the world? It seemed to me, and not only to me, that they knew exactly what was most worth knowing. Unlike our math and science

teachers, who modestly stuck to their subjects, they tended to be poly-maths. Adept as they were at dissection, they would never leave a poem or a novel strewn about in pieces like some butchered frog reeking of formaldehyde. They'd stitch it back together with history and psychol-ogy, philosophy, religion, and even, on occasion, science. Without pan-dering to your presumed desire to identify with the hero of a story, they made you feel that what mattered to the writer had consequence for you, too. (5)

This exalted image of the teacher was true for at least one of my students, who wrote without apparent irony:

When I was younger, I always viewed teachers with the notion that they were demigods. Not in a mythological sense, but in the sense that they were amazing in their own right. Teachers not only possess an im-mense amount of knowledge, but they stand on a pedestal that no one can touch. They never display emotion and they seem to be on top of every situation that comes across their path. Though they can be sym-pathetic and empathetic, their own lives remained shrouded in mystery as they arrived and left each day for class. Teachers never came from the neighborhood; they lived in a distant land unattainable to the normal man. You could even go so far to compare teachers to super heroes. If you lived next door to one, you would never know it. Here they are mak-ing the world better each day and you would have no clue that these were the same people next door. So when you read your eulogy to the class you didn't step off that pedestal. You looked down from it and for once in my life I was able to see you as the person you are underneath the teacher exterior. You will always be Mr. Berman in my eyes, but in my heart I was able to catch a glimpse of Jeff Berman. The emotions that formed in your eyes showed me that you're still a man.

The above response surprised me because I had never imagined teachers and professors having the same prestige as "professionals" such as doctors and lawyers, whose salaries and status are far higher. Nor had I imagined college students being awed by their instructors. Few academic novels describe teachers as demigods to their students: such idealization, when it occurs in literature, usually leads to swift devaluation.

Twelve of the fifteen students reported that they cried during the read-ing, and a thirteenth wrote that "listening to your words was difficult for me; I had a huge lump in my throat for its entire duration." It is culturally more ac-ceptable for women to cry than for men, and in *Empathic Teaching* I reported that over the years I can recall many female students crying in class but no male students. Nevertheless, the men in the class seemed to be equally emotional, as the following description suggests:

> From the very first few lines, some people were tearing. After a couple of minutes, I was crying. Insecurity caused me to check if I was the only male crying. I wasn't. I looked around the room at the faces of my classmates. . . . Many people were crying as if they had known his wife. To be honest, I felt like I knew her. When the eulogy ended, I was speechless. Again, I glanced at my peers. Some girls had their heads buried in their hands. Most were visibly distraught. Professor Berman thanked us, and everyone left the class in silence. Outside, I ran into my friend, and we spoke outside of the bathrooms. Every few seconds, a girl from class would come out, having adjusted their make-up.

Nearly all the students indicated that they could hear the emotionality of my voice. The eulogy would not have been as powerful if they had read it to themselves. "My response to the eulogy would have differed had I merely read it; he bares his soul on paper, but he bares his love when he speaks his words aloud." Remarked another, "If I had read the eulogy myself and had not heard it read to me, my response would undoubtedly have been different. Though I would've cried either way, it was more painful to hear it read by the man who wrote it. To see right in front of you any one person's love, despair, and pain is heart wrenching. To read it on my own, I would have cried for a pain that I imagined. It wouldn't have been the same." One person attributed more emotional control to my reading than I felt. "I can imagine the content was wrenching to write about, but you exercised control over your words. Not once did it sound as if the emotion was overtaking the words, on the contrary, the words held the emotions."

The eulogy reproduced in my students the grief, shock, and horror of my family situation: in effect, my emotions "infected" them. Elaine Hatfield and her associates define emotional contagion as the "catching" of another person's emotions. Their book emphasizes rudimentary or primitive emotional contagion, "that which is relatively automatic, unintentional, uncontrollable, and largely inaccessible to conversant awareness." Implicit is the tendency automatically to "mimic and synchronize facial expressions, vocalizations, postures, and movements with those of another person and, consequently, to converge emotionally" (5). Many empirical studies document the existence of emotional contagion. In general, negative emotions are more "contagious" than positive ones, and gender is a factor in that women are more susceptible than men to "catching" emotions.

The eulogy was painful for all the students. Many felt implicated in my story, demonstrating, as Shoshana Felman and Dori Laub observe in their book

Testimony, that the "listener to trauma comes to be a participant and co-owner of the traumatic event: through his very listening, he comes to partially experience trauma in himself" (58). I don't know whether it would be accurate to say that the students were "traumatized," but some reported feeling physically as well as psychologically distressed during the reading:

> I could feel the shaking resistance against tears I often experience when faced with death. It happens to me every time I go to a funeral. I try incredibly hard not to cry. My lip quivers, my eyes water, and my body shakes. I remember wanting to get up and leave. I envisioned myself running for the door half-way through the eulogy. I knew it would be completely disrespectful so I sat in my seat wiping my nose and eyes with my sleeve. Nothing has ever upset me more in a class. I held my breath so that I would not sob and hyperventilate. I was embarrassed by my oversensitivity. I looked around at everyone else. Some were crying but I truly felt that no one was as upset as I.

Some students reported that they found themselves thinking about class for the rest of the day:

> My eyes precipitated and tears split my cheeks in halves as the sadness irrigated its way to the bottom of my face. I left class screaming at God in my head. Wondering why God does the things he does. The day didn't seem right after your class. Anger and sadness circled around like vultures waiting for me to lie in my pool of thoughts. Sadness claimed my mind for the rest of the day. I went to bed that night wondering about my own life. I wondered what God had in store for me. I wondered what I would do if I was ever in your situation. I thought about your pain.

How did I feel about my students' tears? My purpose was *not* to move them to tears—weepy responses are not necessarily "deeper" or more meaningful than dry-eyed responses. If we judged a story by the quantity of tears it produces in readers or viewers, any television soap opera would be a more profound aesthetic experience than *King Lear*. Nevertheless, I did want to "move" my students, and as the word implies, I sought to transport them to a different emotional realm, one that involved nothing less than the contemplation of life and death.

The adage, "mourners cry for themselves, not for the deceased," is a half-truth. We cry both for ourselves and for those whom we have lost. The most painful aspect of caring for Barbara was watching her suffer; the most painful part of mourning after her death was imagining all that she will miss in life. My tears are as much for Barbara's sake as for my own; and my students' tears were as much for Barbara and me as for themselves.

My students reacted with the sympathy and understanding that every eulogist desires. I hadn't imagined that some might leave class "screaming at God"—something that I had never done either during Barbara's illness or after her death, mainly because I had long ago lost the belief in God. My students' tears are surely understandable, however, and such crying probably occurs frequently in courses on the Holocaust.

What is a writer's or speaker's responsibility to an audience who is moved to tears? My responsibility is to be as truthful as possible, and to convey as many different points of view as possible. There was nothing in the eulogy that I read to my students, or later read to the mourners at Barbara's funeral, that was not truthful when I wrote it, though, as we shall see, some statements I made in March were not entirely accurate a month later. There were, of course, certain subjects about which I did not write, such as sexual intimacy, which was too private to reveal in a eulogy. I was also conscious of not wanting to reveal in too much detail our children's responses to their mother's illness. Neither of our daughters is as self-disclosing as I am, and I did not want to invade their privacy. Nor did I want to include any details about Barbara that I thought she would not want me to disclose. But I did want to tell the truth about Barbara's life as I perceived that truth; that is, I believe, every writer's responsibility.

I can imagine certain subjects that I would not disclose in the classroom. I would be reluctant to talk to my students about undergoing a painful and contested divorce, though I might mention that the experience allows me to empathize more deeply with my students' own experiences with shattered families. I would never speak negatively about another person, especially a colleague, nor would I involve students in bitter departmental politics, as has occurred in my own English department. I would not speak about being involved in a lawsuit, since my point of view would be biased. Nor would I speak about a relative's or friend's difficulties, at least not by name. I would, however, speak about my own difficulties, such as a particular illness or injury—and, should I find myself in Barbara's situation, I would, assuming that I was still able to teach, read to my students my own self-eulogy, celebrating my passion for teaching.

Is It Appropriate to Read a Eulogy in Class?

Hearing the eulogy was painful to all fifteen students, but thirteen implied that it was appropriate for the writing class:

That night, I considered my experience in expository writing. I had never been in a classroom situation like that. I don't think that the eulogy was inappropriate; if a student felt uncomfortable, they were free to leave.

I appreciated your reading of the eulogy; I now find it much easier to share my sensitive disclosures with you.

Yes, I thought it was appropriate for you to read the eulogy aloud, because this is a class where we are all allowed to reveal personal details about ourselves. The teacher should be allowed to do the same and be greeted with the same empathy that we show our fellow students. It showed that you trust us and that we can trust you as well. It is perfectly understandable if you need practice and experience reading it before a public audience before you read it at Barbara's funeral, especially since you had never read it before. I would gladly serve as such an audience.

The eulogy you read was painful, but it wasn't something that I couldn't handle. It wasn't inappropriate in the least. This added a personal touch to the course. I don't think I've ever been in a class where I have felt such a strong range of emotions.

Thank you for being so candid, you have taught me more about life in this one class than I have learned throughout my time in college. It is your own self-disclosures and honesty that make such an experience possible. Thank you.

I think that it was a good idea for you to read the eulogy. This is one of the few times that a professor of mine had done exactly what he/she asks of his/her students. You opened yourself up to your class. I feel that there is even more trust among the class, and perhaps now people will disclose more in their essays and not feel apprehensive about doing so.

I think that it was appropriate to an extent for you to share this with the class. We spend so much time discussing empathy and self-disclosure that it seemed only right for you, as the professor, to share your most personal writing.

From the beginning of your class, I decided that it would be too difficult for me to share personal essays with you and my classmates. I have never been good at expressing my emotions. An extremely difficult topic for me, is my relationship with my parents. . . . I was planning on writing a general essay about parenting and family relations, but your eulogy inspired me to write about my own emotionally charged story.

After hearing the eulogy, I understand this class. You weren't afraid to express your emotions to your relative strangers, which is uncomfortable to do but also extraordinarily relieving. You were the first to dive into the deepest corner of your emotions, and you almost cried. I noticed a few people in the classroom turning red, their eyes watering. You opened the door for other writers to brave similar topics.

I have several times asked myself whether it was appropriate for you to read this material to the class. Every time, I come to the conclusion that it most certainly was.

I appreciate your honesty and trust. I have never had someone close to me die. I do not think that I will take my first experience with death very well. I know that when this day comes I will look back to remember your courage to help me.

When you chose to read the eulogy for your wife's funeral, you were writing about something that was still happening in your life. In your doing this, you gave no separation between the writer and the "character" that you were writing about. Some might say that this dissolves a barrier that should exist in the student-teacher relationship, and that writing teachers should sterilize themselves of emotion. The intimacy that is so dreaded is what I found so helpful for the course. I know that hearing the eulogy has helped me feel more comfortable writing about topics that I would have been too anxious to share.

Someone heard of this, as well as the focus of the class, and while speaking to me about it, said that it was spooky and somewhat voyeuristic on the part of the teacher. I didn't respond, not wanting to alienate this other person but at the same time I was disgusted and annoyed by the comment. I am not sure why I said nothing then, but I want to say now that it was in no way voyeuristic. This person seems to be the kind of person who would keep emotions bottled up inside and that is never a way to deal with problems. . . . It is clear that you understood the finality of death, while at the same time were not able to understand why it was to happen to someone in your life. Though you wonder, you never asked questions of anyone, looking for the answer. You simply detail the life of a remarkable woman.

These thirteen students implied in the quoted passages or elsewhere in their essays that they appreciated the trust I placed in them and now placed greater trust in me. I had opened up to them just as they had opened up to me throughout the semester. "It has always bothered me when a teacher would read hundreds of essays, comment on them, and not read any of their own," wrote one student. "I felt this way regardless of the course topic, whether it be creative writing or literary theory. . . . When a professor reads a work of their own they are putting themselves into the lake of vulnerability." Despite the fact that I had disclosed aspects of myself in *Risky Writing*, my new self-disclosure was different, and they now saw me differently. I was still their teacher, but I had now become another member of the class, one who was struggling, like everyone else, with a personal issue. I had never used the word "intersubjective" in class, but the classroom suddenly became a space where every person, including the teacher, was sharing aspects of his or her own subjectivity with each other. Hearing the eulogy changed my students' perception of and relationship to me, as Jason Tougaw suggests in his discussion of AIDS memoirs: "To be effective as testimony, the narrativization of trauma . . . must alter the speaking subject's relation to an audience, and by extension, it must also alter social relations in general, opening up the possibility for the culture to accommodate the trauma that compels the testimony" (171).

Teachers are not physicians, but a statement made by a doctor who treats AIDS patients strikes me as relevant to educators: "I have learned that the greatest gift that I can give to patients is to allow the awareness of my own pain and loss to deepen my solidarity with them as they face their illness and death" (Selwyn 35). In every minute of every school day, in classes ranging from kindergarten to college, teachers hear and read their students' emotionally charged diaries and essays. Teachers and students who are not ashamed to be moved to tears—who respond to reading and writing assignments with genuine empathy—are those who are most profoundly affected by education.

The remaining two students were unsure whether they thought the eulogy was appropriate to read to the class:

> I do not know if it was inappropriate to read it to the class. I know that I feel it was a little too personal to disclose to the class, but that is partly due to the way in which I was affected by it. I do not think telling the class about his wife, his admiration for her, or her illness were inappropriate; I think his feelings are personal and should be kept private. The eulogy is read in the company of friends, family and loved ones that are gathered to mourn and remember. We are just mere students.

> After you finished reading the eulogy, and class was over, we didn't discuss what you shared with us. I remember walking outside and [hearing] one

of my classmates saying too much was going on in the class. I agreed with this statement because the subjects we were asked to write about were getting more serious, and personal. This seemed to be the climax of the semester. I thought to myself, why did he have to read his wife's eulogy to us. It put a damper on my day because it was so sad. Although I felt this way, I still appreciated you for doing so. I don't look at you any differently; in fact, it gave me more respect for you. For you to be able to talk about something so personal with your students almost put us on the same level and that was nice.

I don't wish to invalidate these two responses—the cornerstone of an empathic classroom rests upon the principle that "feelings are feelings" and not to be disregarded—but I never view members of my classroom as "mere students." They are not exactly "friends," to whom one may make an intimate self-disclosure, but they are more than acquaintances after several weeks of the semester. I don't believe that teachers should unburden themselves to students or seek psychological counseling from them, but I do believe that a teacher's careful self-disclosure can become a profound educational experience for everyone in the classroom. Some of these self-disclosures are sad, and it is certainly possible for students to become depressed by too many wrenching essays, but most of my writing students acknowledged at the end of the semester that there were many more smiles than tears in the course.

Teaching and Writing as Rescue

Family and friends became part of my support system as I cared for Barbara during her protracted illness. Without the help of my children, I could not have cared for her at home, especially toward the end, when she required around-the-clock care. Home-care hospice was also invaluable. Teaching was another support system. It afforded me not only a welcome distraction from the endless and exhausting problems confronted by a caregiver but also an opportunity to forget momentarily the crushing sadness I often felt at home. Throughout Barbara's illness I had my normal teaching load, but I had a compressed schedule so that I could be at home as much as possible. During her illness I missed only one class—when I gave a talk at the Narrative Medicine Conference at the University of Florida in late February 2004. Perhaps what most surprised me about my response to Barbara's illness was the ability to compartmentalize my life. At home I fulfilled all my caregiving responsibilities. There were many times during the final weeks of her life when I felt emotionally and physically overwhelmed. Alice Baker, the hospice case supervisor, suggested toward the end that it might be time to hospitalize Barbara, not for her sake but for our own. I remember feeling so exhausted that I was indifferent to my own health and well-being. I felt that I was dying with Barbara. The early twentieth-century Lithuanian-born Jewish philosopher Emmanuel Levinas would call this phenomenon, which I'm sure many caregivers feel, "dying for the other," when "worry over the death of the other comes before care for self" (*Entre Nous* 216). We all needed a break from the constant caregiving, yet we also felt that we had come this far and could endure a few more days. In the classroom, however, I felt cheerful, relaxed, and in control. I laughed and joked as usual in the classroom even during the last weeks of Barbara's life.

All my books affirm the belief in "writing as rescue," the subtitle of my early study of Joseph Conrad, but equally important is the idea that teaching is also a form of rescue. The "teaching cure" enabled me to remain connected with the outer world of health; teaching served as a lifeline for me at a time when I was struggling to be a lifeline for my wife. Many of my colleagues offered generously to teach my classes during Barbara's illness, and they may have thought that my determination to continue teaching and meeting with students was a sign of strength. The truth was that teaching *gave* me the strength that otherwise I might not have had: as much as I gave to my students, they gave to me and helped me through the crisis. As one person noted, "One thing that touched me as you read your eulogy was that teaching kept you sane. Hearing a professor say something like that made me think, 'That is one more reason why teaching is worth it after all.' It also made me wonder when in my life I will be at the point at which I will be able to say the same thing."

My eulogy was a bridge between the world of the healthy and the sick, the living and the dying; I wrote it when Barbara was gravely ill, but rather than distracting me from taking care of her, the eulogy enabled me to avoid succumbing to despair when she could no longer take care of herself. Taking care of Barbara meant giving her scores of pills every few hours, including two different forms of morphine (one long lasting, the other for breakthrough pain), diuretics, laxatives, antidepressants, and tranquilizers; it meant flushing daily her external biliary drain catheter to lower the toxic bilirubin that was making her jaundiced; it meant squirting liquid morphine into her mouth every hour around the clock when she could no longer swallow a pill; it meant cooking meals for her that increasingly she could not eat; it meant injecting her every eight hours with an antipsychotic so that she would not telephone the police screaming that she was being murdered, as she did on one occasion; it meant giving her water with an eyedropper until she could no longer swallow; it meant carrying her to the bathroom when she could no longer walk and then dealing with her incontinence—perhaps the ultimate indignity of her disease.

Writing the eulogy helped me both to express and fulfill the lifelong devotion that I have felt for her and she for me. The eulogy reminded me of the sacred duty to the other about which Emmanuel Levinas has written. As I note in *Empathic Teaching*, "in Levinas's world, assuming responsibility for the suffering of others reveals mercy, which he sees as part of the phenomenon of love; the origin of love lies in sympathy for the other's suffering" (101). The only absolute value, Levinas concludes in an interview in *Is It Righteous to Be?* is the "human possibility of giving the other priority over oneself" (170), a value that demonstrates holiness, which I tried to convey in the eulogy.

Mourning Loss

Anyone who writes about death and dying will relate to Ruth Behar's statement in *The Vulnerable Observer* about the need to remember those who are no longer here while at the same time recognizing the emotional resistance to confronting unbearable loss:

> Kafka once wrote that he hungered for books "which come upon us like ill fortune, and distress us deeply, like the death of one we love better than ourselves, like suicide. A book must be an ice-axe to break the sea frozen inside us." As Alvin Rosenfeld points out, Kafka was spared the Holocaust, which has made us become readers on the defensive, wanting "to keep the seas of empathy inside us safely frozen a while longer." In our age of "compassion fatigue," I think anthropological writing about death has to be, if not an ice-axe to break the sea frozen inside us, at least an ice pick to chip at the conventional forms of representing and narrating the encounter of the anthropologist with death. Chipping away, reconstituting the dialectic between silence and speech, we will learn to take the deaths that take place over there, across borders, as seriously as we take those that take place here, at home. (86)

Kafka's statement, which I used as the epigraph to *Surviving Literary Suicide*, reminds us of the need to wield axes with special care, lest we injure ourselves as we liberate the sea frozen inside us.

Sooner or later we must all deal with loss, and the eulogy triggered painful memories for members of the class. Several wrote about how hearing the eulogy reminded them about the deaths of relatives and friends, many of which were difficult to mourn:

> I have been trying to write about the eulogy you wrote to your wife. It was difficult for me since I just lost someone close, but I was unable to go to the funeral. I still haven't said goodbye in the formal setting. I don't think that I have to anymore though. Sitting in class and listening to you speak, I felt many of the same emotions and had many of the same

thoughts as if I had been to the funeral. It was a chance for me to say goodbye to her. The most important lesson learned from the experience was the resilience of the human heart. You showed us how we can be strong and I took that as direction for moving on with her in my heart instead of on this planet. You showed us that, with your wife sick and dying, you were able to compose your thoughts and put them into words that conveyed the wonder of a life we all will miss. I never met her or heard you speak of her outside of what you have told us in class, but through your eulogy and the manner in which you speak of her still, I feel as though she was there in some way. You help to bring her into the class, creating vivid images of times you spent together.

I am not very good when it comes to death. My grandfather died when I was ten, and it was my first experience with mortality. He was a double amputee, and suffered the after-effects of several strokes. He used to think that I was my oldest brother. I was only ten, and my brother was twenty-five. He must've thought it was the early eighties. I wasn't close to him because he didn't have the mental capacity to really know me. Last year, his wife passed away. I was very close with my grandmother as a child. After she became frail and ill, my mother had her placed in a nearby home, where trusted friends kept a close watch on her. She managed to live for years after. In those years, I started to prepare myself for her passing. I felt I was ready to deal with it. I wasn't. When I went home for spring break, I found out that she was very ill. That night, my mother called me from the nursing home and told me that Nanny had passed. I immediately began to cry.

It was a very rough night for me. My girlfriend spent the night with me and comforted me. At the wake, I was very composed. I found comfort amongst friends and family. The funeral, however, was a different story. My mother had asked me to read a passage since I was the "family scholar." I told her I was sorry, and that I wouldn't be able to handle it. My brother agreed to do it. When the time came, he lost his composure after the first line. I had never seen my brother cry in my life. From that point on, I was a wreck.

When Professor Berman began to read, I remembered how I couldn't read two paragraphs for my grandmother. Now, here was my professor, reading page after page of his memories with his beloved wife. A few times he came close to tears, but pulled through the wrenching sentences. I found in him an admirable strength which I can only dream of obtaining. . . .

As much as I miss my grandparents, I have not lost anyone very dear to me. I don't know how I will handle losing parents and my older brothers. Hopefully, I will pass before my wife and children. If I do not, however, I hope I have one-tenth the strength of Professor Berman. His wife's eulogy was the most powerful classroom experience I have ever had.

The eulogy spoke to everyone in the classroom, including those who had not yet suffered the loss of a loved one. "Hearing the eulogy did not cause me to reflect upon relatives' or friends' deaths because I have not lost someone close to me. It did make me fear losing the people whom I care about who are still alive. It made me fear losing my future husband, even though I have not met him yet." The same person added:

> So many ideas ran through my head as you read the eulogy. I tried to recall them as I reflected on it in writing a few hours later, but I could not recall everything, nor put it into words. How do I explain this to somebody who was not there in class that day? When you spoke about how much Barbara meant to you, I got scared for myself. You see, for the past several years, I have wanted to be the woman who means just that much to my future husband. I have never been so dear to a man, and it seems impossible that it could ever happen. At the same time it is possible. I am scared that after a lifetime of wanting to mean so much to him, I will mean so much to someone, and years down the road he will be so hurt by losing me. I don't want to hurt my husband like that. I have often said that when I die I don't want people to mourn me. I don't want fanfare. I don't want them to experience pain or hurt. I want them to just move on. My favorite Shakespeare sonnet is #71, by the way. Here as a young person I hope to find strong love, and I fear that love will hit me in the face long before I expect it.

Eulogies are reminders of our mortality, and my tribute to Barbara called attention to the inevitability of future losses. One person who identified herself as female began her essay by discussing her grandmother's weeklong wake three years earlier. The "politics of the funeral disgusted me," she observed, especially the "small talk at the wake," which she felt was "reprehensible." She speculated that "social politics" will require her to "conform" when it is her turn to "host such a 'party.'" She then returned to my reading:

> I was shocked when you told the class that your wife had terminal cancer. I did not know what you held in your hand, and I did not expect it to be a copy of the eulogy you wrote for your wife. I didn't understand at first why you would want to divulge intimate details to your students of only two months. When you offered this assignment, then I understood. Thinking back to that class, I found your reading extremely brave,

and appreciate you trusting us. I had no idea that you did not wear the same smile outside of class, but instead carried a great burden on your shoulders. You read the eulogy as though it were a letter to your deceased wife, which shook me. I was anxious. What if I was writing something like this, something that could make me choke on my own words? I thought about the people in my life I couldn't imagine losing, and how I would feel if I lost them. One of my close friends has experienced tragedy more than once. Two years ago one of my best friends committed suicide, and only last week another close friend drove a car into a telephone pole. His friend is, as I write this, in a coma, and my friend's heartache is my own. You think that it won't happen to you or your friends, but every day it gets a little closer, too close for comfort. I tremble as I type this, worrying that one day I might lose my friend in a similar accident.

I hate thinking about death; I am truly petrified of it. Every day I wonder what would happen if I missed one step on the staircase, if I looked the wrong way in the parking lot, if I walked into a gunfight. All these scenarios appear in my head like alternate endings in a television show, flashing before my eyes. But those are all dramatized visions of death; I have no idea how I will die, and what will happen afterward. It is one of the scariest things I can think about. . . .

My problems seem trite in comparison. It has been three years since my grandmother's funeral, and now I can talk about it candidly, without grief or resentment. Time heals almost all wounds, and then there are some that will ache forever. Reading the eulogy must have been both gut-wrenching and therapeutic. Writing for your class is a form of therapy (when I'm not losing sleep, anyway). I am happy to have, for once, helped with your therapy.

Many students remarked on my "strength and courage," which they hoped they would have when called upon to endure loss. Their perception challenged me, through what is called the "Michelangelo phenomenon," to live up to their ideal. As Tom Cottle explains, "Predicated on interpersonal relationships, the Michelangelo phenomenon represents an attempt by social scientists to describe how the individual self is formed by the perceptions of it of some significant other, as well as by the behavior of this significant other. The essence of the phenomenon rests on the notion that the more the self is affirmed by the perceptions and behavior of the other, the more the individual self 'moves' toward its own conception of an ideal form. Simply put, the more you affirm me in word and deed, the more I imagine that I have begun to reach an ideal form of (for) my self" (24).

Students offered me their own emotional resources during my loss. "I found your reading to be very painful," one person wrote, "but I remained as strong as possible for you. . . . I needed to give you my attention while you read it to the class. I knew this was important to you." They were not only a sympathetic audience but also a supportive group, reaching out to me in ways that seldom occur in the classroom. This supportive group takes on some of the characteristics of a "support" group but without offering the clinical advice that occurs in the latter. Wrote another, "I want to be able to say something truly outstanding, something that will relieve you of your pain and grief; this, I know, is impossible. After listening to your reading I wanted to hug you and say that I was sorry. Sorry is insufficient, this I know."

My self-disclosure narrowed the distance between students and teacher, leading to a more equal classroom relationship based on reciprocity. There was, in Jessica Benjamin's words, mutual recognition: "the necessity of recognizing as well as being recognized by the other" (23). There was nothing transgressive about this narrowed distance, nothing that would be considered unprofessional. I recall two female students hugging me after I announced Barbara's death, and several sent sympathy cards and emails. Many past and present students attended the funeral and later came back to my home, along with perhaps a hundred other mourners. The main effect of the eulogy was internal. "I feel a greater sense of trust and respect now because you have shared your experience with us. By doing so, you have broken down the wall that is usually present in the classroom, separating the teacher from the students." Another student used a similar metaphor to describe our new pedagogical relationship. "You opened the doors of time to your life and led us through the amazing aspects in your life which involved your wife. I felt as if I was there each moment. I felt like a friend watching your life unfold in front of my eyes."

My students' experiences suggest that, contrary to Jonathan Silin's fears, a teacher's disclosure of a spouse's impending death is not an undue burden on them. Rather than burdening students who, in Silin's words, are "struggling to become adults," my eulogy demonstrated the educational and psychological value of talking about death—something that adults, in particular, will find helpful. Reading my eulogy encouraged students to share their own experiences with death—not to "challenge" me but to offer their own points of view. Their concern for me did not require them to become caregivers. My ability to handle the "complex emotions" implicit in the eulogy emboldened them to explore their own complex emotions toward death. I would never suggest that teachers or students should be required to talk about something as personal as death. But I believe that voluntary discussion can be beneficial. And I certainly agree with Silin's concluding sentence: "An open discussion of moments when teachers and students choose to remain silent, a topic about which I am newly curious, may help my own students to understand that profound loss is almost always part of the classroom, whether acknowledged or not."

Barbara's illness affected students from other classes as well. I received an email from a graduate student on October 23, 2003, who commented on the "look" on my face, with which she identified all too painfully:

Dear Professor Berman:

I hope you won't take offense by my boldness of this email. Although I am not fully aware of your wife's medical difficulties, from what you have mentioned they sound serious and, dare I say, terminal.

I write this letter in remembrance of the same "look" I carried around four years ago. You see, I know that "look," I can see that "look" in your eyes, it is the "look" of controlled suffocation. Suffocation in the fact that there are so many emotions running through your mind that it is sometimes overwhelming, controlled because one must maintain and function daily.

Four years ago, as I sat next to my 38-year-old husband, in the cardiothoracic surgeon's office, he told us the lung biopsy was occupational pulmonary fibrosis and that my husband would probably die within the year. I had that same "look."

As I watched my husband go from a strong, hotheaded Italian, down to a weak and struggling man, wheelchair bound and gasping for air, that "look" visited me several times.

The last time that "look" came to visit was on July fourth, 1999. It was the hottest day recorded in Baltimore and as I stepped out of the car to go into Johns Hopkins hospital, you could feel it. All the way up the elevator I had this terrible feeling in the pit of my stomach. My husband had collapsed five days earlier, he was at Johns Hopkins transferring his transplant time over from Pittsburgh to there, when he collapsed in the hotel room. (His chances were greatly improved for a transplant if he did this.) However, the fibrosis was so bad that he was barely alive. They had him in an induced coma and paralyzed so that his lungs would not have to exert themselves anymore than just keeping him alive.

As I came up to his room (the room directly across from the nurses station that is designated for the patients who can die at any minute) and saw my husband lying there gray with lips that were yellow, the "look" exploded.

Oh, they fought valiantly to keep him alive, he was 39 years old, for Christ's sake, he had two boys that adored him. But God thought otherwise and gave him his independence from that awful disease just as this country gained its independence years ago.

As I stood at the nurses station on the phone, teddy bear clutched in my hand, nodding and saying yes as the UNOS coordinator was asking me if I wanted to donate my husband's pericardium sac, the "look" took over.

It was as if the shell of my body was functioning but my brain was anesthetized or like I was sitting in my brain watching these things unfold as if I were an observer in my own nightmare. For days I was in this state. Maintain . . . keep control . . . think of the children.

It was not until I moved with my children up here and signed up for a six-week grief program called "Wave Riders" did I start to lose the "look." I learned that it was okay to be really pissed off at my husband for dying, and in the next thought glad that he was gone and the suffering was over for all of us. For the longest time I tried to maintain that controlled suffocation because I thought it was sinful to have these thoughts prior to, and after his death. Now I'm not saying you should go out and do the jig or come home and scream at your wife, just that it's okay to think these thoughts on top of the profound sadness you already have.

When a loved one is sick and requires constant care and is suffering, we feel helpless and let's face it, we are when it is terminal. The day to day crisis is so tiring that sometimes you just want to run away and never come back.

Please forgive me for my long windedness, I just wanted to let you know that you are not alone. If you ever need to vent, vent away, I can relate oh too well.

I hope you are not offended by my candidness, I know I'm a student and you are the Professor, but we are all human beings.

Since I am Catholic I will say my prayers and blessings for your wife, you and your family.

Take Care.

Self-disclosures are gifts that we entrust to others who we hope will appreciate and respect our private revelations. Barbara's illness was not a secret that I was trying to hide from the world, but I was not willing to disclose it to a group of strangers: I chose my writing class because we had been together for two months and had learned a great deal about each other. Students had disclosed stories about their own vulnerability, and in the process a strong bond had formed. If many of these stories were painful to write and wrenching to read, they nevertheless revealed the writers' and readers' strengths, the ability to survive difficult experiences:

The environment you created in our class is a safe haven for us students to write and speak about things that are very personal and private. I don't think that there are many professors who can do that. It is only fair that your students are accepting of you doing the same. Since that class, I have reflected on the essays that I have written about subjects that I never talk to anyone about. The fact that I feel comfortable in writing about them, reading them in class and having you share your thoughts is a testament to the safe and accepting environment you have created for us in class. The emotions I felt during your reading of the eulogy were ones of love rather than death. I smiled when you mentioned your first date with your wife. I cried when you cried when you said what I think are the strongest five words in the whole passage: "I wanted to be married." You repeated it and I felt the love you had for her, and still have for her to this day. I think your reading of this eulogy to our class is the most brave and courageous act I have ever seen. Your passion for your family and your work has inspired me to write about things in this class that I have never divulged to anyone. And for that, I thank you. Thank you.

Significantly, the students felt that my eulogy motivated them to improve their writing skills. Some wished to become better writers as an act of compassion toward me. "The reading of your eulogy changed my feelings about this course. It made me want to do better in this class. I want to improve my essays so that you don't have to spend so much time to grade them." Others wanted to become better writers so that they could express themselves powerfully and honestly. "I don't think I've ever been in a class where I have felt such a strong range of emotions. When I first signed up for the class, all I could think about was the forty pages I overlooked when I read the course description. Now, all I think about is trying to write a paper that will affect the heart and arouse the mind while trying to remain as true to myself as possible." Paradoxically, although the fifteen essays were anonymous and therefore ungraded, they were among the best written essays of the semester. They contained fewer grammatical, stylistic, and typographical errors than the earlier essays, along with a greater emotional power.

Aesthetic Power

Students responded to the aesthetic and performative aspects of my writing, aspects on which we had focused throughout the semester:

> This was a perfect example of showing rather than telling. In class you stressed this idea, but now it is completely clear to me what you mean by it. I was mesmerized by your words; the class felt the same way. The power with which you wrote was nothing short of astounding. It was as if you were telling a story and you brought the class along with you for the ride. I looked around the room once while you were reading, and not a single student was moving. We were captured by your words.

I think it was a good idea for you to read the eulogy. This is one of the few times that a professor of mine had done exactly what he/she asks of his/her students. You opened yourself up to your class. I feel that there is even more trust among the class, and perhaps now people will disclose more in their essays and not feel apprehensive about doing so.

It was painful to hear you read this. It moved me and many of my classmates to tears. I have not been to many funerals, and therefore have not heard many eulogies. I hope that my future husband writes one for me as beautiful as the one you wrote for your wife. However, I think that it was more meaningful for you to read this to us than if we had read it ourselves. The emotion conveyed in your voice as you read the eulogy would not have been there if we had read it ourselves. We connected with you in a way that would not have happened otherwise. I think that by having students read their own essays aloud to the class we can hear how the students wanted their words heard. Essay reading becomes a performance. We can then feel the emotion the person felt when writing their work.

The aesthetic pleasure of writing sustained me as I was writing the eulogy: the challenge to find the right words to describe my relationship to Barbara, to capture the special qualities that made her unique. I wanted to portray both the lighter and darker aspects of our lives together, including the comic and tragic elements of the story. For it was a story that I was telling, not unlike those that I teach in my literature courses. Whereas "story" is generally pejorative in a court of law, implying fabrication or untruth, the word is honorific in a literature or writing class. We all tell stories, all the time, and the telling of stories allows us to reach insights and interpretations that might otherwise elude us. I was the storyteller, and Barbara was the central protagonist; the challenge was to narrate the story in a way that would be consistent with the expectations associated with the eulogy, a genre with its own formulaic rules. I knew I could be personal but not *too* personal; I did not want to reveal anything of which Barbara herself or our children might disapprove. I also knew that I wanted to end the eulogy on a somber tone befitting the tragic nature of premature death, but the tone could not be so dark that I would be unable to complete my reading.

Writing the eulogy forced me to reflect on the delicate balance between celebrating Barbara's life and memorializing her premature death. Tone, voice, and point of view are essential aspects of all writing, but eulogies pose special challenges, and the decision to write one required me to work through this problem before Barbara's funeral. Solving this "writerly" problem helped me with the larger "life" problem. I had to maintain a double perspective, that of participant and observer. Writing the eulogy forced me to remember details that I might otherwise have wanted to forget. Every detail, no matter how painful, became part of the story I wanted to tell. Writing forced me to shape her life, endowing our relationship with a beginning, middle, and end. Writing forced me to construct a meaning to the unbelievable events that we could not have imagined two years earlier. Writing forced me to give sorrow words, lest silent grief break my heart. Writing helped me to remain focused on Barbara at the same time that it paradoxically offered me a welcome distraction to what was happening to her. I have long known that writing is an excellent form of problem solving, allowing us to put into words inchoate thoughts. "How do I know what I think till I see what I say?" E. M. Forster observed famously. In struggling to capture both the joy and sorrow of Barbara's life, I recalled F. Scott Fitzgerald's "test" of a "first-rate intelligence": the ability to "hold two opposed ideas in the mind at the same time and still retain the ability to function" (69).

It is no accident that I turned to literature to help me write the eulogy and, without knowing it at the time, film. My favorite novelist is Charles Dickens, and during Barbara's illness, we both saw the film *Nicholas Nickleby*, from which I remembered vaguely the quotation about delighting in life's unexpected happiness while knowing the inevitability of loss. Since the Dickens's quote also conveys my attitude about happiness and loss, I decided to use it for the eulogy, and I did a Google search to get the exact words. After Barbara's death, I skimmed the seven-hundred-page novel to get the page number. Unable to find the quote, I reread the entire novel, to no avail. From where did the quotation come? My friend Howard Reiter cleared up the mystery: the quotation comes from the 2002 film adaptation, written and directed by Douglas McGrath, not from the novel itself, as I had thought. Had I not used the Dickens quotation, I would have cited John Keats's insight in "Ode to Melancholy" that "in the very temple of Delight / Veil'd Melancholy has her sovran shrine."

In her book *The Mourner's Dance*, Katherine Ashenburg suggests that the "telling and retelling of a terrible event seem to have a certain anesthetizing effect, while they also make the death incontrovertibly real," both of which, she adds, reveal two other tasks of mourning: "to accept that the death has truly happened and to begin to carry on in spite of it" (220). While writing the eulogy, I often found myself immersed in what the psychologist Mihaly Csikszentmihalyi calls "flow," in which we lose all sense of time. These flow experiences, which correspond to Ashenburg's "anesthetizing effect," involve painful, risky, difficult activities that challenge one's imagination. Flow experiences resemble what Norman Holland calls, in his book "The Brain and the Book," a "trance-like state of mind we get into when reading or in a theater when we lose track of our bodies and our surroundings."

I found Barbara's perfectionism difficult to live with, but I am a perfectionist about writing. I struggle to make every sentence as lucid as possible. Writing the eulogy became as important to me as designing Arielle's wedding gown became to Barbara four years earlier: every detail needed to be right.

Hundreds of people gazed at Arielle's wedding gown, and hundreds—including many of the same people—would listen to my eulogy. This was no ordinary essay but a tribute to the most important person in my life. Part of Barbara's anxiety was that she had never designed a wedding gown before; part of *my* anxiety was that I had never written and delivered a eulogy. Both of us spent countless hours thinking about the projects. Both of us suffered from hyper-criticism, never satisfied with our work. Barbara was constantly redoing the gown's buttons, hem, train, and veil, just as I was constantly revising my words and thinking of new details to add. Barbara could visualize the entire gown before she started to work on it, whereas, by contrast, I could not begin to see a structure for this book until I had written rough drafts of several chapters. Despite these differences, the paradox of art, whether it be designing a wedding gown or writing a book, is that what appears natural, graceful, spontaneous, and seamless is almost always laboriously crafted and recrafted. This is why my students and I spend so much time in class discussing revision. And just as Barbara felt that creating her daughter's gown was a spiritual experience, inspired by intergenerational memories of Barbara's mother and grandmother, so did I believe that writing the eulogy was a sacred rite, inspired by a lifetime of love and devotion.

My students' comments about Barbara, whom they had never met, were uniformly respectful, but there was one comment that I wish were true:

> I did not have a copy of your eulogy to follow, but there was one sentence that has been glued in my mind since hearing it. By stating "She never gave up on life, but life gave up on her," you summed up the battle of cancer. Those people who are struggling with cancer still manage to thrive on life and refuse to let their illness shatter their will to live. They continue to live each day as though it was the first day of the rest of their lives, seeing a lifetime ahead of them rather than a few months, weeks, days. They seem to have a happier life when living with cancer because, with the illness, they gain a new perspective on life. Up to the day they lose this battle, they hold their heads high and strong. While cancer is a cruel and drawn-out battle, it creates a strength in its carriers that cannot be compared to any other. They don't give up on life. Life gives up on them.

Those who survive deadly diseases like cancer may well experience an elation that those who have never been seriously ill do not feel. For such people, my student's observation is probably correct. But no one can hold his or her head high and strong who is in the final stages of terminal cancer.

It's certainly true that Barbara and I gained a new perspective on life. Two momentous events occurred during this time that brought intense joy to both of us: the wedding of our younger daughter, Jillian, in October 2002, two months after Barbara's diagnosis, a time when she was still feeling physically well, and the birth of our older daughter Arielle's son in August 2003, almost exactly a year after the diagnosis, a time when Barbara began a new experimental treatment with thalidomide, which made her feel so sick that she had to end treatment after only ten days. From that moment on she was held captive by the plunging roller coaster. There was nothing joyous about the perilous descent, nothing that brought her more than a few moments of respite from excruciating physical and psychological pain. And so it would not be true to say that she enjoyed a happier life as a result of cancer. From the moment she felt a large mass in her liver, even before her diagnosis, she began to experience severe depression, anxiety attacks, and panic attacks. Despite all my cheerleading, my efforts to kindle a sense of hope that I did not feel, she viewed everything through a glass darkly. I did too. Cancer indeed transforms one's perspective, but it is important not to romanticize suffering.

Barbara tried valiantly to hold her head high and strong, but it was a daily struggle to resist the temptation to sleep as much as possible to escape the nightmare that life had become. In the final weeks of her life, when she took ever-increasing doses of morphine to manage the horrendous pain of pancreatic cancer, which affects the entire gastrointestinal system—pancreas, stomach, liver, and bowels—she was tormented even during what had once been merciful sleep by wildly violent dreams of the death of her family—dreams that were so real that she would often wake up agitated and demand to see my hands, which she was certain a madman had chopped off.

Death is an everyday reality in literature and life, but despite its ubiquity, few teachers encourage students to speak or write *personally* about death. Our intellects remind us of our mortality; our emotions convince us that we are exempt from finality. Sometimes this is healthy denial, while other times it is not healthy. Unhealthy denial is the theme of Tolstoy's great cautionary tale *The Death of Ivan Ilych*. Barbara and I struggled to accept the inevitability of death, and in the end we finally succeeded.

If the reality of death is difficult to accept for those approaching sixty, how much more difficult is it for undergraduates? My students' anonymous responses indicated the fear that they will be unable to cope with a loved one's death. As one wrote, "I am not very good when it comes to death." Few of us are. Part of the educational value of my eulogy may be that it demonstrated that we can indeed survive a heartbreaking loss. Before Barbara's diagnosis, I would not have thought this possible. Now, thanks in large part to the support of family, friends, and hospice, I know that it is possible. I hope that my self-disclosure will make it easier for my students to survive their own future losses.

Barbara, at two months old, with her mother, 1946.

Barbara in high school (*above and facing*).

Coney Island, Brooklyn, 1967.

Barbara and Jeff in Ithaca, late 1960s.

Barbara and Jeff in Ithaca, late 1960s.

Ithaca, late 1960s.

Arielle, at about six months, with Barbara, 1973.

Barbara, upon receiving her master's in computer science, with Arielle (*right*) and Jillian, Albany, 1984.

Barbara and her best friend, Ellen Gootblatt, at a Broadway play, 1988.

Barbara and her parents, Morris and Jean, at Arielle's college graduation, 1995.

Left to right: Arielle; Barbara; Jeff's parents, Roslyn and Isadore; and Jillian at Arielle's college graduation, Ithaca, 1995.

Barbara's sister, Karen, her husband, Moshe, and their children (*clockwise from top*) Rafi, Gabe, Shane, and Peter, 1995.

At Mount Rushmore, 1997.

Jeff and Barbara at Yosemite National Park, 1998.

At Squaw Valley, California, 1998.

Barbara and Caleb, 1998.

Arielle and David at a wedding in California, 1999.

Left to right: Lynn Willscher, Alex, Jillian, and Barbara at University of Chicago Law School Graduation, 2000.

Attending a baseball game in Chicago, 2000. *Left to right*: (*first row*) Jeff, Larry and Marilyn Albert, Barbara; (*second row*): Alex, Jillian, David, Arielle.

January 16, 2004

This is such a special day ~~that~~ day that I couldn't ~~let~~ it pass without writing. It's so difficult for me to combine letters and words. We've ~~we~~ shared a ~~spectacular~~ life together, ~~a~~ love for one another that has ~~anb~~ ~~stretch~~ stretched by time. I

Barbara's last written words, January 16, 2004 (Jeff's fifty-ninth birthday).

Arielle and Nate, 2005.

5

THE OTHER EULOGIES

Barbara died on April 5, a month after I read the eulogy to my students. I added three paragraphs to the eulogy, which I read at the funeral on April 9:

Indeed, long after her physicians and nurses had predicted her death, and long after she had embraced death as an end to unbearable suffering, Barbara's heart continued to beat. There are many explanations for why she clung so tenaciously to life, ranging from fear of death to unfinished business, but the explanation that I would like to believe comes from my friend Anne Jung, who said: "Barbara's heart is clearly beating for all of you—a testament to her strength as a person and the intensity of her spirit. And if you think about it, why would she be willing to let go and leave the life of love and devotion she has had with all of you? It makes perfect sense to me."

I should add that we are grateful to the many people who helped us during the past twenty months: to Barbara's sister, Karen, who repeatedly traveled back and forth between Florida and Albany, and who has been with us for the past two weeks; to Ed Dick, our psychotherapist, who helped us to accept the inevitability of death; to Herb Weisburgh, a retired social worker who mobilized Barbara's energy fields through the art of therapeutic touch; to everyone associated with hospice, especially Geraldine Breitenstein, who began as Barbara's nurse and ended as a family friend; and to the many friends and colleagues who offered their prayers and loving thoughts. I am also grateful to my dear friend Dr. Jerome Eckstein, the founder of the Judaic Studies program at the University at Albany, for conducting this memorial service.

Barbara died hours before the beginning of Passover, and the hospice chaplain who was with us during her final moments commented on the religious significance: "She passed on Passover, and her long bondage is over." Her death was peaceful—the only peaceful time of the long ordeal. We were all at her bedside, talking to her and stroking her arms, and it was impossible to tell the moment she expired. For the first time in months she looked like she was truly at rest. She would have worried much less about death had she foreseen her serene ending. I won't comment on the symbolism of her burial on Good Friday except to say that this entire week has great significance for her Jewish and Christian friends.

One sentence was partly true when I wrote it in January but untrue when she died three months later: "*She had a natural, unself-conscious beauty that never faded, not even after her illness.*" It was hard to recognize that lifelong beauty during the last weeks of her life, when her body was ravaged by cancer. She looked like documentary footage of Holocaust survivors, with her sunken cheeks, yellow complexion, emaciated arms and legs, and dazed eyes. In contrast to her atrophied legs, arms, and chest, her abdomen was cruelly distended, as if she were nine months pregnant, both from the cancer and from the fluids that her kidneys could not eliminate from her body. It was difficult to find muscle in her thighs when we injected her every eight hours with antipsychotic medication. I had no intention of adding these graphic details to the eulogy, but I did want to include two other sentences that my children persuaded me to omit when I read the eulogy to them the night before the funeral: "For the last two weeks of her life she was unable to eat or drink. We were told that the limit for most people is six days without water; Barbara lasted for eleven days without a drop of water." I agreed eventually with my children that these words were too disturbing. Nevertheless, they are part of the story of my wife's illness, and I include them here because they dramatize her indomitable will to live.

Our children, Karen, and Jerry Eckstein offered their own eulogies at the funeral, and each saw Barbara in a special way. Unlike me, to whom delays of any kind are anathema, my older daughter, Arielle, is a notorious procrastinator, a character defect that drove me crazy when she was younger. (My compulsive need to finish a project ahead of time drove her crazy.) And yet I must admit that although I warn my students not to wait until the last moment before writing an essay, Arielle has become proficient at working under pressure. Nor has procrastination prevented her from high academic achievements and a Ph.D. in clinical psychology. She was unruffled as she began writing the eulogy the night before the funeral. By contrast, her sister Jillian, less gifted at procrastination but no less academically talented, was distressed by the possibility that she might run out of time.

There was one moment when family tension, which had miraculously vanished during Barbara's illness, reared its ugly head. When Arielle stated earlier in the afternoon that she intended to write about how her mother created her wedding gown, I replied, "Sorry, that's in my eulogy." Instantly she became indignant and reminded me that it was *her* gown and, therefore, *her* material. "Too bad," I said pitilessly, "I used it first." "Well, then," she added, "at least I'll use mom's statement in her journal." "Sorry, but I used that too." We argued back and forth until I agreed magnanimously to let her use the wedding gown material for her eulogy, at which point she said, "Forget it, I'll use something else." Both she and her sister wrote eloquent tributes to their mother, loving, thoughtful, funny, and truthful.

Jillian's Eulogy

On October 17, 1946, a precious baby girl was born to Morris and Jean Kozinn of Borough Park, Brooklyn; she was named Barbara Dona. On April 5, 2004, Barbara passed away. Though she departed too soon, during her fifty-seven and a half years she had a full and rich life. From the very beginning, Barbara was doted upon. Her parents, who had difficulty conceiving, called her a miracle child. By all accounts, she was a wonder.

I learned more about her youth when my mother took me back to her old neighborhood six years ago. My mom lit up as she showed me her building on Thirteenth Avenue and Fifty-first Street, and the places in the neighborhood where she used to play. She was a lively storyteller, and it was like we were reliving favorite events from her childhood: the lunches at Horn and Hardart automat, the kosher pizza at Bella's, trips to buy penny candy at Pete's, and those hot dogs that she loved so much at Nathan's at Coney Island.

At the age of sixteen, Barbara left Brooklyn and moved to Buffalo to start college. Our parents met there, married shortly after college, and moved to Ithaca where our dad began grad school and my mom taught first grade. Most importantly, when they got to Ithaca they started their family.

Barbara was a terrific mother. If you were to list every quality you'd want in a mom, she had them all. She was gentle and nurturing—tending to our cuts and bruises, listening when someone made us cry. She was supportive, and encouraged us to try different things—yet she respected our decision not to pursue something. For example, both Arielle and I took piano lessons from an early age, something we both enjoyed and which was important to mom. But after seven or eight years when we turned our attention to sports, she respected our decision to stop the piano lessons, and she became our biggest fan from the sidelines. When I was in fifth grade, my best friends joined a basketball team and, of course, I wanted to join too. But it was a church basketball team, for Christ the King. My mom was initially opposed to my participation, but she relented when she realized how important it was to me. For the next eight years she attended just about every basketball game I had.

I think our parents agreed on just about every matter of importance regarding their children's upbringing, but they had very different styles. When they wanted us to do something that we weren't keen on doing, my dad resorted to bribery. To prevent me from quitting band in the ninth grade, he offered to buy me scuba diving gear to use in the swimming pool. When he wanted Arielle and me to apply to Cornell early decision, he bribed us with cars. My mom's style was very different. She was quieter and more subtle; she didn't always make her opinion known, but it was very clear that she didn't support my dad's tactics. But she was forceful in her own way.

My mom always encouraged my sister and me to experience life and take risks. She made clear to us that the world was full of responsibilities, which we should seize. She encouraged us to study abroad and travel, to enter professions that were challenging and rewarding, and to live in new places. She led by example, for she was always experiencing life, traveling to new cities and countries. Mom and dad visited us wherever we lived. When my sister and I were both in Ithaca and Chicago, we had great times with our parents exploring these cities, taking in the restaurants, museums, and parks, and just being together. Mom and dad were also always taking trips to new places; in the last few years they went to Prague, Vienna, Budapest, Santa Fe, Yosemite, Yellowstone, Colorado, and Utah.

Our mom was also smart. She excelled not only as a parent, but also as a computer analyst for the New York State Department of Social Services and then the New York State Division of Criminal Justice, where she worked for over twenty years. She loved her work, mostly because she made wonderful friends there.

Though not all of you know this, in addition to being a computer analyst, our mom was an accountant, a plumber, an electrician, a handyman, and a lawyer. In her mind, there was nothing she couldn't do or fix. Most of the time she was right, and if you inspect our parents' house closely, you'd find all kinds of strange gadgets holding things in place. When the toilet would break, she would scoff at the idea of hiring a plumber. Instead, she would take the toilet apart, inspect it, and repair it. She was the only person we know who not only did her own taxes, but who began the process by first deciding how much money she wanted to get back from the government, and then proceeding accordingly. She was so self-reliant that she never left home without her compass, map, and tape measure.

My mom was a perfectionist in everything she did. She always supported our efforts to learn her skills, but we didn't share her perfectionist tendencies. For example, for years now, I have been bringing home pants that were too long and that I needed my mom to hem. Though she always hemmed them, she would suggest that I learn how to do this myself. Several months ago I took her advice and with her consultation I hemmed a pair of pants. After I finished, she inspected them, commended my efforts, and said, "Great. Next time, go to a tailor."

Even during her illness, our mom continued her tradition of trying to live life to its fullest. Despite being diagnosed only two months before my wedding, she continued to plan and oversee every detail of the event, and it was a truly joyous occasion. Subsequently, she spent her time knitting clothing for her future grandchildren, attending Arielle's baby shower and the birth of Nate, visiting her parents in Florida, traveling to Acadia National Park and to Newport, Rhode Island, and visiting Alex and me in Washington, D.C., and New Hampshire.

As many of you know, my mom did not want to let go. She was devoted to her family and friends, and she had an amazing will to live and a love for life. To the end, she was interested in our future, even though she could not be part of it. For example, as my dad did more and more of the cooking, my mom would teach him her recipes and critique his work. She loved his chicken and matzah ball soup and conceded that it was better than her own. She helped him improve his hummus, which at first was a little dry. About a month before she died, I asked her if she was ready to go. She replied: "Yes, I think dad has learned all of the important recipes."

Barbara died the way she lived, exemplifying devotion, strength, courage, and strong-mindedness. She was a woman of amazing character, whose footsteps her daughters are trying to fill. She was the best mother a girl could have, and she will live on through her family and friends.

As Jillian notes, Barbara was a perfectionist in everything. Perfectionism is both a blessing and a curse, as the "incident with the bricks" demonstrates. Several years ago I was backing our old Ford (which my parents had given to us when they bought a new car) out of the driveway during winter. The driveway was icy, and the rear-wheel-drive car had terrible traction. In an effort to make sure that the car didn't get stuck on a particularly treacherous part of the driveway near the garage, I gunned the accelerator and then cut the wheel prematurely. The right front bumper hit the brick wall just to the right of the garage door, pulling the two-foot section of wall away from the rest of the house. The bricks on the wall remained intact, but the wall itself swung open and closed, like a door, and had to be rebuilt. We hired a mason to repair the wall using the same bricks. He disassembled the wall, brick by brick, and then reconstructed it. It took him several hours, and the repaired wall looked fine to me. For much of that time I watched him, complimenting his work. It did not look fine to Barbara, though she wasn't sure why. A couple of weeks passed, and she suddenly realized the problem: the mason had not used the same bond pattern in the repaired wall to match the rest of the house. As one of Barbara's do-it-yourself books points out, "The bond is the pattern formed by the courses in a brick wall. Courses are laid on top of each other so that the vertical joints in one course never fall directly above the vertical joints in the course below." There was no structural difference between the repaired wall and the rest of the house, but there was a slightly different aesthetic appearance.

And I mean slight. During the next months I would invite relatives and friends, who were having lunch or dinner with us, to inspect the brick wall, and none could detect the problem. Even El Adams, who was a teacher by vocation and a mason by avocation, had trouble finding the difference. It did not matter to Barbara that she alone detected the imperfection: not only was the mason incompetent, she fumed, but I should have noticed the problem as he was rebuilding the wall. Her anger increased when I told her that she was overreacting. Now she was furious at me for three reasons: for knocking down the wall, for telling the mason that he had done a good job, and for not supporting her. The incident with the bricks turned out to be one of our worst marital fights. She never forgot it; as my friend Barbara Adams (El's husband) quipped, "A good memory is the bane of friendships and marriage." I became so concerned that I called Barbara's parents to enlist their help—a mistake, since they understandably sided with their daughter, not their son-in-law. I couldn't hear what Morris was saying over the phone, but I could tell from Barbara's reactions that he agreed with her decision to take the mason to court. She did, and the judge ruled in her favor, requiring the mason to return the four hundred dollars we had paid him. Barbara decided to bank the money without repairing the wall, though she told me that she was never going to look at it again.

The following summer Barbara's parents visited us, and I asked Morris if he could detect the error. He looked and looked and looked. "The bricks are a different color," he said. "Nope, they're the same bricks." "The bricks are cracked." "They were cracked before." "Some of the bricks are discolored." "They were discolored before." "The bricks are darker." "I told you, Morris, they're the same bricks as before—they've been cracked and discolored for years." Finally I told him the problem. He didn't say anything—which was highly unusual for him—but I sensed that he was surprised by how upset his daughter was at the mason—and me.

In retrospect, I'm sorry that I did not support Barbara on this issue. Had I done so, she would not have become so upset. But her perfectionism was difficult at times for me to live with, especially since I could rarely do a job "right" in her eyes. Ironically, several months after her diagnosis, she had her own driveway accident. As she was getting out of the car, she forgot to put the transmission in park and turn off the engine; the car, which was still moving, crashed through the garage door and almost smashed through the back of the house. Neither of us had much to say about the incident. We both realized, as our therapist said on more than one occasion, that terminal illness forces people to decide what they want to hold onto and what they must be prepared to let go of. It was easy to let go of perfectionism.

Just as Jillian learned more about her mother's life by visiting the Brooklyn neighborhood in which she grew up, so did I learn more about Jillian by reading her eulogy. It was no surprise that she spoke about her mother's nurturing qualities, but I had forgotten that Barbara was opposed initially to Jillian's participation in a CYO league when she was in middle school. My recollection is that *I* was opposed, not Barbara. I am not proud of my opposition, which was based on prejudice. I recall telling Jillian that I was uncomfortable with her participation in a Catholic league because she was Jewish, and I especially did not want her to wear a T-shirt to school emblazoned with the words "Christ the King." "Dad, I know who I am," she exclaimed indignantly. She finally overcame my opposition. I also recall, with shame, attending one of Jillian's basketball games in a church and then engaging in a shouting match with a volunteer who asked for a two dollar "contribution," which I declined to pay because by definition a contribution is voluntary, not mandatory—another decision I later regretted.

It is true, as Jillian reports, that Barbara and I agreed on nearly everything with respect to parenting though our styles were different. What Jillian describes as my use of "bribery" I would characterize as "positive reinforcement," a euphemism for my controlling behavior. I was a controlling father in some ways—in *many* ways. But Barbara was stricter with the children on certain issues. I didn't have a problem with their boyfriends sleeping over during high school, an idea which Barbara vetoed without the possibility of my override. She spent far more time with our children and their friends than I did. They loved to shop together, bake cookies together, plan parties together, watch television together. Barbara was rarely if ever heavy-handed: she valued academic achievement as much as I did but placed less pressure on the need to excel.

There is only one sentence in Jillian's eulogy with which I partly disagree, when she observes that her mother encouraged her children to "experience life and take risks." Barbara certainly urged them to experience life, as she had done, but she was not a risk taker when it came to adventurous activities such as parasailing, rock climbing, and bungee jumping, all of which Jillian has done. Despite growing up near a world-famous amusement park at Coney Island, Barbara did not enjoy riding on roller coasters or Ferris wheels because the motion and height scared her. She was a "delicate" child and assumed that her own children would also be delicate. I remember that when Arielle and Jillian were young, I would lie on my back in the living room and toss them into the air, catching them in the nick of time. The girls loved this physical activity and always demanded "more," even if the roughhousing sometimes resulted in minor bruises and tears. Barbara was only slightly more approving when she saw a childhood friend's husband, a physician, throw *his* children into the air. If the girls hurt themselves while we were playing "catch the spider," she would look at me accusingly, even if the next moment they wanted to resume the game. Many forms of physical play that I initiated with the girls usually made Barbara nervous. Perhaps because she grew up in an age when girls were treated differently from boys, she felt uneasy with this kind of risk taking. She never participated in high school sports, and though she encouraged our children's participation—Jillian played tennis, basketball, and softball throughout high school while Arielle was the captain of the cross-country running team—she fretted that they would injure themselves, something about which I did not worry.

Barbara was far more adventurous than I, however, when we went to Bryce National Park in Utah in the summer of 1996. One morning we decided to sign up for a mule ride down the canyon, which turned out to be one of the scariest experiences of my life. The mules were not only huge, much larger than they looked on television, but they also seemed to have a will of their own. My mule was directly behind Barbara's as we slowly descended the rocky trail. I was certain that I would do something stupid that would spook the beast, causing him to crash into Barbara's mule, resulting in the four of us plunging off the cliff. I held both my leather reins and my breath as we made our way to the canyon floor. The few times I could see Barbara's face, as we went around a turn, she was smiling, while I must have looked ashen as I was contemplating a violent death. Nor was I reassured when the tour guide stated that the mules are frightened only when something unexpected occurs, like seeing a rattlesnake—I learned the word "ophidiophobia" in high school because it was my number one fear. Afterward, when we finished the ride, Barbara said it was one of the high moments of our Southwest trip. I have a color photo of her sitting proudly on the mule, wearing a cowboy hat, looking like Dale Evans, who, along with Roy Rogers and Hopalong Cassidy, was one of her idols while she was growing up in Brooklyn.

Barbara could be adventurous when she wanted to, and she was always encouraging when it came to meeting personal and professional challenges. Both by word and by deed, she urged our children to have a family and a career. She acknowledged that she became an elementary school teacher because she followed her mother's advice that "good Jewish girls become teachers," but she changed careers a few years later and chose computer science, a field that was then uncommon for women.

Arielle's Eulogy

A few weeks ago, my family and I began looking through some of my mom's old belongings. I found myself drawn to her letters and keepsakes. Looking through them was a way for me to learn more about my mom. It also helped me to remember her as she was before her illness—a vibrant, energetic person.

I first peered through her baby book and found a handwritten letter that was written by my mom's pediatrician shortly after her birth. The letter was addressed to my grandmother. It read:

"Care of Baby"
1. Never permit to lie in wet diaper.
2. Use alcohol on gauze pad to cover navel.
3. Do not bathe baby until three days after navel has fallen off.
4. Use baby oil over entire body.
5. Use powder sparingly. Do not cake!
6. On or about the fourteenth day, baby may be taken outdoors, providing weather permits. Baby is not a curio—keep everyone away!!! Listen to all "yentas" and you are sure to get into trouble.

Continuing to search through my mom's mementos, I found a collection of letters she had tucked away. Included in them were letters my grandparents had written to her when she left home to attend college. Shortly after my mom left for school, in the fall of 1963, her mother wrote to her: "The school looks nicer each time that I see it and I trust that you will avail yourself of all the opportunities it offers you. Home is quite empty without you, but once we are all back at school, time will pass quickly. Remember not to look ahead too far. Please take care of yourself and get as much sleep as you can. Also, have as good time, socially, as is possible."

By October 1963, my grandma appeared to have become slightly more irritated with my mom. She wrote to her daughter: "Daddy and Karen and I want you to know what a pleasure it was to have you home for even a little while. We enjoyed every moment and hope you did, too. How was the trip back? My one complaint is: Why are all of you college students dressing so sloppily? If you think it makes you look smart, the answer is No! Blouses and skirts are much more appropriate."

Several days later, as my mom was preparing to visit home, her mother wrote: "Barbara, dress with slacks for traveling and comfortable shoes or sneakers. Don't take them off, as your feet swell on such a long ride and you may not be able to put them on again. Hope you get some sleep on the ride. Love, Mother."

Following college, my parents were separated for a short period of time while my dad studied at Cornell and my mom attended graduate school at Hofstra. A letter dated July 30, 1967, revealed a side of my mother that I had never seen—cute, playful, flirtatious. In it she wrote: "Baby, I'm really tired now, but I don't want your mailbox to get lonely, so here I am. Life is draggy here—I keep thinking about your coming home. . . . Tomorrow it's up bright and early for school. I keep wishing school is over, yet I know that when it is over it will be almost time for you to go back. So at the same time I wish to prolong the time till the end of August to be with you. I'm going to write every day this week. I want to be around in your hour of need and to brighten up your day of studying. A bientot, mon amour (a little French to change the pace)."

Even when Jillian and I were young, we knew how lucky we were to have our mom. On August 14, 1982, I wrote a note to my mother: "Dear Mommy, Thank you for all you've done. You've sure done a lot. And now I think I can start helping you and working for you, like I did in the morning. Remember, I made my toast. Now that I'm getting older, I think that it's time for me to cook some things—like toast, bagels, crescent rolls, and other stuff. I'd like to start today or tomorrow or sometime pretty soon. And mommy, I forgot to tell you, I love you very much."

Jillian of course felt the same way as I did about my mom. On April 29, 1985, she honored my mom by writing a letter for mother's day. She was ten years old at the time. She wrote:

Dear Mom,
Mother's day is nearing and it's time to start thinking about you. I'll have to buy you a present and get you a card. But I'm sure as you're reading this you're saying, "It's not the present but the thought that counts." Well, I know that too but I thought you might like a present anyway. Maybe it's just because I love you and admire you. You're smart and talented. Everything just comes to you naturally. You know I'd love to be just like you when I grow up. For instance, you didn't know a thing about stained glass but after a few weeks of learning, you had it down pat. I wish everything came to me naturally. Maybe I'll be like that when I grow up. I hope so. Where you find the time to do everything, I don't know. I mean, with your job and all. Most people don't have time to do other things if they have a job. But you have a job, you have hobbies you do, and you have time to help Arielle and me. It really surprised me how you do it. I can't imagine someone doing all that. But now I know it's possible.

It's true that my mom was able to do so many things, and have so many interests. In May of 1996, she traveled with my dad to the Southwest.

She sent me this postcard from New Mexico: "Arielle, we're enjoying every moment of our trip. We're now in Sedona, Arizona, surrounded by beautiful red rock mountains and unusual formations. It's a geologist's dream. Between my love of geology and anthropology and crafts, I'm in constant fascination. Today we're off to the Grand Canyon, then back to Santa Fe, and then home, when we'll need a big rest."

My mom also has a good sense of humor, even about her own tendency to worry. In a letter she wrote several years ago, she remarked: "Tonight is dad's birthday. Tomorrow Ellen is coming to speak at Schenectady County Community College. Then we'll spend the day together and she'll sleep over. I get to show her the necklace she bought me for my birthday. I had a dream the other night that the stone fell out of it and that she didn't like it. Maybe I should double my Paxil!"

After I graduated from college, I moved to Boston, where I worked while applying to graduate school in clinical psychology. I must have talked with my mom about my future plans, because I found the following letter that she had written to me afterwards: "Dear Arielle, that's the first time I sent mail to you at your new address—strange writing Massachusetts. I was sorry that you didn't stop on Sunday because I wanted to tell you how impressed I was with you on Thursday night when you were talking about your plans, and your terrific attitude. You seem really organized and in control of things, and you look absolutely beautiful also. You're really a special person—even if you weren't my daughter I'd think so. Just wanted you to know how proud I am to have you as a daughter. Love, mom."

As I read through her letters, I am keenly aware of what I will miss over the years—the opportunity to sit next to my mom and have her teach me about herself, myself, and the world. But I know that as a new mother myself, I will continue to learn from her and *about* her over time—through the experiences she has given me, the values she has taught me, and the comfort she has provided me.

It is hard to imagine a contemporary pediatrician offering the same advice that Barbara's mother received in 1946, especially the admonition to "keep everyone away" from the newborn baby for an unspecified length of time. The "Care for Baby" letter dramatizes not only the dramatic changes in baby care in the last half century but also the rigid guidelines in effect at her birth, when mothers had a long list of dos and don'ts.

Barbara was a collector, and so it is not surprising that she saved the college letters written by her mother. I recall the stringent dress code in effect for female students during our freshman and sophomore years, when women had to wear skirts and nylon stockings to dinner, and when they had evening curfews in the dormitories. I haven't reread the letters we sent to each other from the fall of 1967 through the spring of 1968, when we were studying at different universities, but I remember that it was the only time we were separated, and the only time I felt lonely since meeting her—until her death.

Arielle included in the original draft of her eulogy Barbara's wry reference to doubling the dose of her antidepressant, Paxil, in anticipation of a small party in her honor. Arielle later decided to omit this sentence from the eulogy, believing that the detail was too private to be disclosed at the funeral. I think it would have been both appropriate and funny to have included the sentence. Neither Barbara nor I had reservations about telling relatives and friends that we were on an antidepressant, and I don't think she would have been upset by the inclusion of that detail in the eulogy. She and I were both catastrophizers, and we both took antidepressants for several years preceding her diagnosis, she for anxiety and depression, and I for a sleep disorder. We often said that if we could change one aspect of our lives, it would be to worry less. Our poet-friend Judith Harris called Barbara a "worrier-warrior," an apt term for her ability to live with fear and dread during her illness. Interestingly, most people were unaware of Barbara's tendency toward anxiety and depression, since she usually appeared so calm and serene.

Several of our relatives have suffered from anxiety and depression, including my mother, and that's one of the reasons why I have devoted so much of my teaching and writing to a discussion of how creative writers have portrayed mental illness. I taught a course called Literature and the Healing Arts in 2002 in which we focused on the literature of depression. We read Leo Tolstoy's *Death of Ivan Ilych*, Albert Camus's *Plague*, Primo Levi's *Survival in Auschwitz*, William Styron's *Darkness Visible*, and Lucy Grealy's *Autobiography of a Face*. Styron's observation, following his suicidal breakdown and recovery, that "I began to see clearly how depression had clung close to the outer edges of my life for many years" (78) would also be true, to a lesser extent, for Barbara's life, though unlike him, she never abused alcohol. It is ironic that so many novelists, poets, and playwrights are wary of taking an antidepressant, fearful that it will destroy their creativity, but they do not hesitate to self-medicate with alcohol—the "liquid muse."

As a father, I'm proud of my children's love and devotion, their many achievements, and, most of all, their goodness. As an English teacher, I'm proud of their excellent writing skills, which they use every day in their chosen professions: clinical psychology, for Arielle, and law, for Jillian. Decades ago I recall a colleague saying that children of academics are often subjected to intense academic pressure, a statement with which I agree. I try not to place too much pressure on my students, but some of them tell me that it's difficult to live up to my expectations. Our children have *exceeded* our expectations. If, during adolescence and early adulthood, they could not utter a single sentence without prefacing it with the word "like," they have become, either because or in spite of their father's constant corrections, articulate young women. Their devotion to their mother during her illness went beyond filial duty. They were both remarkably poised when they delivered their eulogies, and they both captured so many of their mother's wonderful qualities. Indeed, they embody their mother both in appearance and talent. I recall my mother saying to me many times while growing up, in response to whatever act of insensitivity I was guilty of at the time, "I hope you have sons just like yourself." Instead, Barbara and I have been blessed with daughters of whom any parent would be proud.

Karen's Eulogy

I believe that Barbara's energy is with us here now, and that she would want us to celebrate her life, rather than mourn her passing.

When Barbara was asked what she might be learning from this difficult struggle with cancer, she replied, "I realize how much I cherish life, how much I love it. Don't waste a moment, since you don't know what tomorrow might bring."

My sons found their Aunt Barbara's calm demeanor so comforting. When they were young, a simple phone call to Aunt Barbara always helped to ease the jitters before that first day of school. Soon after my son Peter planted his first vegetable garden, I remember Barbara walking out there with him to admire his work, or how can I ever forget how she massaged my infant son's head while in the hospital recovering from open-heart surgery. She just had that way of making others feel so special and comforted, simply by her words of encouragement, acknowledgment, and praise.

Barbara could get along with anyone. She was always easy to talk to, with an insatiable curiosity about everything. This curiosity was, and is, an integral part of her very essence, her undying spirit. I remember hearing stories about Barbara's and Jeff's travels: Barbara leading the way, with map in hand, trying to squeeze in umpteen sites of interest, while Jeff's stomach would be grumbling, hoping that some time would be allotted for meals. For Barbara, eating was just a waste of time, when there was so much more to see and do!

What seemed like insurmountable tasks to most of us were no big deal for my sister, whether it be tossing together an impromptu meal for company, or doing a wide variety of home repairs. She never turned her back on a challenge.

Barbara's creativity never ceased to amaze me—quilts, Tiffany-style lamps, sweaters, even paisley polyester ties during those flower-power days of the '70s.

When Barbara taught first grade in Ithaca, New York, the little kids and their parents adored her. As a computer programmer, Barbara shined.

If there was a problem, she inevitably found a solution. By nature, she was a problem-solver. Even with the cancer, she viewed it as a problem, for which she would exhaust every possible means in order to find a workable solution.

It was very difficult for Barbara to lose the fight to this disease, and fight she did with every bit of energy left in her body. Throughout the struggle, Barbara was gracious, so very thankful and appreciative for everyone's encouragement and love.

Not too long ago, when one of my sons remarked, "We love you, Aunt Barbara," she quietly responded, "I love you too," and added, "Talk to your children about me." Barbara will not only forever be in our hearts, but in our daily lives for as long as we live.

Arielle and Jillian need only replay the videos of their weddings to witness the expression on their mom's face, an expression of exhilaration that words can never adequately express. Your happiness is your mom's happiness, and that will prevail. Believe it when your mom told you not to worry, because she reassured you that she will, in fact, be with you whispering in your ears.

Barb, you're a part of me and that will never change. You understood in a way that only a sister can. I will still be reaching out to you for advice and, you know, your special way of just "seeing" the obvious which goes unseen by many.

I love you, Barb. You'll always be my role model and hero.

Karen visited us frequently during Barbara's illness, and they spent countless hours reliving their childhood together and talking about their own children. Karen's strength and courage never faltered during her sister's illness. Feeling strongly about the tradition of saying Kaddish for the eleven months following the first month of mourning, Karen went regularly to Friday night services at her temple, where she derived comfort from thinking about her sister's life. "Barbara is constantly with me, in my thoughts," she wrote in a recent email. "I try to listen really closely after communicating with her telepathically, waiting to 'hear' her response. I am continuing to learn from her."

Jerry's Eulogy

We did not ask to be born, and we do not normally wish to die. Consciousness of this absurdity gives rise to a metaphysical loneliness. So, how are we to make sense of life? Would we now choose to be born, having experienced life? The schools of Hillel and Shamai debated this question for more than a three and a half years in the first century CE, and though they generally disagreed on matters of Jewish law, they finally

agreed on this: it would have been better had we never been born, but
now that we have been born, let us look to our deeds. This pessimistic
outlook can be attributed to their experience of the Roman destruction
of Jerusalem, its Temple, and thousands of Jews.

Barbara, I believe, would have answered differently. She made sense
of life mainly through love. She was extraordinarily devoted to her family and friends—and to her dogs; and her love was reciprocated. Barbara delighted in the goodness and accomplishments of Jeffrey, Arielle,
and Jillian, to whom she contributed so much, and she was content with
her own considerable attainments. She was sophisticated in the arts and
humanities as well as computer science; but her paramount virtue was
love, and in this she followed the Golden Rule: *Love your fellow as yourself*. The great sage, Hillel, born in 60 BCE, said that this rule "is the
whole Torah and the rest is commentary; go and study it." Ben Azzai, a
Talmudic sage of the second century CE, found a rationale for the
Golden Rule in the Torah's tracing of all humanity back to a common
parentage, to Adam and Eve, thus establishing the unity and equality of
the human race as created by God. But even unbelievers have reason
to recognize the primacy of the Golden Rule, for a lonely and mean-
ingless universe cries out for mutual love as much as God and a common origin do.

Barbara's deeds and sentiments embodied the Golden Rule. Her good
cheer and wisdom, her laughter and compassion, have entered our soul.
She will be remembered always, and with love.

I have known Jerry Eckstein for more than twenty years, and he has become a father figure and mentor to me. I admire his intellectual boldness, his
vast learning, his philosophical rigor, his graceful prose style, and, above all, his
humor and humanity. He is sensitive to the many conflicts in human nature,
and he has the courage to acknowledge his disbeliefs. Shortly before he was
to be ordained as a rabbi, he realized that he could not go through with the process, since he had lost his belief in God as a result of the Holocaust. Instead,
he earned a Ph.D. in philosophy at Columbia University, driving a taxicab in
New York City to support himself and his family. His loss of belief in God, however, did not prevent him from founding the Judaic Studies Department at the
University at Albany, where he taught for many years before his retirement in
2000. Jerry's books—*The Platonic Method, The Deathday of Socrates, Metaphysical Drift*, and *On Meanings of Life*—reveal his profound synthesis of religion, classics, and philosophy. His definition of "metaphysical loneliness" is
the best that I have come across:

Metaphysical loneliness is a feeling that existence is nobody's friend,
that we are all vagrants in the universe. It emerges with an awareness

that human existence is inherently conflicting, unable to support happiness for long, and that, ultimately, every person is alone. Such loneliness is not a mere accompaniment to personal tragedy, to the absence of friends; it is an obbligato to the consciousness of the human condition, arriving with the understanding that all blessings are hexed—that Utopia is "no place," as its Greek etymology signifies, not because it is imaginary, but because it is unimaginable. Those who have lost faith are especially susceptible to this sadness. (*Metaphysical Drift* 36)

Jerry begins *The Deathday of Socrates*, his second book on Plato, with an observation about the importance of reflecting on death. "Montaigne says that 'practice cannot help us' to prepare for death; 'we can try it only once: we are all apprentices when we come to it.' But he also says that 'there is a certain way of familiarizing ourselves with death and trying it out to some extent.' Indeed, in the *Phaedo*, Socrates contends that the function of philosophy is to 'train' us for dying and death" (3). Jerry reads the *Phaedo* not as a straightforward philosophical dialogue but as a dramatic play that reveals Plato's true philosophy, and he argues that, contrary to conventional wisdom, Plato disapproves of Socrates' "heroic suicide." In Jerry's words, "Plato agrees with Socrates that 'the unexamined life is no life for a human being,' but the playwright considers the perpetually examined life as also not worth living; Plato discriminates between obsession and passion. Furthermore, Plato sees the moderate person as taking excessive positions and actions on occasion, for the one who always follows the middle course is as radical as those who never deviate from the extremes" (57). Through a careful analysis of Socrates' flawed logic, Jerry shows that Plato wishes readers to see his opposition to his master's suicide—an opposition that for two thousand years has remained unnoticed.

In an example of life imitating art, Jerry returns reluctantly to suicide in the epilogue to his next book, *Metaphysical Drift*, in which he comments on his writer-friend Bruce, who took his own life three weeks earlier. In the suicide letter to Jerry, Bruce lists his recent failures, including the collapse of a multimillion-dollar contract to produce a television series based on several of his novels and the rejection of his latest manuscript. "You're the philosopher," Bruce wrote in his letter, "you're the one who can understand the one thing a dreamer needs are his dreams. Take them away and you [are] an empty shell. A good thing perhaps that most people aren't dreamers" (206). Addressing a letter to his deceased friend, Jerry notes that although Bruce mentions reading Plato's *Phaedo* the previous week, he apparently did not read Jerry's commentary on it:

> You knew that in my view, unlike traditional ones, Plato does not consider Socrates' suicide to be an act of noble martyrdom; that Plato is not

only grieved, but angered by the act; that he condemns the act as selfish, as unconcerned with its consequences on family and friends; that
he makes Socrates' defense of suicide obviously invalid, while providing
the interlocutors' opposing arguments with better logic. But you had already closed your mind to opposing arguments. You saw yourself as
similar to the traditional Socrates, who chose death over exile when no
longer able to teach Athenian lads his truths. At least Socrates was an
old man when he chose death, very old in his time, and some say quite
ill, but you are only fifty-four and in good physical health. In my judgment, though, Socrates was not a martyr to Truth, and you are not a
martyr to Art. (207)

Jerry suggests that his friend's suicide was motivated not mainly by philosophical renunciation of life but by clinical depression, which is often alleviated by psychotherapy, medication, or the passing of time. Jerry then ends his
book with an eloquent affirmation of life: "Love, creativity, beauty, friendship,
justice, reason and compassion seem to me all the more important in an absurd world; to maintain one's humanism while approaching eternal blackness
is a great dignity. I do not know whether my end will be violent, like yours,
Bruce, or whether destiny will allow me to fade out in peace; but I do know
that I miss you" (209).

Jerry's book-in-progress, "An Atheist's Bible," not only exposes the problems and wisdom in the Hebrew Bible but also offers his own vision of spiri-
tuality. "The ultimate mysteries," he affirms at the beginning of the book, "are
not about whether God exists and what His nature is. They are, rather, why
there is anything, including God, instead of nothing at all; and why is anything,
in the end, not otherwise. Reason brings us to the border of these unknow-
ables. Existence is suffused with mystery." Jerry argues that no less than religious humanism, atheistic humanism "affirms the innate dignity of all humans,
and cherishes its manifestations as ultimate values."

Jerry and I have lunch together regularly and debate a wide variety of
subjects; he is a political conservative and loves to poke fun at my liberalism.
I always defer to his knowledge of the Jewish Bible and Talmud, of which I am
so ignorant; he defers to my understanding of literature and psychology, which
is less deep than he thinks. I always ask Jerry to read a manuscript before I
submit it for publication; I jokingly refer to him as my proctologist in that although it is painful to have him examine every word, I know afterward that he
has spotted every potentially malignant problem.

I asked Jerry to conduct Barbara's funeral service and to offer his own
eulogy. He approached the bema slowly, and for a moment he seemed so overcome with emotion that I thought he was going to faint. Just as I started to rise
to steady him, he regained his composure and gave the eulogy, but he was

visibly shaken throughout the service. I asked him, months after the funeral, to explain why, in light of our metaphysical loneliness, we should have children. He responded with the following note:

> The question put to me is: "If it would have been better not to have been born than to have been born, as the school of Hillel and the school of Shamai concluded in the first century CE after the destruction of the Temple of Holiness, Jerusalem, and thousands of Jews, then are we not morally obligated not to produce children, not to bring them into a hateful world?" These Schools would have rejected this consequence, however, for they also concluded that "now that we have been born, let us look to our deeds," and thus we must follow God's command to be fruitful and multiply (Gen. 1:28, 9:7). Presumably, God has a purpose that justifies such suffering.
>
> The question put to me pertains not only to particular persons, but to all persons; it is a question that also suggests our discontinuing the human race. Still, the suggestion would not have been unthinkable to the Schools of Hillel and Shamai, since God, Himself, had contemplated such action: "The LORD saw how great was man's wickedness on earth, and how every plan devised by his mind was nothing but evil all the time. And the LORD regretted that He had made man on earth, and His heart was saddened. The LORD said, "I will blot out from the earth the men whom I created—men together with beasts, creeping things, and birds of the sky; for I regret that I made them. But Noah found favor with the LORD" (Gen. 6:5–8). And so God changed his mind. He saved only Noah, his family, and representatives of all living species from the Flood in order to give life a fresh start.
>
> Hence, widespread evil and suffering must not cause us to cease producing children, whether as individuals or communities; the principle of life as well as the life principle should dominate. Indeed, these principles ruled even after the Nazi Holocaust's destruction of millions of Jews, when Jews continued to have children, some as many as possible, and when they strove to establish the State of Israel. How could they have been justified apart from religious considerations? Mainly, because it would have been false and arrogant for them to think they could know that future generations would prefer not to be born. This assumption is always arrogant and mostly false. There are other reasons for not having children, however, which are valid.

While looking through my file cabinet for Barbara's writings, I came across a handwritten statement of Jerry's from the late 1990s entitled "Yet." The statement may be viewed as his "credo," affirming his life beliefs. He has allowed me to reproduce it here:

It was hard for me to be born and to be conceived, but creating concepts and nurturing them have been one of my two greatest joys—giving
meaning to my life. It still does, though I am old. Home life with immi-
grant ultra-Orthodox Jewish parents was hard—emotionally confusing
and depressing; but for some time, now, emotions have been fairly clear
and bright.

God deserted humanity in the Holocaust, especially the Jews, so,
though hard, I relegated him to a delusion. My adolescent children
forsook me thirty years ago after I divorced their mother, so, though occasionally failing, I have gradually hardened myself against the pain. Fortunately, Mari stepped into their place fourteen years ago.

The approach was arduous, but my chosen career has been fulfilling.
The move from philosophy to Jewish philosophy, to creating a Judaic
Studies Department, afforded a fuller Jewish identity—one with integrity.
Teaching has also partially satisfied the need to nurture adolescents.

Love, the other major source of my life's meaning, has been less constant and harder to achieve. I have loved and been loved by two of my
three wives, but with Kathy [Mari's mother] I enjoy also the deep security that she will not abandon me. Friendships, too, have contributed
much to the meaning.

Yet life is absurd. Rationally, it is as Camus said: "The absurd is lucid
reason noting its limits." But the absurdity is more than facing ultimate
mystery, or yearning for certainty or immortality and knowing that they
are unavailable. It is a feeling that existence is nobody's friend, that we
are vagrants in the universe. Still, there is great dignity in living and de-
fying the absurd. Curiously, though, I am becoming somewhat resigned
to death.

Jerry's answer reminds me of a stanza from a poem by W. H. Auden, who
also argues that since it is impossible not to have been born, the best one can
do is to live as fully and intensely as possible:

The desires of the heart are as crooked as corkscrews,
    Not to be born is the best for man;
The second-best is a formal order,
    The dance's pattern; dance while you can. (Qtd. in Arendt,
"Remembering" 183)

Barbara danced throughout her brief life, and those who eulogized her
affirmed her goodness and grace. Like every person, she was complex, yet Jillian, Arielle, Karen, Jerry, and I all saw her in largely the same way. She had so
many talents, interests, and hobbies that she could do almost anything well—
she was perhaps the most self-sufficient person I have known. As I suggested

in my eulogy, it is hard living with a perfectionist, and now that she is gone, I see that my dependency on her was something both of us should have resisted. I *can* do many of the things that I thought only she could do, such as keeping track of the finances, caring for the dogs, loading software in my computer, finding my way while driving. No one would have been prouder of me for performing these tasks than Barbara. She urged all of us to do our best, as she did. She followed instinctively the Golden Rule, and love guided her spirit in life and in death.

6
STUDENTS READING ABOUT BARBARA'S LIFE

U ntil the day of the funeral I did not know whether I would be able to read the eulogy. I had rehearsed it so many times that I had almost memorized it, yet my voice was shaky when I read it to myself the morning of the funeral. That shakiness intensified when I walked into the funeral chapel. How, I wondered, could I maintain my composure amid so much sorrow? From the moment of Barbara's diagnosis I had found myself unexpectedly bursting into tears, my entire body convulsing; I knew that I would be keenly disappointed if words failed me now. I tried to remain positive and focused, reminding myself that, just as I was able to read the eulogy to my students, so would I be able to read it now. Perhaps it would be easier now since, unlike my students, the mourners, who numbered close to 250, would not be surprised to hear a eulogy.

Months before the funeral, when Arielle, Jillian, and I visited the funeral home to select a casket, we were told that we could play music during the service. Many compositions came to mind, including "Dance of the Blessed Spirits" from Gluck's opera *Orpheus and Eurydice*; Mozart's resplendent Concerto for Flute and Harp, K. 299, truly heavenly music; Ravel's "Pavane for a Dead Princess"; Samuel Barber's "Adagio for Strings"; and Ralph Vaughan Williams's haunting "Lark Ascending," all of which Barbara loved. But I decided to play, with her approval, several of Debussy's short compositions: "Maid with the Flaxen Hair," "Claire de Lune," "Reverie," and "Prelude to the Afternoon of a Faun." Debussy's dreamy, exotic, shimmering music, ravishingly beautiful and other worldly, has always reminded me of Barbara. The music now had a soothing effect on me, helping to evoke her presence as the mourners streamed into the funeral home.

As the service began, I sat next to Arielle, Jillian, and Karen in the first row and listened to their tributes to Barbara, which they delivered in strong voices that faltered only momentarily. Finally my turn came. I walked to the bema and started reading, slowly and deliberately, feeling like a professor addressing a large audience. (Most of the academic talks I have given have drawn only a handful of people, one of whom was always Barbara.) I felt strangely composed, as if I were on automatic pilot: my voice broke only once, when I read the sentence about catastrophe befalling us the day of her diagnosis. I was able not only to complete the reading but also to establish eye contact with the relatives, friends, coworkers, and students who came to honor Barbara's memory. (By contrast, I did not look at my students when I read the eulogy in class.) After I finished my eulogy, Jerry delivered his, and we then drove to the cemetery.

I had asked my brother to be one of the pallbearers, but several of the cars, including his, became separated from the funeral procession and never made it to the cemetery. I decided, at the last moment, to help carry the casket, which at least gave me something to do. The ceremony was brief. I knew in advance that watching the casket descend slowly into the ground would be the most wrenching moment of the day. I clutched my children's arms for comfort and could feel my face contorted by grief.

My reaction to the many mourners who attended the funeral startled me. I have not always attended friends' or colleagues' funerals in the past, believing that what is most important is not how one is treated in death but in life. I still believe that, but I was surprised by the depth of my appreciation for the many people who attended Barbara's funeral. I had told out-of-town friends that I didn't expect them to attend the funeral, but many came nevertheless, for which I was deeply grateful. Colleagues with whom I have not been collegial in the past appeared both at the funeral and at the cemetery, and I remember thinking that whatever conflicts we had in the past seemed trivial in light of the respect they were now paying to Barbara and our family. I resolved to attend funerals in the future: they have greater significance than I realized. I felt the same gratitude upon receiving hundreds of condolence cards.

During the funeral I did not recite Kaddish, the ancient mourner's prayer that is recited for eleven months, nor did I later observe the other rituals, such as covering mirrors, wearing a black armband, or "sitting shiva," the Jewish seven-day mourning period that helps survivors confront the loss of a loved one and continue with their lives. Nor did I observe the other rituals of mourning, such as lighting a *Yahrzeit* candle on the anniversary of a death. I thought then, as I think now, that it would have been hypocritical to pray to a God in whom I do not believe. Yet I asked Glenn to say Kaddish, and he was glad to do so. Months later I read Leon Wieseltier's *Kaddish*, a diary of his yearlong mourning for his father, and I came across a rabbinic statement with which both he and I disagree. "The rabbis famously say that those who cannot pray for the sake of praying should pray anyway, because it will bring them to pray for praying's sake. I never liked this statement. It is behaviorism or it is opportunism, since it finds a religious utility for faithlessness, and thereby steals the thunder from belief and unbelief" (322).

Every culture and religion has its own death rituals, and as Katherine Ashenburg points out in her book *The Mourner's Dance*, "Of all Western cultures, the Jews have preserved the fullest repertoire of post-burial customs. They underscore the perplexity of the first days and weeks of mourning: something is irrevocably finished, while something else, the adjustment, is beginning" (111–12). Like so many books, including this one, *The Mourner's Dance* came into existence as a response to a death in the family, in Ashenburg's case, the death of her daughter's fiancé in a car accident. I was struck by the observation that there are many psychological and anthropological explanations for death rituals, including darker motives of which most people remain unaware:

> We may observe certain customs—wearing dark clothes to the funeral, speaking only about the dead person's good qualities, holding a wake, erecting a tombstone—believing we do so out of respect if not affection. Certainly I did. So it was disconcerting to discover that anthropologists see most of the traditions and rituals around death as born out of fear and self-protectiveness. We have rationalized and sentimentalized them since, but as the anthropologists tell it, they began as something more craven. The dark clothes hide the living from the malevolent spirit. Crying and speaking well of the dead persuade him that he is regretted. Holding a wake reassures him that he is not forgotten, perhaps even deludes him into thinking he is still living. The tombstone is an attempt to keep the spirit under the ground, where he can do less harm. So, symbolically, are the small stones Jews leave on tombstones when they visit a cemetery. (11)

"A foolish consistency," Emerson writes in his essay "Self-Reliance," "is the hobgoblin of little minds." Ashenburg's last sentence reminds me that although I did not observe most of the Jewish rituals, I do observe a few, such as placing small stones on Barbara's gravestone whenever I visit the cemetery. Apparently some of the death rituals persist even when we believe that we have rejected them. Death rituals die hard deaths.

I was grateful for the relatives, friends, colleagues, and students who came to our house for lunch following the funeral service and burial, and we shared memories of Barbara. I remember vaguely that we had a great deal of food, most of which was consumed, confirming one of Ashenburg's more surprising observations: "Caterers will tell you that people eat much more at a funeral than at a wedding" (25). Glenn and his daughter, Rachel, slept over at our house following the funeral, as did my daughters and sons-in-law, and all of them gave me comfort and support, as I tried to give them. Friends continued to bring over meals that they cooked. More than eighty families made contributions in Barbara's memory to hospice and the American Cancer Society. One of our friends, Professor Sherman Raskin, longtime chair of the English Department at Pace University and the founder of Pace's Master's Program in Publishing, named a graduate fellowship in Barbara's memory. Within a few weeks I contacted a monument maker for Barbara's headstone—I ordered a double stone, one for her, the other for me. I did not wait eleven months, the required period of time in the Jewish religion, when the gravestone is unveiled; instead, I visited the cemetery as soon as the stone was completed in the early fall and set into place. I visit the cemetery every few months, but I don't feel closer to Barbara when I'm there. Philip Roth's observation about visiting his mother's grave characterizes my own feelings: "I find that while visiting a grave one has thoughts that are more or less anybody's thoughts, and leaving aside the matter of eloquence, don't differ much from Hamlet's contemplating the skull of Yorick. There seems to be little to be thought or said that isn't a variant of 'he hath borne me on his back a thousand times.' . . . What cemeteries prove, at least to people like me, is not that the dead are present but that they are gone. They are gone and, as yet, we aren't. This is fundamental and, however unacceptable, grasped easily enough" (*Patrimony* 20–21).

Writing and Grief Work

Can writing be considered a "death ritual"? I began writing about Barbara almost immediately after her death—most of the eulogy was written before her death. Perhaps unconsciously, I wrote the eulogy in preparation for this book. Leon Wieseltier began *Kaddish* soon after his father's death, and though he is, unlike me, an observant Jew, I identify with his need to read and write about death: "One of the most dreaded eventualities in a man's life has overtaken me, and what do I do? I plunge into books! I can see that this is bizarre. It is also Jewish. Anyway, it is what I know how to do" (172).

I can't recall the exact moment when I decided to write a book about Barbara: that idea evolved from the first essay I wrote for my students in April, when I described their reactions to the eulogy. I wasn't sure, in the beginning, whether I had enough "material" for a book. As it turned out, I had more than enough to write about her. Daily writing became a solemn duty. Months after I started writing, I read Parkes's *Bereavement* and was startled to discover that his definition of grief work—"the process of learning by which each change resulting from the bereavement is progressively realized (made real) and a fresh set of assumptions about the world is established" (141)—describes uncannily my feelings while writing about Barbara. Parkes suggests that grief work consists of three components: (1) "there is preoccupation with thoughts of the lost person, which . . . derives from the urge to search for that person"; (2) "there is painful repetitive recollection of the lost experience, which is the equivalent of worry work and which must occur if the loss is not fully accepted as irrevocable"; and (3) "there is the attempt to make sense of the loss, to fit it into one's set of assumptions about the world (one's 'assumptive world') or to modify those assumptions if need be" (77–78). Writing was my grief work, and while it was indeed hard work, it was harder for me on those days when I was *not* able to write because of my teaching responsibilities.

I didn't know it at the time, but my decision to write about Barbara demonstrates two essential features of grief work: "obsessional review" and "distancing." In *The First Year of Bereavement*, Ira Glick, Robert Weiss, and Colin Murray Parkes define obsessional review as "going over and over the same scenes," which is an integral part of the mourning process. "It was distressing to the widows [in their research project] that they were so absorbed by the review and could not simply recognize their loss and be done with it. But they seemed unable to stop" (126). Writing about Barbara was my way of engaging in obsessional review. I searched all our file cabinets and dressers for anything that she wrote, and I grew excited whenever I came across writings that I had not seen before, such as the statement about getting Pandora after Cybele's death, or the letter to her father. I felt elation when I read her cancer diary, realizing that it would help me bring her to life with her own words. I treated the diary as if it were a lost Shakespeare manuscript, something to be preserved and studied. The diary affirms her ability to live with pain and to pursue every avenue of treatment. My obsessional review did not extend to her clothes, which remain in her closets, untouched, nor to our daughters' wedding videos, which I am not yet emotionally ready to view; but it did extend to her writings; her crafts, which I dust conscientiously; her recipes, which I am now making; and her photos, which are everywhere in my home and in my university office.

Writing about Barbara was also a form of distancing, which Glick, Weiss, and Parkes define as the "avoidance of unmanageable distress by the device of keeping disturbing thoughts away from the focus of one's attention. Many of our widows, and somewhat fewer of our widowers, tried at first to fend off disturbing thoughts and memories. Some kept busy and some avoided people or situations that would remind them of their loss" (295–96). It seems counterintuitive to believe that writing about Barbara was a way to *avoid* thinking about her, but the paradox may be understood by Parkes's observation in *Bereavement*: "*In order to avoid thinking about something we have to think about it*" (41; emphasis in original).

Obsessional review diminishes but apparently never ends, as Lily Pincus points out in her own and her clients' mourning experiences:

> Most people are not aware of their need to search but express it in restless behavior, tension, and loss of interest in all that does not concern the deceased. These symptoms lessen as bit by bit the reality of the

loss can be accepted and the bereaved slowly, slowly rebuilds his inner world. Yet I wonder whether the impulse to search for the lost person ever completely disappears. Even for those bereaved who have successfully built a new life, search for the lost love object persists at moments of great strain, weakness, or illness, just as the dying person often recalls memories of his childhood and appears to be searching for his first love objects, his parents. (116)

My colleague Ronald Bosco, an Emerson scholar, gave me a striking example of how the memory of loss lasts a lifetime, even in a mind otherwise ravaged by dementia. Ralph Waldo Emerson married Ellen Louisa Tucker in 1829, but she died sixteen months later from tuberculosis. Emerson loved her dearly and idealized her throughout his life; his second marriage, to Lidian Jackson, was based upon affection and respect but not the same deep love. (He named their daughter after his first wife.) Emerson suffered from dementia during the last years of his life, but he was lucid enough to record in his pocket diary for 1879 the date of his first marriage and the anniversary of Ellen's death on February 8, 1831.

I knew when I started writing the eulogy that I was trying to work through my grief, but only after reading Parkes's book did I realize the motives or "components" behind my "grief work." I was obsessed with Barbara, and I did everything to hold onto her in life. My writing began when I realized I was losing her. This search for a dying woman compelled me to look everywhere for her. Joan Didion describes the same phenomenon in her memoir *The Year of Magical Thinking*. When I thought about Barbara after her death, I could only brood over my loss, painfully and repetitively fixated on her absence, like a broken record that keeps returning to the same spot; but as soon as I began writing about her, I felt close to her again, reconnected, *almost* as if I had never lost her. Writing helped me make sense of my loss, enabling me to construct a new image of her that was now safely—and imperishably—inscribed on paper, a beloved presence I will never lose again.

The pleasure I derive from working on this book, shaping every sentence until it is as clear and compressed as possible, parallels the satisfaction that members of a bereavement support group experience from narrating their losses to each other: "Paradoxically, the telling and retelling of a terrible event seem to have a certain anesthetizing effect, while they also make the death incontrovertibly real" (Ashenburg 220). "At times I felt guilty," Ashenburg acknowledges, "that I was so gripped (dare I say entertained?) by their sad stories and these brave people. Then I would remind myself that the widows and widowers were also enjoying one another's company. There was a certain richness, not surprising in a group where everyone had sustained a loss and gathered together, committed to a notable level of openness" (221).

How odd to experience satisfaction if not pleasure when talking or writing about death. Yet such feelings originate, I believe, from the effort to maintain control in the face of suffering and death, and to construct an interpretation that can explain an otherwise inexplicable event. If the dying are unable to find the words to describe the moment of death, those who care for them do; and when these stories are well written, evocative, and meaningful, we call them art. Death is, paradoxically, the undying muse of art.

Responses to "Dying to Teach"

Shortly after Barbara's death I wrote a twenty-five page, single-spaced draft of "Dying to Teach" that included my students' responses to the early draft of the eulogy I read in class in March, the completed eulogy I read at the funeral in April, and my daughters' eulogies. (I had not yet included Karen's or Jerry's eulogies.) I then gave a second assignment, optional and anonymous, like the first:

> I'm giving each of you a copy of "Dying to Teach." It is a first draft; I'm sure I will continue to revise and develop it. It contains the eulogy I read in class, a later version of the eulogy that I read at Barbara's funeral, my two daughters' eulogies, and a discussion of how your class responded to the eulogy I read in class (based on the fifteen anonymous essays I received). You can keep the copy. I would like you to read the essay closely. I have quoted passages from each of the fifteen anonymous essays I received. On a separate piece of paper, would you please answer the following questions:
>
> 1. If you submitted an anonymous essay, did I accurately represent your point of view? If not, please explain.
> 2. Are you comfortable with allowing me to use the quoted passages for a possible article or book? If not, circle the passage from your essay that appears in "Dying to Teach," and I will delete that passage. It would be helpful for me if you explained why you are withdrawing permission.
> 3. Please offer your impressions of "Dying to Teach." Be as specific as possible. What surprised you most about the essay? What will you most remember about the essay?
> 4. Is there anything in "Dying to Teach" that you believe I should delete?
> 5. Is there anything that you believe I should add to "Dying to Teach"?
> 6. Speculate on how reading the essay has affected your thinking about death.
> 7. If you were one of the fifteen people who submitted anonymous

responses to the eulogy, would you like readers of "Dying to Teach" to know anything additional about yourself?

8. If you were not one of the fifteen, were your responses to the eulogy different from your classmates' responses? If so, please explain.

Ten students turned in responses to the first draft, and while few answered all eight questions, those who answered the first question all believed that I had accurately represented their points of view. They were comfortable with the way I had used and contextualized their words. No one asked me to delete his or her responses.

Several themes characterize the students' responses to the first draft, beginning with their appreciation that I was interested in learning their point of view. "I liked how you included essays from the class. I liked reading the opinions of my fellow classmates and seeing how they differed from my own. I was one of the fifteen that responded to the eulogy you read in class. I thought that you summarized what I thought accurately and the parts you chose to quote were appropriate. I've never had a teacher quote what I had to say in an essay that may be published; I am honored that you quoted me." The same person felt that it is better for teachers to ask their students how they feel about a particular issue than to speculate on their feelings. "Very rarely do teachers ask their students to comment on something they have written; I don't think I've ever been asked to give my opinion on such a matter. This is crucial for an essay of this nature in which you quote your students' essays. I realize legally you may need our approval, but I'd like to think that it is more a form of respect." Students also agreed with my decision not to edit their language. "I think it is important that you didn't revise or change what we wrote. This way, you are showing exactly how your students felt. If you had corrected or changed our words, there may have been a bias present."

Some students explained why they hadn't turned in the first optional essay, and their writings give us insight into the challenge of responding to death. "I did not respond to 'Dying to Teach.' I had a lack of words every time that I sad at my computer and started to write. I had so many thoughts that wouldn't translate to my fingers. The computer screen stayed black for four days. I decided then to stop trying. I knew that I wanted to tell you that I was sorry. I wanted to be able to let you know that my heart was aching for you and your family. My heart was aching for your wife. It never came to me. I never handed the assignment in. I wish I had. Now that I think back on the day that you wrote the eulogy, words have started to come to my hands." Although the above student intended to write "sat" instead of "sad at my computer," the latter dramatizes the difficulty of finding the right words to express sympathy. Now, a month later, the writer has found appropriate language to express condolence, perhaps as a result of newly acquired empathy. "I have always lacked the characteristic of being able to put myself in someone else's shoes. I have always wanted to be able to do so, I just have never before. That is until I participated in this class; now your essay and my classmates' essays all bring me to tears." The writer ends the essay by returning to the "lack of words" to convey grief despite the fact that, paradoxically, the entire response essay has been a moving expression of grief:

> I feel that my response to "Dying to Teach" would have been a combination of all the responses that you're received; mine would have been a jumbled response at best. As I explained earlier my response did not come, no matter how hard I tried I could not find the right words to say at the time. I recently tried to write it again; after your wife died. The words again were not there. How do you console a person after such a loss? My only answer is that you don't. You can try and your words may mean a great deal and they may not. But I can't bring back your wife, as much as I would like, and I can't find a replacement to fill your void. I can only once again tell you that I am sorry. I am sorry that I could not find the right words that you wanted to hear and I am sorry that you even have to go through this in the first place. I hope after this class ends that you find a way to share your story with classes in years to come. I guarantee that your students will benefit in knowing their teacher is human.

Those who were absent from class when I read the eulogy appreciated the opportunity to read about their classmates' reactions:

> I was not present in class the day you read the eulogy aloud. When I was told about the events that occurred in class that day, I wished I had been there. I am sure that many of my classmates, myself included, did not expect you to share such a personal disclosure with us. There were several moments when I wanted to ask you for a copy so that I may read it. I was ashamed and embarrassed; I never asked. After reading your essay, a part of me felt relieved. I finally read the eulogy.
> When you handed out the eulogy to the class, I wanted to begin reading it. I placed the packet in my bag and anxiously waited. I waited for the perfect opportunity to read it. Silence was needed. I wanted to be able to read through the essay and not be disturbed. I decided to take the essay with me to work. My office is generally quiet in the morning so I seized the opportunity. Despite a few phone calls, I was able to read the essay thoroughly. Reading the eulogy made me quite upset. I was angry with myself. I wished I had been present in class when the eulogy was read. I will never be able to describe or feel what my classmates felt.

Had I been present in class during the reading of the eulogy, I would have felt and looked the same as my classmates did. . . . I appreciate that you were able to disclose this information to us. As one of my classmates stated, "I know I find it easier to share my sensitive disclosures with you." You made it easier for the class to write about sensitive topics without the fear of reading it to others. I do not think the class would have been as trusting if you had had not the courage to read the eulogy to us.

Two students identified more closely with my daughters' eulogies than with my own, mainly because they were closer in age to Arielle and Jillian and could imagine losing a parent. One noted that although she was one of only two people who did not know whether my reading of Barbara's eulogy was appropriate, she was glad that I represented her point of view. She then commented on how my daughters' eulogies affected her:

I especially liked Jillian's. The way in which she encompassed her mother as an individual, and then as a mother, and managed to conclude with a circle by bringing it back to her mother was powerful. I admired Arielle's ability to incorporate solid evidence of Mrs. Berman's life into her eulogy. Without these two eulogies I do not think the essay would have the same effect. It gives the reader a vivid picture of how much Mrs. Berman was loved.

The other student explained why she could "barely make it through" my children's eulogies:

I had to keep stopping to wipe my eyes. The words would become so blurry under my tears that it was hard for me to proceed through the text. I could imagine myself dispelling similar feelings about my own mother. I put myself in their shoes the whole time I read their eulogies. It crushed me. Even now as I type this part of my response I am sobbing over my keyboard. I cannot even imagine the day when I have to do this for my mom. The parts of Jillian's eulogy that touched me the most were when she was hemming her pants under Barbara's supervision and when she asked her mother if she was ready to go [and] she replied: "Yes, I think dad has learned all the important recipes." That made me cry the hardest because my mom always asks me to watch her do things and I always whine and moan. She always responds with the question: "What are you going to do when I'm not here to show you?" Until I read Jillian's eulogy, this had never affected me. I never envisioned my mom being gone. This made me realize that I should start paying a little more attention to my mom before that luxury is gone. The parts of Arielle's eulogy that were equally as moving for me to read were examples of her and Jillian's childhood letters and a compliment her mother makes in a letter.

The letters reminded me so much of all the handmade cards and letters I have made for my mom over the years. My mom has shown some of them to me and I laugh every time I read one. They are stored away in her closet along with the many creations my brothers have made for her. The compliment that Barbara made to Arielle that moved me to tears was as follows: "You seem really organized and in control of things, and you look absolutely beautiful also. You're really a special person—even if you weren't my daughter I'd think so. Just wanted you to know how proud I am to have you as a daughter. Love, mom." I thought that these were the most loving, wonderful words a mother could ever say to her daughter.

This essay has definitely made me more aware of the fragility of life. I have a hard time dealing with death, but I think this essay has made me face some of my fears. Reading this has especially made me face the fear of my mother dying. The death of my mother is a fact with which I cannot come to terms. This essay has given me a glimpse of what it will be like to lose my mother. This is why I had such a hard time getting through Jillian's and Arielle's eulogies. Reading this has opened my eyes to the reality of death; it has made me more appreciative of what I still have and who I still have the luxury to enjoy in my life.

As the above passage suggests, the eulogies reminded students of their own mortality and the fragility of life. The eulogy affected them powerfully because it was not an abstract, theoretical truth they could dismiss, as in the statement, "all men are mortal," which Ivan Ilych fails to heed at the beginning of Tolstoy's famous story. Rather, my eulogy was an emotional truth that hit close to home. I was writing about my own experience, which then became part of their own experience. They realized that death can strike at any time, in any place, in any way, to any and every person, and that we must endure inevitable losses with as much fortitude as possible. Without exception, the students acknowledged that death is devastating regardless of whether it is expected or not. Indeed, no one seemed to know how to respond to death. It mattered little whether the deceased was a relative, a friend, or a friend's parent. Each death produced shock, disbelief, and confusion:

My friend's father died unexpectedly a few months ago. Along with two friends, I took a trip downstate to attend the funeral and pay my respects. The funeral was not what I expected. In the church I was raised in, no one stands up to speak of the deceased. My grandmother passed, and no one talked about their own experiences with her either during the wake or funeral. When the priest gave the floor over to people who wanted to talk about my friend's father, I was unprepared.

My eyes welled up with tears, shed for a man I've never met. My friend gathered the strength to sing a song in memory of her father. Her strength bewildered me. A few days later, she returned to Albany. Even though she was immensely saddened by her father's death, she managed to return to her studies nonetheless. I didn't understand it. Growing up, I don't think I had the best relationship with my father. Things have been better since high school, but it still isn't the father/son relationship I would like. However, if he were to die today, I wouldn't know what to do. My trip home for the services would be preceded by me deregistering myself for the semester.

Students cannot predict how they will respond to a loved one's death, and some of them assume that they will find themselves "deregistering" from their college courses. The above student acknowledges that reading "Dying to Teach" was an educational experience: "The essay has caused me to continue thinking about death. I hope that when faced with losing my first loved one I will be able to find the strength that you found." Others in the class felt the same way:

Reading this essay has given me a different outlook on death. You show how your attitude changed as your wife's illness progressed. Most people are afraid of death, yet in situations such as this, death becomes a welcomed change. That thought still scares me and the death of younger people from illness is terrifying. No one should have to suffer in this way. I have seen people pass away in the prime of their life, and it is never easy. The only factor that helps to ease my pain has always been knowing they are no longer in pain. Along with knowing that they will suffer no more, the song by Billy Joel, "Only the Good Die Young," always fits in with an unwanted death. I am still afraid to die, but you showed how your entire family stood by your wife until the very end. This aids in re-assuring me about death, knowing that loved ones stick together until the end.

Many students stated in their second response essays that "Dying to Teach" enlightened them about the darkest of subjects. "Reading the essay gave me a greater insight in to how the loved one begins to cope after the loss. I realized while reading your essay that death is often a long and grueling process. The moments before appear grueling and trying, the moments after seem silent and blank. However, you have also made it apparent that you can make someone live on through your words. Barbara lives in your mind, and through this essay she lives on in your writing. I can now see that even when we lose someone, that despite the physical absence, they will always be with us in our memories. Not only will Barbara forever live on in your mind, but in the mind of each student within our expository writing classroom." Another remarked on our family's changed attitude toward death. "'Dying to Teach' has given me a greater sense of how death is welcomed after a long period of suffering. I remember sitting in my room praying for an hour each night. I remember how you told us that you're 'waiting for her to die.' When you said that, I thought about miracles and how I could possibly achieve one by praying every night. When I received word of her passing via email, I felt let down. It is still hard for me to look at someone's passing as relief. Reading your essay has given me a view into a window I have refused to look into. I started to feel that death isn't always bad. It can provide relief." Another person was struck by the ways in which I coped with Barbara's death. "Previously I viewed the death of a loved one as something from which you would never recover. You have shown me that there are ways to cope with the death of someone close to you other than drug therapy. You said that coming to school every day helped you retain your sanity. I don't mean to say that you were unaffected by Barbara's death; on the contrary, you coped with the grief astonishingly. You like all of my classmates, possess an inner strength that I can only hope to have one day."

It would be more accurate to say that "drug therapy" helped Barbara and me to cope with her illness, for without the tranquilizers and antidepressants she took every day for panic attacks and depression, and the antidepressant I took to help me sleep, coping would have been much more difficult. Until the final weeks of her life, when she was semicomatose, the psychological challenge of her illness was as formidable for both of us as was the physiological challenge.

For nearly all the students, reading "Dying to Teach" raised more questions than answers. "After reading this essay and the eulogies, I have thought a lot about death. I wonder why people die. Or rather, why do they live? I would not trade living for having not lived, but death is so painful. A young girl from my neighborhood died this past winter. At the bus stop where she was killed there is an enormous arrangement of everything from flowers to candles to huge stuffed animals. I wonder why people die if it brings so much pain to others. Yet, who would truly want to live forever?" Those who are religious acknowledged that death has tested their faith. "After reading 'Dying to Teach,' I was speechless. I have dealt with the passing of a close relative. I had no emotion nor do I deal well with death. During the different stages before burial, I felt as if God had betrayed me. It has now been ten years since the passing of my relative; I have only attended a funeral service once since then. The passing of my grandfather took place during spring break. I had to attend the wake.

Darkness fell upon me. I was scared. I imagine the same feeling fell upon you as you entered the service." Those who were not religious continued to search for answers. "I, like Professor Berman, am not religious. I consider myself agnostic and maintain that view. Though I was brought up Christian, traditions and all, I do not believe in fairytales. I wish that I could. I wish there was a 'paradise.' It would make death, not easier, but acceptable. It would make life and death make sense. I want there to be a paradise, more so than before having read 'Dying to Teach.' I want there to be a place for Professor Berman and Mrs. Berman to be together again. I believe that people like them deserve a place like that."

Regardless of their religious views, the students read "Dying to Teach" as a cautionary tale, reminding them of the mystery and inevitability of death:

> After reading your essay I came to the conclusion that at one point in our lives we are all going to have to deal with death. In some cases it is easier to deal with death before it happens, rather than if death is unexpected. I have experienced both. They are both hard and heartbreaking. When I knew that death was evident, I woke up every morning fearing the day. I lived life in a bubble just wishing it would happen so it would all be over with. On the other hand when death was unexpected it left me to wonder why? Why do people have to die? I guess that is one of life's unexplainable. Like how we stand straight if the world is a ball and is constantly rotating. I constantly ponder such issues, and every time I fail to find the correct answer. So death is another one of the unmentionable; along with the concept of after life and trying to come to closure with death.

"I Wasn't Ready"

All ten students stated in their response essays that they benefitted from reading "Dying to Teach." An eleventh response essay, representing a different point of view, appeared in my university mailbox a week after I received the others. Unsure whether I had permission from the author, whom I will assume is female simply because there were many more women in the class than men, to include the response in my next revision, I told my students during our next meeting that I wanted to represent this point of view in the writer's own words. "If the author does not wish me to use the response essay, please leave a note in my mailbox." Since all the students were present in class when I made the announcement, and since no note appeared, I quote the response in its entirety:

I did not submit an anonymous response to the eulogy. It is not because I didn't write one. I wrote a full page of my reactions and views, but decided at the very moment I was asked to turn the paper in, that I should not do so. I should not turn the paper in because my views were so strongly opposed to those of most of the class. I didn't want anyone's feelings to be hurt.

I was reluctant to read "Dying to Teach" and I am even more reluctant to discuss my feelings about it. I skipped over the actual eulogy; once was plenty. "Dying to Teach" confirmed my suspicion that I was in an extreme minority who believed that a eulogy belongs among friends and relatives and not among strangers in a classroom.

There are enough catastrophes in everyday living that I do not need to carry anyone else's burden. I felt like I was being imposed upon by that eulogy, and feel doubly so in "Dying to Teach." Please don't think that I mean to disrespect you. I don't. I feel very very sorry for you. No one should have to endure what you have gone through so valiantly. I cannot imagine having to wake up without my companion beside me. I think of it often, and I need no other reminders that life is fragile.

However, with the exception of coursework, I choose my reading material like I choose my movies. If I think it will be upsetting then I avoid it. It was horrible enough to sit through class while you read that eulogy, seeing so many people affected by it, while feeling nothing but aggravation within myself. I counted floor squares; I contemplated my pen. I did whatever I had to in order to distance myself from the situation that I had been thrust into unknowing, unwilling, and unprepared.

I suppose that at the heart of the matter my biggest issue with the whole thing was that I wasn't ready. I knew from the outset that I would be expected to write about personal experiences and listen to the personal experiences of other students. I was not, however, prepared to hear a eulogy for a, then, living person written by my professor.

I wonder if I will turn this in. I am certain that a student's writing style will give them away whether the paper is anonymous or not. Here it is anyway. I am truly sorry for your loss.

This essay must have been difficult to write and even more difficult to submit, especially since the author believed she was in an "extreme minority." That she did, in fact, turn in the essay demonstrates her respect for herself and for me.

Although she may have been the only one in the class who felt burdened first by hearing the eulogy and then by reading "Dying to Teach"—I say "may" because I don't know whether the others who did not submit response essays shared her point of view—many people will agree with her position. I can understand her desire to avoid feeling burdened by another's problems. Mental health professionals have told me that they are exposed to so much sadness in their everyday professional work that they don't like to see gloomy films or read dark novels. As I discuss in *Surviving Literary Suicide* and *Risky Writing*, reading depressing literature may place certain readers at risk; the contagion or "Werther" effect, in which readers overidentify with depressed or suicidal fictional characters, is well documented. Traumatic literature may traumatize certain readers, especially if they are not prepared for wrenching events: this is indeed the above student's criticism, and my brief comments preceding the eulogy made it impossible for her to prepare herself for the emotionally charged reading. Citing an observation made by Terrence des Pres—"What others suffer, we behold"—Geoffrey Hartman uses the term "secondary traumatization" to describe "a guilt, perhaps a shame, implanted by becoming aware of evil or simply of such suffering" (78). Empathy has its limits, Hartman adds, and the "management of empathy is not easily taught" (79).

Teachers cannot prevent students from becoming at risk, but they can observe the protocols that I discuss in *Risky Writing* to minimize this possibility. These protocols include alerting students in advance to emotionally charged essays, allowing students to leave the classroom when they feel distressed, balancing assignments on painful topics with lighter ones, encouraging students to meet with their professors during office hours to discuss problems with the course, giving students the option not to write on any topic that they deem too personal, and knowing how to make appropriate referrals if they believe that students are at risk. I hope that the above student did not suffer permanent harm from hearing the eulogy and reading "Dying to Teach," and I appreciate her willingness to allow me to represent her point of view in her own words. She apparently viewed the eulogy mainly as a story of suffering rather than, as I intended it, a story of a beautiful, courageous life ending prematurely.

Ironically, I suspect Barbara would have agreed with the above student's argument, for she did not want to read anything sad during her illness. Until the final month of her life, when she was rarely conscious, we would watch rented videos together every night. I tried to choose movies that would be funny and upbeat, but even some of the comedies contained characters who were dying of cancer. (We didn't watch any Woody Allen films, but I wonder how she would have responded to his sardonic observation that "I'm not afraid of death. I just don't want to be there when it happens.") Sometimes she became upset or angry with me when the grim reaper made an unexpected appearance. For example, while watching an episode of the *Sopranos*, we were jarred when "Uncle Junior" (Dominic Chianese), the elderly mob boss, develops the same kind of cancer that Barbara had, adenocarcinoma—his was in his stomach, not pancreas. Nor was she cheered when his cancer went into remission. She wanted to watch films that would allow her to escape, if only momentarily, from the knowledge that cancer was ravaging her body. She could not bear to see a movie that reminded her of impending death. She did not mind my reading the eulogy to my students, but she did not want to know their reactions to it.

If our situations were reversed and I were dying, I doubt that Barbara would have wanted to deliver a eulogy at my funeral. A private person, she would have grieved silently, believing that death was an unspeakable subject. She planned every detail of Jillian's elaborate wedding, which occurred two months after her diagnosis, but she did not want to think about her funeral. Three months before her death, our daughters and I purchased a burial plot for her in a rural cemetery, and although she was glad that I would be able to visit her grave often since it was close to home, she had no interest in seeing pictures of it. She mentioned her funeral only a few times. She wanted to be buried in the Mount Rainier T-shirt she had bought a few years earlier when we visited the Pacific Northwest; she wanted a plain casket, which was to remain closed; she did not want her parents to attend; and she wanted to be buried with our dog's cremated ashes, which she had saved in an urn that we kept in the garage. Apart from expressing these wishes, she never spoke about the funeral, and knowing how she felt, we did not refer to it in her presence.

I do not mean to imply that Barbara did not do everything that had to be done regarding her death. She accompanied me to see a lawyer about drawing up a will, a health proxy, and a durable power of attorney, and she invited a financial planner to visit us at home so that we would choose the best pension option for me. Despite her worsening health, she delayed her retirement by several months to qualify for an incentive that would increase my survivor benefits. She also taught me her favorite recipes, as Jillian says in her eulogy. And she was always helping me to learn to do what she alone did throughout our marriage: how to do the taxes (which I later decided was far too complicated for me to understand), how to distinguish the perennials from the weeds in our garden (which I promptly forgot), how to unclog the drains and repair leaky faucets (which I now pay a plumber to do), and how to groom the dogs (which I can do, though I'm afraid to cut their nails). She was a supremely practical person, and to the end of her life she tried to help us cope with her death. But she was reluctant to talk about dying or death, and she would have agreed with my student's statement that one needs "no further reminders that life is fragile."

And yet I believe that Barbara would be pleased with my decision to write this book, and I also believe that she would be pleased to hear that her life has become part of my students' education. In her eulogy Karen quoted Barbara's statement—"Talk to your children about me"—and I believe that, like

most people, Barbara wanted to be remembered. She was a teacher before becoming a computer analyst, and she loved to read serious literature, as the list
of the novels at the end of her diary indicates. She had a far better memory
than I for remembering birthdays, anniversaries, and deathdays, and I know
that she did not want to be forgotten. I never spoke to her about writing a book
about her, but she would have helped me write a good book, as she did in the
past with my earlier books. She read all of my books in manuscript except for
the last one, *Empathic Teaching*, which she started to read but could not finish.
Knowing her as I did, I am certain she would have insisted that all the facts
about her life be correct. And she would have supplied me with countless details of the past that only she could have remembered.

Counterphobic Motivation

Unlike Barbara, I cope by confronting my ghosts head on, beginning with the
effort to read everything I can about whatever problem is upsetting me. Counterphobic motivation appears in my earliest published writings. The opening
paragraph of my first book, *Joseph Conrad: Writing as Rescue*, depicts a cartoon
that I had saved years earlier from the *New York Times Book Review*:

> The cartoon I came across several years ago illustrates, with startlingly
> literal gallows humor, the grim predicament of a man at the end of his
> tether. As he glumly piles one book upon another to reach the noose that
> dangles ominously above his head, he accidentally gazes down upon an
> opened page. He pauses. Riveting his attention upon the book, he stays
> his self-execution. By losing himself in the story, he seems paradoxically
> to have rescued himself from the anguish that prompted him to repudi-
> ate his life. The noose continues to dangle above his head, serving as a
> reminder of his vulnerability to self-destruction; the man's interests, how-
> ever, are now elsewhere—at least until he completes the book. (11)

I argue in the book, which was based on my 1971 doctoral dissertation,
that the high suicide rate in Conrad's fictional world—higher, indeed, than that
of any other major novelist—can be traced to his own abortive suicide attempt
in 1878 when he was twenty years old. Information about the suicide appears
in a long-lost letter written by Conrad's uncle and guardian, Thaddeus Bobrowski, which was published in 1957, thirty-three years after the novelist's death.
The letter, which Bobrowski wrote to a friend of Conrad's deceased father
in 1879, describes the events leading up to his nephew's suicide attempt, including heavy gambling debts, a failed love affair, and the inability to secure a

permit that would allow him to serve on a French ship. "Having managed his affairs so excellently," Bobrowski writes sarcastically, "he returns to Marseilles and one fine evening he invites his friend the creditor to tea, and before his arrival attempts to take his life with a revolver. (Let this detail remain between us, as I have been telling everyone that he was wounded in a duel. From you I neither wish nor should keep it a secret.) The bullet goes *durch und durch* [through and through] near his heart without damaging any vital organ" (31). Conrad later showed the wound to many people, without telling them, however, that it was self-inflicted.

Years later he wrote a purportedly autobiographical novel, *The Arrow of Gold*, in which the hero, Monsieur George, which was the actual name Conrad called himself while living in Marseilles in the late 1870s, incurs a wound as a result of engaging in a duel to defend the honor of a shadowy woman. No mention of suicide appears in the novel, but self-inflicted death, in both ambiguous and unambiguous forms, appears in many of his stories, including *Heart of Darkness, Lord Jim, Nostromo, Under Western Eyes, The Secret Agent,* and *Victory*. By creating and killing off fictional characters with whom he identified, Conrad was able to hold in check his own suicidal urge. To this extent, I suggest, he was an escape artist, more successful than other extremist writers, like Virginia Woolf, Ernest Hemingway, Sylvia Plath, and Anne Sexton, who could not finally exorcize their own self-destructive impulses:

> Unlike the others, he was able to exploit a private weakness into enduring artistic strength; and from this artistic success he gained personal strength. His commitment to work, the greatest of the Victorian verities, enabled him to control the tensions which might otherwise have led to paralyzed introspection. Just as Marlow's retreat into the mindless but therapeutically efficacious riveting of the torn steamer's hull in *Heart of Darkness* has the effect of rescuing his inflamed imagination from Kurtz's unspeakable horrors, so did Conrad's pursuit of art allow him to maintain a commitment to an ideal greater than the solitary self. As the Marlow of *Chance* shrewdly observes, "to be busy with material affairs is the best preservative against reflection, fears, doubts—all these things which stand in the way of achievement. I suppose a fellow proposing to cut his throat would experience a sort of relief while occupied in stropping his razor carefully." It is a startling metaphor, filled with fascinating biographical ironies. Given the pervasiveness of the destructive element in his novels, Conrad's work involved a continual sharpening of his razor—and the use of that razor against his fictional characters. But as long as he was engaged in the sharpening of the blade, and as long as his reading public could admire the deadly beautiful bite of the blade, he gained enough

relief—though at times he surely nicked himself—to keep it away from his throat. (*Joseph Conrad* 27).

Neither in my doctoral dissertation nor in the Conrad book did I mention the reasons for my preoccupation with suicide. It was only in 1994, when I contributed an essay to *Self-Analysis in Literary Study*, edited by Daniel Rancour-Laferriere, that I discussed how the suicide of my college mentor, Len Port, has affected my life and work. The discussion, which I included at the beginning of the chapter "Suicide Survivors" in *Diaries to an English Professor*, explored the aftermath of suicide, which may haunt relatives and friends for decades:

> Suicide creates intense, long-lasting guilt, grief, and anger among family and friends, and Len's death overwhelmed me. By literally hanging up on him, cutting him off, I felt like I betrayed his friendship. He had forced me into a Catch-22 situation: had I remained on the phone, as he urged me to do, listening without intervening, I would have respected his wishes but felt greater disloyalty, blaming myself for not having done everything in my power to save his life. Years later I discovered that my situation was by no means unique: approximately one in four suicides occurs in the presence of another person or while the suicide victim is speaking over the telephone—a phenomenon that emphasizes the interpersonal nature of suicide and the crucial importance of the role of the other. ("Grief" 38)

I felt so guilty over my failure to save Len's life that although I attended the funeral in New York City, I did not seek out his parents to tell them how grief-stricken I was over his death. I regret that omission deeply. Nor did I attend his wife Phyllis's funeral. I was unable to face another death.

It took me several years before I was able to talk openly about Len's suicide, and once I started, I could not stop. My response to grief is to talk about it, to analyze it, to research it, to write about it, and to find ways to connect it with the stories I teach in the classroom. Or, as Martin and Doka would say, my style of coping with grief is "intuitive" insofar as I experience loss deeply and gain strength and solace by openly sharing it with others, especially other grievers. Writing cannot undo the past, cannot bring the dead back to life, cannot avert tragedy and suffering, but it can give us greater insight into ourselves and, equally important, help us to take charge of our lives. Writing reveals not only what we *consciously* know but also, if we are attentive to our words, what we *unconsciously* know. Writing is both grief work and rescue work, enabling the writer to change a passive situation—that of a victim or a mourner—to an active one. Writing restores one's self-control, focuses one's energy, and overcomes feelings of hopelessness. As Martha Wolfenstein observes,

Speaking about the disaster, in contrast to being haunted by memories that come against one's will, provides the possibility of turning passivity into activity. In retelling an experience, we voluntarily reevoke it. Narration is thus like play in that one can assume control over the repetition of an event which in its occurrence ran counter to one's wishes. While, alone at night, one may dread the vivid revival of the experience, when telling it to others one wants to evoke it as vividly as possible. Here is again the turning of passivity into activity: from being the helpless victim one becomes the effective storyteller, and it is the others, the audience, who are made to undergo the experience. (139)

"Every novelist only writes one novel," the writer Bernard Malamud observed to Norman Holland. So, too, do literary critics keep writing the same book. I do. I return in every book I write to traumatic subjects, foremost of which is suicide, in an effort to confront and master my fears of death. Perhaps this is why Freud's book *Beyond the Pleasure Principle* speaks so powerfully to me, not in its highly speculative "death instinct," which has never received clinical or empirical support, but in its "repetition-compulsion principle," which has proven enormously helpful in understanding the reliving of traumatic events. My earliest writings and, presumably, my latest writings all reveal an effort to master fear. Freud's description of his eighteen-month-old grandson's "fort-da" game—throwing a spool of thread away and then reeling it in, in a manner suggestive of loss and recovery—describes much of the underlying motivation of my teaching and scholarship: "At the onset he was in a *passive* situation—he was overpowered by the experience; but, by repeating it, unpleasurable though it was, as a game, he took on an *active* part" (16; emphasis in original).

One of Freud's most magisterial essays, "Mourning and Melancholia" focuses on the role of loss in both phenomena. "The distinguishing mental features of melancholia are a profoundly painful dejection, cessation of interest in the outside world, loss of the capacity for love, inhibition of all activity, and a lowering of the self-regarding feelings to a degree that finds utterance in self-reproaches and self-revilings, and culminates in a delusional expectation of punishment" (244). All of these symptoms, Freud argues, with the exception of the disturbances of self-regard, by which he means self-esteem, are present in mourning as well as in melancholia (depression). In this essay Freud investigates the dynamics of identification and internalization—how we take qualities of others into ourselves and become like them—and, in a famous statement, declares that we find the "shadow of the object" falling upon our selves when we lose a loved one. Freud does not pathologize mourning, but it is curious that he categorically rules out the possibility that mourning can become so intense as to lead to illness: "although mourning involves grave departures from the normal attitude to life, it never occurs to us to regard it as a pathological

condition and to refer it to medical treatment" (243–44). He also unequivo-
cally rules out unconscious factors in mourning, apparently not realizing that
those who consciously mourn loss may also be unconsciously mourning earlier losses.

Freud published "Mourning and Melancholia" in 1917 and *Beyond the
Pleasure Principle* in 1920, shortly before the two most painful losses in his life:
the death of his twenty-six-year-old daughter Sophie Halberstadt in 1920 and
then the death of her four-year-old son Heinz in 1923. Freud's early biographer
Ernest Jones reports that the death of his beloved grandson had a devastating
effect on the psychoanalyst: "It was the only occasion in his life when Freud
was known to have shed tears. He told me afterward that this loss affected him
in a different way from any of the others he had suffered. They had brought him
sheer pain, but this one had killed something in him for good" (3:92). Freud
confided to Heinz's father, "I have spent some of the blackest days of my life
in sorrowing about the child" (Breger, 306). In 1930 Freud revealed to the
American psychiatrist Smiley Blanton his obsession with death: "I think about
the possibility of death every day. It is good practice" (Breger, 267–68).

Freud stoically endured these and other losses during his eighty-three
years, but he might have theorized mourning differently had he suffered these
losses earlier in his life. And yet he did experience major losses in his early
childhood: the death of a younger brother, Julius, when Sigmund was two;
the probable depression of his mother, Amalia, whose brother died at the age
of twenty; and the sudden departure of his nursemaid, a maternal figure who
was caught stealing, arrested, and sent to prison. Freud apparently did not explore these losses sufficiently. The most controversial thesis in Louis Breger's
biography is the assertion that these early losses had a traumatic impact on
Freud, resulting in his "lifelong preoccupation with illness and death—both
his own and of others close to him" (17). These losses produced, in Breger's
view, his fainting spell in the presence of Carl Jung, his phobia about traveling on trains, and his superstitious belief that he was destined to die at a particular age, such as fifty-one or sixty-two, in conformity to his friend Wilhelm
Fliess's theory of periodicity. Peter Gay states in his biography that Freud's
mourning over his father's death was "exceptional in its intensity. It was exceptional, too, in the way he put it to scientific use, distancing himself somewhat from his loss and at the same time gathering material for his theories."
Gay adds that "one phenomenon that he observed in himself, and named,
during these sorrowful days was survivor guilt" (88). To the extent that every
interpretation reveals something about the interpreter, much of Freud's psychological theorizings reflect his efforts to master his fears—staving off death,
paradoxically, by constantly writing about it.

One could not have predicted that I would write a book about Barbara's
death, in the same way that one could not have predicted that she would die

of cancer at the age of fifty-seven, but in retrospect, my decision to write this book is consistent with my lifelong identity theme. As Holland states in "The Brain and the Book," "Writers have a compulsion to write because a particular medium or sensory modality became part of that identity theme. When this acting-out succeeds, it fulfills identity and is therefore a source of great pleasure. When it fails, it is a source of equally great unpleasure because identity re-creation has failed. Hence the creative urge acquires its compulsive quality." This helps to explain why it was so important for me to read the eulogy first to my writing students and then to the mourners at Barbara's funeral. A "successful" reading, which required maintaining composure to speak the words, would affirm my identity theme of confronting and mastering loss; an "unsuccessful" reading would disaffirm my identity theme.

It is not just "suicidal" writers, or those who attempt to come to terms with traumatic subjects like suicide, who seek to transmute painful personal experience into artistic or scientific discovery. George Pickering has coined the term "creative malady" to describe how psychological illness was the driving force behind the creativity of Charles Darwin, Florence Nightingale, Mary Baker Eddy, Sigmund Freud, Marcel Proust, and Elizabeth Barrett Browning. "The illness was an essential part of the act of creation rather than a device to enable that act to take place" (19). Pickering speculates that most of their achievements would not have taken place were it not for their psychological illness. Writing in the mid 1970s, Pickering states that to his knowledge, there is "no convincing evidence of exceptional creativity among psychoneurotics in general" (288). Since the publication of *Creative Malady*, several researchers, including Kay Redfield Jamison in her book *Touched with Fire: Manic-Depressive Illness and the Artistic Temperament*, have demonstrated persuasively that there is a much higher incidence of mood disorders in creative writers, artists, and musicians, particularly depression and manic depression. Grief and loss, then, like psychological illness, may be the catalyst behind a wide variety of artistic and scientific creativity. Death itself may be a dark muse, as David Aberbach suggests in *Surviving Trauma*, with the "love and care lavished upon the work of art serving as a permanent testimony to the artist's attachment to the lost person" (23).

Kay Redfield Jamison is a striking example of a writer who has devoted herself to the study of an illness that affects her own life. The best-selling author of several books on manic depression, she is professor of psychiatry at Johns Hopkins University. I attended her lecture on March 8, 2005, at Hudson Valley Community College. After speaking about depression among college students, she discussed her own history of manic-depression, going into more detail than she had in her memoir *An Unquiet Mind*. During the question-and-answer period, she revealed that she had suffered a severe suicidal breakdown when she was an assistant professor of psychiatry at UCLA. Unsure whether

her illness would prevent her from fulfilling her teaching and clinical responsibilities, and whether she needed to hide the fact that she was bipolar, she
sought advice from the chairperson of her department, who told her, suppor-
tively, "Learn from it, write about it, teach from it"—advice that she has followed, with spectacular results.

The teacher's challenge to students, like the writer's challenge to readers,
is to narrate painful stories that are not overwhelmingly traumatic. Many
people remain ambivalent about traumatic stories, as Nancy K. Miller and
Jason Tougaw suggest in the introduction to their edited volume *Extremities*:
"A reader's involvement with the painful details of another's story entails both
the pleasures of the imagination and the defenses of personal boundaries—
and these reactions shape the exercise of identification across the borders of
the unfamiliar. Accounts of extreme experience set in motion an ambivalent
desire to look, to grapple with real suffering, and at the same time to look away—
to put the book down, including this one" (19–20). Stories can wound just as
they can heal; indeed, they *must* first wound if they are to heal. Since different
people have different thresholds of pain—and different patterns of grieving—
what may be tolerable to one person may be intolerable to another. Moreover,
a person's threshold of pain may change throughout his or her life. A reader's
response to a traumatic story like a eulogy is roughly analogous to a patient's
response to a terminal illness: readers need time to move from initial shock
through anger, bargaining, depression, and final acceptance.

My students' involvement with the painful details of Barbara's story does
not confirm the "pleasures of the imagination," since no one commented on
this—such pleasure, I suspect, may produce too much guilt to be acknowledged publicly. But we can see the students' psychological defenses, which in
nearly every case were threatened by the presence of death in the classroom.
Hearing the eulogy and then reading "Dying to Teach" evoked, not surprisingly,
profound ambivalence: the desire to grapple with death and the need to look
away. We were all literally looking away when I read aloud the eulogy in the
classroom. Their identification with my story created both disconnection and
connection: each felt alone, unable to help me, but they also felt bonded to
each other and to me, offering me their heartfelt sympathy. My story wounded
them but also helped them, if not now, then in the future, when they too will
experience loss. My story heightened their awareness of the fragility of life but
also affirmed the need to seize the day before it is too late.

7

LIFE AFTER BARBARA

Following her diagnosis, scores of relatives, friends, neighbors, colleagues, and students sent Barbara "get well" cards. I was so grief-stricken that, after showing them to her, I filed them away in a large cardboard box, without reading them carefully. Following her death, hundreds of condolence cards began pouring in. I had neither the time nor the concentration to give them the attention they deserved, but I wrote thank-you cards to the more than eighty families who made contributions in honor of Barbara's memory to hospice, the American Cancer Society, or other charitable organizations. Seven months after her death I spent an entire weekend reading and reflecting on each card.

The Language of Condolence

How does one speak about the unspeakable? How does one find words to express the inexpressible? And how does one convey condolences to those who are inconsolable? Writers have struggled with these questions from time immemorial. I have no philosophical answers to these questions, but I can talk about the condolence cards that were most meaningful to me.

I valued every expression of sympathy, regardless of how it was expressed. We received more than 250 condolence cards and letters, most of the generic "with sympathy" kind. Cards with handwritten notes were always better than those without handwritten notes. Many began their brief notes by writing that "there are no words to express our sadness," but in doing so, they were, paradoxically, finding the language to convey sadness, even if only formulaically. The best condolences were the letters that spoke specifically about how Barbara's life affected the writer.

Barbara valued those cards written by people who were successfully battling cancer themselves and who could therefore understand her fear. One of the most memorable cards came from a retired member of the English Department, Ted Adams, whose eccentric humor always delighted us:

Dear Barbara,

I've had cancer on and off for 18 years, but I am still here and having fun. The aftermath of kidney-ectomy (I guess the right word is nephrec-tomy) was grim but when the doctor told me to go home, I refused. He granted me one more day so I could have more strawberry ice cream and on TV see the rest of the Joan Crawford Festival.

Science keeps stepping ahead, and there are many medical miracles.

Many people told us that they wanted to help us in any possible way, but only a few offered specific suggestions. My longtime editor at the University of Massachusetts Press, Clark Dougan, wrote from Amherst: "If Barbara's treatment regimen brings her to Boston, I hope you will bear in mind that we are along the way. It would be a long round-trip, and our guest room is always available. (If you'd like, I'll even throw in that long-promised Czech meal.) My one other thought, Jeff, is that if there is anyone who can find a solution to Barbara's medical condition, it is Glenn Dranoff. As my son Michael keeps telling me, he is simply the best—but I suspect you already know that." (Clark's son Michael is an M.D./Ph.D. student at Harvard Medical School and train-ing with Glenn.)

The condolence letters were longer than the "get well" letters, and many writers recalled Barbara's acts of kindness, which in some cases changed their lives. Some of these letters focused on the act of writing, as Barbara's colleague Kim Bauer recalls:

> I just wanted you to know that I will never forget Barbara's kindness, or yours, towards me. I worked with Barbara for the Department of So-cial Services at 67 North Pearl Street. When I had first started there back in the early eighties, I told Barbara that I was interested in writing and she told me her husband was an English professor at SUNY Albany. She offered your services to critique a short story that I wrote, which you did. Your encouragement, and Barbara's too, spurred me on. This past Sep-tember I graduated from Empire State College with a degree in Literature and recently, I have joined a writer's group that I really enjoy. I haven't had much time to pursue my writing because of work and family re-sponsibilities, but I'm finding more time now. Whether I publish or not doesn't really matter to me, what does matter is the pleasure I get from writing.

Store-bought "get well" cards express the hope of recovery, but sympa-thy cards offer a different type of hope, the joyful remembrance of those who have departed from life. A quotation from Emerson appears on one of these cards: "Nothing is ever wholly lost. That which is excellent remains forever a part of this universe." Several people used their sympathy cards to describe how they remember Barbara. Thus a member of the Albany Obedience Club writes: "We have a lot of people coming to our classes and joining our club and it is impossible to know everyone. However, I was the asst. instructor in the Beginners class when Barbara joined AOC so I had the privilege of getting to know her. We gauge people on how they treat their dogs and Barbara was *first class.*"

Sandy Morley, Arielle's high school cross-country coach and my running partner, recalled seeing Barbara during our early morning runs: "The memories which will always stay with me are very small ones in comparison to yours but are special all the same. In the early mornings as Jeff and I would be running we would overtake Barbara walking the dogs. She was usually bundled up to the hilt in the cold weather but always had a brilliant smile and cheery 'hello' as the dogs strained at their leashes! It is a tiny 'picture' but very much the way I will remember her." Our friend Ellen Lundell, who lived with her husband Ed next door to us in Ithaca in the early 1970s, recalled a statement that I had made to Barbara that reveals one of my best qualities, being a neat freak: "Most people have big blind spots. I can think of none with Barbara—a childlike trust. She's the only friend I know who never complained about her married spouse. The only time, and it was light-hearted, is when she said you were so neat & clean that you didn't want her to do [arts and crafts] projects & their temporary mess in [your] apartment & that you should 'go to Ellen where the mess wouldn't matter.'"

Some people were careful to note that they could not fully imagine my situation because they had not lost a spouse. "This will be one of very many notes of condolence you receive," wrote Gene Garber, a former chairperson of my English Department. "Few of us have sustained anything like your loss, or persevered through a time of such long care, and so our sympathies fall short. For all of that, you will know that they are heartfelt." Those who have lost a spouse, such as an elderly widow whom we often saw at chamber music concerts, made reassuring statements based on their own experiences of grief: "Life can be rough—it can be so very sad—but somehow we manage to struggle through—and you will. You'll never really forget—each day you'll think of her— but it does get easier. I know." A former graduate student of mine, Maryanne Hannan, reminded me of a statement I had made to her several years ago, when her husband died. "Once, during one of my hard times, you said to me that Beauty and Art would sustain me. While, at the time, it didn't seem likely, to some extent it has proven so. I wish the same for you." Now happily remarried, Maryanne heard from a colleague of mine that I was writing a book about Barbara, and she closed her letter by writing that my tribute "will be full of both Beauty and Art." Barbara embodied beauty and I contributed the art, Maryanne elaborated in an email when I asked for permission to quote her words.

Many of the condolences came from former students who had read Barbara's obituary in the newspaper. Some had battled cancer themselves. "I wanted to let you know how sad I was to learn that your wife had died. I have thought of you often since I heard of Barbara's illness and wish the outcome had been more positive. Sometimes it seems that cancer is everywhere—it's just a matter of which one we will be forced to contend with. I was very 'fortunate' to have been diagnosed with thyroid cancer 2 years ago, and, post surgery & radiation, have been healthy since. I'm sorry that all cancers can't be treated as easily as my personal situation. I'm sure that your daughters and that new grandson of yours are providing you with solace and comfort. I know you are blessed to have known the happiness & love which you and Barbara so obviously shared and I wish you peace and healing."

Some students had taken courses with me thirty years ago, and upon receiving their condolence cards, I regretted that I had not remained in touch with them. One person implied that she had not lived up to my expectations. "Let me tell you now that I have been dreadfully proud of having been your student, of having taken every course you taught! I have found journal writing such a helpful habit over the years, especially during times of distress. However, I have suffered from not having attained to teaching college English or publishing anything—how could you have felt gratified with my lack of performance after all the wonderful opportunities I had at SUNY? Well, I will not let this keep me from sending this note to you, Jeff." Her card saddened me because I was unaware of her feelings of self-failure. In a holiday card to her, I wrote that my feelings toward students have nothing to do with whether they pursue teaching careers or become published writers.

I received several condolence notes from students who had heard me talking in class about Barbara's illness or death. A former undergraduate, Julia Florer, sent me a note indicating that she had run the Susan G. Komen Race for the Cure in memory of Barbara. "I will continue doing so every year for as long as I can until they find a cure." Another woman offered her condolences while suggesting that my words would be a consolation to her in the future, when she suffered loss:

> I want to offer my deepest condolences for the loss of your wife. You have always spoken so highly of your relationship and marriage with her, and because of that, I can only begin to imagine what a great loss she was to you. It means a lot to me that you confided in the class about something so personal. I'm honored to know that teaching us was helping you through hard times. I hope it comforted you to know how much I was helped by your sharing with us. You told us that one day we will mourn the death of the most important person in our lives, and when that happens, I will think back to your words of knowledge and understanding.

I cannot prevent the inevitable loss of loved ones in my life, but somehow I feel consoled in advance by the words of a caring, open teacher and role model.

Students were conscious—in some cases, self-conscious—that they were sending cards to their English professor. These cards were, without exception, well written, including those penned by students who feared that their writing skills were unsatisfactory:

> I cannot imagine the pain that you are going through but I do think about what would happen if my grandparents died. You spoke so highly of your wife and the class could see your true love for her. You said a lot in class regarding the death of a loved one, especially the fact that if you keep them in your thoughts and hearts, they will never die. I don't know how I am going to react when someone close to me passes away, but I know that I will always keep your words with me. You are one of the best professors that I have had in Albany and it is due to your openness and honesty. I am truly sorry for your loss. However, you really helped me to be able to deal with situations in the future. For that I am truly grateful. P.S. Please don't look at the grammar and punctuation. They are probably horrible.

Just as Barbara valued survivor stories, which gave her hope until the end, so did I value cards from people who have found the strength and courage to survive the loss of a beloved spouse. One of these cards was written by Randy Craig's brother, David, an English professor at Clarkson University, whose earlier words I quoted in the eulogy. In that letter, written not long after his wife's death, David recalled how he and Kristin "both said that we were happier and more contented with our lives and with each other after she got cancer. Her cancer brought everything close up, made it easier to concentrate on what was important to us and what wasn't. . . . I hope that the two of you have something of the phenomenon. God knows there is enough difficulty, confusion, and trouble that come with the disease." David sent us a card on November 1, 2003, in which he reveals a form of grief work similar to my own—writing:

Dear Jeff and Barbara,
    Given a summer in which Randy gave me such promising reports, I was especially sorry to learn that you are again dealing with the complications of a flare-up. To deal with such flare-ups in the mid-fall strikes me as especially difficult—or at least it was for Kristin and me. To rekindle hope and perseverance as skies lower, light fades, and intimations of cold set in takes a special act of will.

Yet from what Randy tells me about you, Arielle, Jill, and their spouses, it seems as if you are weathering this "stormy weather" as you have passed through the earlier stages of the cancer. Holidays, family anticipations, and much else still pull you forward.

I am passing through my own mid-fall transition, a change in one of my own coping with difficulty patterns. At one point in our marriage, I had vowed to write Kristin 1,001 love letters in 1,001 days. I actually wrote 787 letters and have been rereading them at the rate of 2 a day since she died. Friday I ran out of letters, but by coincidence I ended with letters that you two more than most people can appreciate, letters written in May and June of 1995—mid-400 love letters—when Kristin had her second cancer. While the letters were filled with worry, uncertainty, and concern, their tone was hopeful, even happy. And that's what I hope for you and your family—the consolation that only family, love, and difficult times can bring.

Wishing you well,
David

David's reference to 1,001 letters reminds me of the *Thousand and One Nights*, the classic medieval Islamic story, commonly known as *The Arabian Nights*, in which a daring young woman named Scheherazade has a plan to dissuade a king, betrayed in love by one of his wives, from putting to death each bride whom he marries daily. She tells her father, who is the king's executioner ordered to behead the unlucky new bride on her wedding night, that she will marry the king herself and then read to him a story so beguiling that he will fall asleep at dawn, without ordering her execution. She does this for 1,001 nights. During that time she tells more than six hundred stories, some short, others long, breaking off each one shortly before daybreak, when the exhausted king falls asleep. Scheherazade's storytelling skills enable her to live for another day, when she will continue the story or begin a new one. The king becomes so enamored of these stories that he cannot live without them. The stories are themselves irresistible; as Padraic Colum remarks, "*The Arabian Nights* is not a book merely, but a whole literature, having everything that a complete literature must have—character, pathos, humour, poetry, tragedy, wisdom, piety—the complete reflection of the variegated life of a people" (vii). Of all the stories, none is more enchanting than that of Scheherazade herself and her masterful storytelling ability, which testifies to the power of art to sustain life, the same theme on which Maryanne Hannan comments in her condolence letter to me. Scheherazade's own story ends happily with marriage to the king, who has decided to end the barbaric practice of putting his wives to death.

Scheherazade's story demonstrates that words are "speech acts," as J. L. Austin theorizes, performative utterances in which the "issuing of the utterance is the performing of an action" (6). Words not only *describe* but they also *do*. Randy Craig has written an important book on the "promising" aspect of language in Victorian law and fiction, showing how major nineteenth-century British novelists "conform to, circumvent, and modify the conventions of betrothal" (x). Noting that the marriage proposal is perhaps the most problematic promise, Randy quotes a statement from Plato's *Symposium*: "What is strangest of all is the popular conviction that a lover, and none but a lover, can forswear with impunity—a lover's vow, they say, is no vow at all" (xii).

David and I have both turned to writing to express love for our wives. We both wrote daily: he wrote letters to Kristin when she was still alive, and I started writing this book immediately after Barbara's death. Our words could not prevent Kristin and Barbara from dying, but they expressed our undying love and, by doing so, provided us with the strength to persevere after their deaths. This is perhaps the main purpose of a condolence: it testifies to the power of love to survive any loss.

An overwhelming majority of the earth's population believe in God, and most condolences offer religious consolation, but other consolations must suffice for the agnostic or atheist. The ones that have helped me suggest that the deceased still dwells in the memory of the living. Personal and familial memory is short, however—I have only dim recollections of three of my four grandparents, who died when I was young. This is why writing is so important: the writer inscribes the deceased's life in books, which last, if not for eternity, then for decades or centuries. There are several anthologies of remembrances, but the one that I have found especially valuable is Sidney's Greenberg's *Treasury of Comfort*. Reading these remembrances, one becomes a student of sorrow, learning how others have endured loss. Particularly striking is Washington Irving's statement about the eternal sorrow of the bereaved. "The sorrow for the dead is the only sorrow from which we refuse to be divorced. Every other wound we seek to heal—every other affliction to forget; but this wound we consider it a duty to keep open—this affliction we cherish and brood over in solitude" (qtd. in Greenberg, 22). The statement implies not that we must be married to suffering but that love inevitably leads to loss. Morris Adler offers a similar thought. "Sorrow is the obverse side of love. To ask for immunity from sorrow is to ask for more than a special dispensation granted no other. It is to ask that we love not, gain no friends or devotedly serve any cause. To enter into any relationship of deep meaning is to run the risk of sorrow" (qtd. in Greenberg, 44).

Sidney Greenberg offers three principles for coping with sorrow. The first is the value of expression, written or spoken. "The poet in a romantic mood may speak of the 'silent manliness of grief' but it is hardly evidence of manliness to remain silent in grief. Such silence, such repressed emotions, may be most dangerous to the mourner when they erupt at some later day in a more violent and damaging form" (120). The second principle is to avoid excessive grief or self-pity. "Grief in moderation is beneficial and healing. Taken in excess, it can destroy our will to live and rob us of our initiative" (121). And the third principle is to "accept bravely what we cannot change, to go out of ourselves to transmute sorrow into service, to pass from feeling sorry for ourselves, which paralyzes, to feeling concern for others, which heals" (121).

I found one other passage in *A Treasury of Comfort* helpful, a statement by Albert Einstein that affirms the interrelationship between past and present, death and life:

> What an extraordinary situation is that of us mortals! Each of us is here for a brief sojourn; for what purpose he knows not, though he sometimes thinks he feels it. But from the point of view of daily life, without going deeper, we exist for our fellow-men—in the first place for those on whose smiles and welfare all our happiness depends, and next for all those unknown to us personally with whose destinies we are bound up by the tie of sympathy. A hundred times every day I remind myself that my inner and outer life depend on the labours of other men, living and dead, and that I must exert myself in order to give in the same measure as I have received and am still receiving. (1)

The editor does not acknowledge the source of this passage, but with the help of a Google search, I located it in *The World as I See It*, which I then read. Einstein believed in a cosmic rather than a personal God. "I cannot conceive of a God who rewards and punishes his creatures, or has a will of the type of which we are conscious in ourselves. An individual who should survive his physical death is also beyond my comprehension, nor do I wish it otherwise; such notions are for the fears or absurd egoism of feeble souls." Disbelief in a personal God, however, did not prevent Einstein from affirming the mystery and sacredness of life—an affirmation that an agnostic or atheist can also accept. "Enough for me the mystery of the eternity of life, and the inkling of the marvellous structure of reality, together with the single-hearted endeavour to comprehend a portion, be it never so tiny, of the reason that manifests itself in nature" (5).

Einstein believed that the "life of the individual has meaning only in so far as it aids in making the life of every living thing nobler and more beautiful. Life is sacred—that is to say, it is the supreme value, to which all other values are subordinate." Barbara also believed this, and I have tried to hold onto these words following her death. Life is different for me now, and I find myself struggling to survive without her. Grieving the loss of a loved one represents nothing less than what Thomas Attig calls "relearning the world," and teachers find themselves students again, compelled to seek out new answers to the question of how to live. "Bereavement jolts us off the path we have learned to follow in life and leaves our lives in disarray. As we relearn our ways of being in the world, we identify, explore, test, and ultimately appropriate new ways of going on" (Attig, 19).

Gratitude

I did not need to relearn the importance of gratitude, expressing thanks to the many people who helped our family. I consider myself a grateful person, but I never "theorized" the subject until I read *The Psychology of Gratitude*, edited by Robert Emmons and Michael McCullough. The volume consists of eighteen essays on a wide range of topics. Robert Solomon notes in the foreword that "one could . . . look at gratitude as one of the essential but usually neglected emotions of justice" (x). Emmons states that a "distinguished emotions researcher recently commented that if a prize were given for the emotion most neglected by psychologists, gratitude would surely be among the contenders. In the history of ideas, the concept of gratitude has had a long life span, but in the history of psychology, a relatively short past" (3).

Defined by the *Oxford English Dictionary* as the "quality or condition of being thankful; the appreciation of an inclination to return kindness" (1135), gratitude is considered one of the empathic emotions, a way to acknowledge the existence of the other. In his essay "Gratitude in the History of Ideas," Edward Harpham acknowledges that some philosophers have taken a dim view: "Gratitude," observes La Rochefoucauld in his *Maxims*, "in the generality of men is only a strong and secret desire of receiving greater favours" (qtd. in Harpham, 19). Seneca's view, by contrast, is more representative: in Harpham's words, "Gratitude does not arise as a result of an exchange in which one individual gives another a gift with the expectation that something of equal value will be given as a return. On the contrary, gratitude arises in response to a gift freely given by another" (24). Solomon Schimmel points out the close relationship between gratitude and humility: "One who is humble rather than arrogant tends to appreciate how much he or she owes to others—God or humans—for which he or she is grateful, and this gratitude will instill a desire to continue the chain of benefaction by helping others in need" (55). Dan McAdams and Jack Bauer suggest that, like guilt and empathy, gratitude functions as a moral barometer, a moral motive, and a moral reinforcer. "As a barometer, gratitude provides a reading of the moral significance of a situation, signaling a perception that one has been the beneficiary of another person's moral actions.

As a moral motive, gratitude urges the grateful person to respond in [a] gracious and prosocial way. As a moral reinforcer, gratitude functions as a social reward and continues to encourage moral action in a social community" (87).

One of the paradoxes of gratitude is that we indirectly help ourselves when we thank others for their help. A strong relationship exists between gratitude and happiness; many studies demonstrate, as Philip Watkins states, that "grateful people tend to be happy people" (175). Gratitude contributes to one's subjective well-being in that "the more grateful individuals report themselves to be, the more they express satisfaction with their lives" (Watkins, 169). Watkins adds that the expression of gratitude may serve as a coping mechanism during adversity: "If he or she tends to view life as a gift, the grateful person may be able to find benefits even in unpleasant circumstances" (178).

As Karen said in her eulogy, throughout Barbara's illness, she "was gracious, so very thankful and appreciative for everyone's encouragement and love." Barbara and I both acknowledged our gratitude to the many people who went out of their way to help us, and after her death, I wanted to give thanks publicly for the help that hospice provided to us. To do this, I wrote a letter to our local newspaper, the *Albany Times-Union*, which was published on June 1, 2004.

Compassion of Hospice Eases a Trying Time

Until my beloved wife, Barbara, was in the final stages of pancreatic cancer, I knew little about hospice. The word itself scared me, mainly because I associated hospice with the dying. But hospice consists of a large support system that helps caregivers in their devotion to loved ones. And home hospice allows the terminally ill to die with dignity in their homes, in a familiar and comfortable setting.

Once my wife was eligible for hospice, a caseworker, Alice Baker, visited us and determined Barbara's medical needs. Alice made sure Barbara always had adequate medication—a daunting challenge since each day she would take between 30 and 50 pills.

A home health aide, Geraldine Breitenstein, who was also a trained nurse, came Monday through Friday for an hour and a half. She bathed Barbara, dressed her when she was still able to get out of bed, and read to her when she couldn't walk. Gerry began as Barbara's aide and soon became a trusted family friend.

A chaplain, Joel Janzow, came every week, spoke with Barbara about spiritual and existential questions, and, toward the end, when she was in a semicoma, sang songs to her and played his guitar. A social worker, Jill Iversen, called regularly to make sure our family was coping with the situation, and a massage therapist, Carrie Hogan, came regularly.

Whenever a medical emergency occurred—and there were many—a hospice nurse was only a telephone call away. Many times a hospice nurse came late in the evening with new medication, medical equipment, or, shortly before Barbara's death, oxygen—not to prolong her life but to make her remaining days as comfortable as possible. And after Barbara's death, hospice sent us helpful pamphlets on bereavement.

Without exception, the many hospice staff people and volunteers whom we met were compassionate and empathic. They didn't talk about empathy; they practiced it. Indeed, I have never met so many compassionate people in my life.

There were many worthwhile organizations to which we considered inviting friends to send donations to honor Barbara's memory, including the American Cancer Society and St. Peter's Hospital, but we finally decided on the Community Hospice of Albany County, to which we will always be indebted.

Now I know that hospice is not only for the dying but also for the living.

Jeffrey Berman
Guilderland
jberman@albany.edu

Most of the people whom I named in the letter called or wrote me to express *their* gratitude. I hope that my letter helps to educate the public about this compassionate and worthwhile organization.

Only a handful of past and present colleagues failed to attend Barbara's funeral or send a condolence card, and I found myself unexpectedly angry at them. I confided to a friend that a retired colleague, with whom I have been on good terms, had failed to acknowledge Barbara's death, and I was told that "he couldn't find the right words to do so"—a comment that only increased my anger because he was a charismatic teacher, never at a loss for words, and a scintillating conversationalist. I remind myself that I too have failed to mark colleagues' deaths (or those of their spouses or companions), and that if I can forgive myself for past omissions, I should forgive others. I must also remind myself that even English professors find it difficult to express condolences, as was demonstrated when I received a note from Art Efron, one of my undergraduate professors:

Dear Jeff,

I was terribly saddened to learn of Barbara's death. Your letter reached me in February, and I put off answering. Then [my wife] Ruth and I went on a long trip to Japan, and I put off answering even longer when

I returned. At one point I actually wrote an answer and then realized it was so inept that I chased after the mailman who had picked it up from our box and retrieved it, then tore it up.

I'm very sorry that Barbara died.

Ten weeks after Barbara's death, Arielle, Jillian, and I flew to Fort Lauderdale, Florida, to visit her elderly parents, who were too frail to attend the funeral. The last time I had seen Jean and Morris was in January 2003, when Barbara was still feeling well enough to travel. I knew that Jean was suffering from Alzheimer's disease, but I was nevertheless shocked by the degree of her memory loss. She has not displayed the temper tantrums, bursts of irrationality, and hostility that usually accompany Alzheimer's, but she is no longer able to drive, go for walks by herself, prepare meals, or use the telephone. She looked weaker than I remembered her, but she was smiling throughout our visit. She seemed to know who I was: she called me "Jeff," and she asked how my teaching was going and whether I was writing another book. She didn't appear to know my relationship to her family. She doted on ten-month-old Nate and said how thrilled she was to be a grandmother. "Great-grandmother," we reminded her gently.

As we saw in her letter to Barbara, Jean is a deeply religious woman who for decades has thanked "Mr. GOD" for her happiness. She has always expressed how blessed her life has been, but now she repeated this statement so often that it sounded like a mantra. She acknowledged having memory problems and that she was suffering from dementia, but she was still able to play the piano. She paused only momentarily before she played the two songs we requested, "New York, New York," from *On the Town*, and "Sunrise, Sunset," from *Fiddler on the Roof*. There was nothing wrong with her "music memory," which, as Oliver Sacks notes in *The Man Who Mistook His Wife for a Hat*, can remain intact even after nearly everything else is forgotten. Apart from playing the piano, however, there was little about her past with which she seemed familiar. She was delighted to be with my children, with whom she has always been close, but she didn't know their names nor did she ask anything specific about their lives. I was reluctant to bring up Barbara's name, fearful that it would upset her—and fearful that I would start crying. "I'm Arielle and Jillian's father," I said, "and Barbara was their mother." "That's nice," Jean replied, still smiling but without a flicker of recognition.

For months Karen had told me that her mother couldn't recall her other daughter, and that she has tried to disguise her memory loss, but seeing this in person was so disturbing that I could hardly maintain my composure. As we were leaving, Jean asked me, with a placid smile on her face, how I was doing, and I could respond only with the forced word, "great," which seemed to please her. Barbara's father, Morris, keenly aware of the double loss of both his daughter and now his wife, kept repeating that this was the worst year of his life, a statement with which my daughters and I silently agreed. Unlike Morris, whose health problems, including congestive heart failure and emphysema, have darkened his worldview, Jean's appreciation for life apparently has not diminished. For years she has volunteered in a nursing home, playing the piano for Alzheimer's patients, and soon she may be one of those patients, deriving comfort from hearing another pianist. There is no effective treatment for her disease, just as there is no effective treatment for pancreatic cancer, but at least she has led a long and good life. Despite enduring several tragedies, including the suicide of her father when she was a young girl, the death of a young daughter, and now the death of Barbara, she has never lost her joy in existence.

Only when we returned to Karen's house in Cooper City, a twenty-five-minute drive from her parents, did I break down in tears and sob uncontrollably. I thought of Brabantio's statement in *Othello*: "for my particular grief / Is of so flood-gate and o'erbearing nature / That it englugts and swallows other sorrows / And it is still itself" (1.3.55).

I was almost as confused by my own behavior as I was by Jean's, and it is still not clear to me why I felt so devastated. Alzheimer's has robbed Jean of a lifetime of her history, and most of her memories of Barbara seem to have been erased. In one sense this was fortunate, in that it spared Jean from the pain arising from her daughter's death, but in another sense it was horrifying, since it meant that she could not remember the joy Barbara had brought to her. With the loss of Jean's memory came the loss of her selfhood, of nearly everything that had contributed to her history and identity. I couldn't stop myself from wondering how Barbara would have felt about the situation were she still alive and ill: she would have felt both anguish and relief. For months she had tried to soften the news of her terminal illness for her parents, and now nature intervened in a way that would have been unimaginable two years earlier. Alzheimer's has fulfilled life's promise of tragedy.

A few weeks after Barbara's diagnosis, Jillian learned that her law school roommate, Brooke Snyder, had been killed by a hit-and-run driver late one night in San Francisco. Barbara broke down in tears when she heard this, saying, "What's happening to me is sad, but what happened to Brooke is tragic." Like most parents, our greatest fear was that our children would die prematurely. I wanted Jean to be spared the knowledge of her daughter's death; yet at the same time I wanted her to acknowledge *my* pain, the enormity of *my* loss. Barbara's death has felt like my own death, the loss of the center of my life, and I wanted Jean to cry for Barbara and for me. I realized, then and now, that I was indulging in self-pity, an emotion that, contrary to what Sidney Greenberg implies, cannot simply be willed away.

Jean *was* blessed, in so many ways, but she would have been more blessed had she been able to remember her daughter's beautiful life. Without the understanding of both delight and sorrow, pleasure and pain, we cannot fully appreciate the beauty of life: this Keatsian knowledge was now sadly lacking in Jean. Barbara brought great joy to her parents throughout her life, as well as to her children and me, and that joy is etched in the minds of those who remember her. Perhaps it still exists somewhere in her mother's mind, in a region, perhaps, that not even Alzheimer's can erase. In an email written shortly after the first anniversary of Barbara's death, Karen told me that her mother "noticed a blinking light close to the ceiling in their room, and she told my dad that that was Barbara. Perhaps she's aware of the time of year and remembering what happened."

The week before I saw Barbara's parents I visited my own mother in Long Island, at whose house I also broke down in tears, though for a different reason. My mother had not attended Barbara's funeral, not because she was in frail health, like Barbara's parents, but because she said that she was emotionally unable to endure the ordeal. I was relieved by her decision not to attend the funeral, for I knew that her presence would have made it more difficult for me to maintain composure while reading my eulogy. I often find myself crying when my mother cries, as in entrainment, or sympathetic vibration. When I returned to the house in which I had grown up, I realized how much Barbara had transformed my life from the moment we began dating forty years earlier. Suddenly I felt like a child again. It was almost as if our life together had never existed. My mother could not understand this explanation when I tried to convey it to her. Perhaps she felt dismayed by the implication that my life before Barbara was unhappy, which was not the case: my life before Barbara was remarkably ordinary. But my loss felt greater in my parents' house than in my own in Albany, where Barbara's presence surrounds me in countless ways in every room.

An Absent Presence

I have continued to live in the same house into which Barbara and I moved in 1981. The house has a million joyful memories of our life together. We had decided to renovate our old kitchen shortly before her diagnosis, but I have lost interest in this project—perhaps I will feel differently in the future. I have not disposed of Barbara's clothes, which hang in the closets just as she left them. I have made no changes outside or inside the house except to buy a new vinyl fence to replace the aging basket-weave fence in our backyard, new toilets, an Oriental rug to replace the old one in my study, a new refrigerator, and a new love seat to replace the one in which Sabrina had chewed a hole. Nor do I intend to stop all the clocks inside our house, the way Miss Havisham does in Satis House in Charles Dickens's novel *Great Expectations* to mark the time when she was jilted by her fiancé. An angry, embittered woman, she stops all the clocks at twenty minutes to nine, the time when she opens a letter on her wedding day only to be informed that the scheming Compeyson has no intention of marrying her. "The marriage day was fixed, the wedding dresses were bought, the wedding tour was planned, the wedding guests were invited. The day came but not the bridegroom" (205). Miss Havisham freezes time in order to define her identity around victimization and betrayal, signifying that she will spend the rest of her life married to suffering and revenge. I will always regard Barbara as my wife but not in a morbid or pathological way, and I have no intention of remaining fixated on the past. I suspect that in time I will make changes to the house: it won't be a shrine or a mortuary. Donald Hall's observation about his deceased wife's presence in his house characterizes my feelings about Barbara's: "Your presence in this house / is almost as enormous / and painful as your absence" (51).

In subtle ways, however, I find myself unable to let go of the past. I needed to "keep busy" immediately after Barbara's death to avoid brooding excessively over loss, and so I decided to paint the inside of my house, including several rooms that had not been painted in fifteen years. I spent nearly a week, from morning to night, painting the walls and ceilings, using the identical colors of the past, mainly a neutral beige. The freshly painted rooms looked cleaner than before, but our children did not notice a difference until I pointed it out to them. Months later Arielle and Dave moved from an apartment in Cambridge to a home near West Hartford, Connecticut, and they selected bold, vibrant colors—yellow, green, and blue. I am not yet ready to use such lively colors in the rooms that still need to be repainted. But perhaps I have this chicken-and-egg situation backward: painting these rooms cheerful colors might hasten my own cheerfulness.

Many of the changes in my life have been easier than I anticipated. I have no trouble cooking for myself. I know the difference between good and mediocre food, but I can enjoy the latter almost as much as the former. I would describe myself as a "low maintenance" person, as Barbara was, but I have much lower standards than she did, and therefore I never complain about food unless there is too little. I don't enjoy cooking, but I have learned several of Barbara's recipes. I prepare large quantities of chicken cacciatore, beef stew, chili, pasta, lentil soup, and lima bean soup, which I then freeze in plastic containers. I will typically make a quadruple portion of chicken cacciatore and then freeze it in dinner-size portions. It tastes as good the seventh night as it does the first: indeed, I could eat chicken cacciatore every day for a week without growing tired of it. (Barbara never cared much for this dish and did not make it often, which is perhaps why I now eat it with a vengeance.) Or I'll buy five pounds of fresh salmon on sale, which I then cut into half-pound sections and freeze. That's ten dinners in a row. I hope that the health benefits of omega-3 oil outweigh the health risks of PCBs, which must be floating through-out my body. I suppose I'll need to expand my repertoire when I invite friends over to dinner, unless they're as fond of chicken cacciatore or salmon as I am. In the winter, I made chicken with matzah ball soup, which helped me through the long, frigid nights. The irresistible flavors wafting from my slow-cooker can make coming home at night to an empty house less forbidding.

I also discovered why my family was critical of my hummus, as Jillian complained in her eulogy. Only when I bought a new bottle of sesame tahini did I realize that it should be soft, moist, and easily spoonable, not the dried up, foul-looking tahini that was sitting in our refrigerator for years. I now believe that my hummus is as good as Barbara's was in her prime. I have also expanded my chicken dishes, thanks to the recipes Randy Craig has given me from his *Silver Palate Cookbook*.

One problem having dinner by myself most nights is that I tend to gob-ble down my meal in ten minutes. This is not a problem when I eat by myself, but a couple of times a week I will have lunch or dinner with friends or col-leagues, and I'm generally finished almost before they begin. My social skills, never strong to begin with, have deteriorated, though my dining companions have politely refrained from criticizing me. I do try to remember to use a fork and knife when I'm with them, something that I do not always do when eat-ing alone. Why dirty silverware when fingers are just as good? Why dirty a plate when I can eat out of the pot? Why dirty a glass when I can drink out of the bottle?

Mourning Sickness

Until Barbara's death, I never experienced loneliness as an adult. Now it is a constant companion. (Once I heard myself blurt to my students that now I am "married to sadness and loneliness," but I have been careful not to repeat that melodramatic statement.) "There is no lonelier man in death, except the sui-cide, than that man who has lived many years with a good wife and then out-lived her," Hemingway writes in *Death in the Afternoon*. "If two people love each other there can be no happy end to it" (122). Married four times, Hem-ingway predeceased all his wives and thus was not talking from his own expe-rience. Perhaps Dante was talking about his own experience when he observes in the *Inferno* that "there is no greater sorrow than to be mindful of the happy time in misery" (Canto 5, 121–23).

Early morning, when I wake up, and evening, when I go to sleep, are the loneliest times of the day. As soon as I awake, I go running with our dogs, and in a few minutes I feel better. After breakfast and a cup of coffee, I begin to feel optimistic about the day's events. I spend most of the day working—

preparing for my classes, grading papers, writing recommendations, meeting with students, reading, or working on a book or article. This aspect of my life has not changed at all. But whereas I would spend nights with Barbara—having dinner together, talking about the events of the day, watching a video together, or simply being together, without doing anything—now I spend most nights alone, generally reading. This is when I miss Barbara the most. Weekends—when Barbara did not work—are now harder than weekdays.

Barbara and I were close without suffocating each other. She fulfilled my need for intimacy with a woman along with my desire for meaning and beauty in life. Each of us could experience aloneness in the presence of the other without the feeling of loneliness. Before her death I had only an intellectual understanding of metaphysical loneliness; now I have an emotional understanding. Leroy Rouner has helped me to grasp the many ambiguities of loneliness:

> So what shall we say about loneliness? That it is a virtue? That it is something to be overcome? That it is the source of creativity? That it is the agonized cry of the heart from philosophers and poets who seek to say the unsayable about the agony and ecstasy of life, and the awesome unspeakableness of death?
>
> Perhaps all of the above. Or perhaps simply that it is a precious bane; an inescapable part of the human condition; a blessing and a curse; a burden of all our days and, at the same time, a resource for bearing that burden? (12)

I can understand the potentially creative implications of loneliness, but it remains for me a feeling I do not like, and I seek to transform it into a more positive feeling or state of mind. I agree with Eliot Deutsch's statement that "loneliness is not only an awareness of a present state of being unhappily or irreducibly alone, but is an awareness of a future that is empty and disconnected. Loneliness, one might say, is a state of being lonely toward the future" (118). One may be lonely either when one is alone or in the company of others. Some of my loneliest moments occur when I am in the presence of couples, especially those with whom Barbara and I were close friends. Loneliness is painful, but it can be endured, and, as Wesley Wildman suggests in his study of the ancient Gilgamesh epic, we should allow loneliness to "have its seasons in our lives": in this way, "as with Gilgamesh, loneliness slowly transforms us into compassionate rulers, humble listeners, great adventurers, truer companions, freer wanderers, and deeper grievers" (37).

I loved sleeping with Barbara, having her warmth and body next to me. She had curious night rituals. She would fall asleep with her "filter"—a small piece of tissue placed over her nose, so that she wouldn't sneeze. Sometimes she would sneeze even with her filter, and since she always sneezed in pairs, I would—to be mean—shake her so that she would lose the second sneeze. Every night she would place a tiny strip of adhesive tape on her forehead, so that she wouldn't develop a wrinkle, a practice she ended only a few weeks before her death. We always had the same position in bed, even when we would stay in hotels or motels—I slept on the right side, she on the left. I would mischievously encroach on her space and would return to my own side only when she complained that I was "hogging" the bed. Sometimes I would lie on my left side and rest my right leg on her body—until she protested that I was crushing her body. The dogs would usually lie on the bed beside us, but when I turned the light off, they would jump off the bed, despite Barbara's pleas for them to remain. When I would wake up in the middle of the night to go to the bathroom, one of them would usurp my position. Sometimes Barbara would tuck one of them underneath the sheets, and together they looked like the Wolf and Little Red Riding Hood.

The happiest time in my life, I believe, was when our children were younger, and I would check to make sure they were sleeping before I went to bed. Knowing that my wife and children were asleep gave me a feeling of security and happiness that has never been equaled. Now I sleep by myself in an empty house. Many nights I sleep fitfully, and I don't allow myself to remain in bed after I awake in the early morning. I make the bed as soon as I rise, even before I go running with the dogs; I now associate an unmade bed with Barbara's illness. One night, while sleeping, I felt Barbara's presence next to me, and she felt so warm and soft that I woke up, expecting to see her. Instead, my arm was embracing one of the sleeping dogs.

I have been trying my best to take care of the dogs, as I promised Barbara, but it has been an ongoing struggle. They seemed to know instinctively when she was growing sicker, for not only was she unable to walk them every morning and late afternoon, as she had always done, but gradually she stopped playing with them. For six months before Barbara's death, the dogs expressed their distress by relieving themselves inside the house at all hours of the day and night. After her death, I consulted our vet, who suggested that we neuter our male, who would become so frantic when I went to walk him that I could barely put on his leash. An antibark collar helped considerably after a neighbor complained to the dog warden, but it no longer works with Caleb, who isn't deterred by its slight shock. I now run with them every morning and, following Glenn's suggestion, take them for a long walk in the early evening whenever possible. Nevertheless, it was a long eight months after Barbara's death until they stopped leaving me unwelcome gifts on the floor, where I have learned to step cautiously. They know that I am not Barbara, nor am I Jillian, who loves them as much as her mother did.

Crying is still a problem, not when I'm alone and don't mind it, but when I'm with other people. I have become, like Pippa Brentwood, the undergraduate who grieves her father's death in May Sarton's academic novel *The Small Room*, a weeper. Lucy Winter, the young assistant professor of English who is Pippa's teacher, is unnerved by her student's flood of tears, which she regards as an inappropriate "plea for sympathy":

> "I know this is a hard year for you, Pippa, but I think the less you dramatize—" How harsh it sounded!
> "It's real suffering," Pippa wailed, and the tears poured down her cheeks like summer rain. "You can't say it's not real!"
> Face this, Lucy admonished herself. Be kind. After all, she's only a child. "Of course it's real. The loss of one's father at any age . . ." But where to go from here? (49).

As I suggest in *Empathic Teaching*, throughout *The Small Room* "Lucy struggles to empathize with her students without being overwhelmed by their problems" (67). Sympathetic in other ways, Lucy—and Sarton—cannot accept that tears, no less than smiles, are appropriate both inside and outside the classroom. Nor can they accept the fact that sometimes it is better to cry than not to cry. Many times I have apologized to friends and strangers for crying in their presence, only to be told by some mourners that they wish they could cry for their lost loved ones.

I struggled to hold back tears when I read Barbara's eulogy to my students, who responded more empathically than does Pippa's professor, and later I struggled to hold back tears when I delivered the eulogy at the funeral. I don't fear crying as much as exploding into tears, my body convulsing, as happens often now, when I least expect it. I did not cry when I watched videos of *Wit* and *One True Thing* at home by myself. I steeled myself in advance, knowing that both films are emotionally wrenching. But as I was walking out of a movie theater with Randy and Jane after watching *Vanity Fair*, I burst into tears and cried all the way back to their house. In her film memoir *Crying at the Movies*, Madelon Sprengnether explores her inability to weep over her own losses, including the death of her father when she was nine years old. Yet she would often sob over fictional tragedies in the safety of darkened movie theaters. "Stories and fantasies we normally labor to suppress or forget appear, writ large, before our eyes in Dolby sound and full-screen Technicolor" (11). I too have cried in movie theaters, yet I still don't know what in *Vanity Fair* triggered the eruption. Tears pour down my cheeks not only like summer rains but also like freezing rain, and I can never predict when these storms will occur. I feel like I am living in a strange body, never knowing what emotional waves will sweep over me. I seldom cried before Barbara's illness, and perhaps decades of un-expressed tears have caught up with me. "The bitterest tears shed over graves," Harriet Beecher Stowe observes, "are for words left unsaid and deeds left undone" (128–29). Crying is "involuntary self-disclosure," as Judith Kay Nelson suggests (177), and for this reason we may feel that our body is betraying our desire for self-control, but Nelson also reminds us that crying is a sign of attachment behavior "designed to signal those around us that we are in distress and in need of care and comfort. . . . The connection and comfort that crying helps to bring our way, in reality or symbolically, may help to make our bodies feel better and heal sooner" (137).

I have learned most of the household tasks that Barbara had always performed. They turned out to be easier to learn than I anticipated. Barbara could remember when each bill was due, and she would wait until the last day before mailing the payment lest we lose interest on the money in our checking or savings account. By contrast, I pay bills the day I receive them, so that I don't have to worry about them. Better yet, most of these bills are now paid automatically online. I will never have Barbara's sense of direction, but with the help of MapQuest and, when that fails, a cell phone, I have managed eventually to arrive at all of my destinations. I value neatness over cleanliness, but I have adopted several of her practices that I resisted when she was alive, such as drying the stall shower with a towel so that mold doesn't grow. I now clean the bathrooms regularly, something that she used to do. (I once failed the "feminist test" when I admitted to a female colleague decades ago that I never cleaned the toilets.) I also occasionally dust the house, though not carefully enough to earn my children's approval.

Anger or Acceptance

Leon Wieseltier's observation about the wisdom of accepting death, without anger, characterizes my own feelings. "I have been slapped by the nature of things. I have a choice between anger and acceptance; and I would like to be angry. But I would not like to be stupid. So I must begin the labors of acceptance" (54–55). The only times I become angry at Barbara are when I find myself unable to perform those tasks that she did effortlessly. When I was driving for the first time from Albany to Brooklyn to visit Jillian and Alex in their new apartment in late October 2004, I became hopelessly lost when I inadvertently traveled over the Williamsburg Bridge and entered into unfamiliar territory in lower Manhattan. That was Barbara's fault. When I couldn't remember where I parked my car in a large underground parking lot, despite reminding myself that this would be a test of my independence, that was Barbara's fault. When my new Dell computer crashed and I was told that I lost everything on my hard drive, that was Barbara's fault. When I couldn't thread a needle to sew a button on my shirt, that was Barbara's fault. And when I couldn't figure out how to submit my students' final grades online, that was Barbara's fault.

Anger is as much part of death as it is part of life, yet it was not one of the predominant emotions that I felt during Barbara's illness. Perhaps I did not allow myself to feel anger, or perhaps I couldn't find an appropriate target for it. Nor did I see anger within her; as I wrote in my eulogy, "she felt little anger and no bitterness." Yet I must acknowledge Ellen Gootblatt's statement to me after reading a draft of this manuscript: "Barbara was very angry, very upset, very bitter about her illness." Perhaps Barbara did not express these feelings to me because she knew I would be upset, or perhaps she *did* express these feelings but I chose to ignore them. As I remarked earlier, she did not write about anger or bitterness in her cancer diary: about that I am certain. Was she reluctant to express these feelings in writing because she did not want readers to remember her in this way? Did she believe that "negative emotions" would make recovery more difficult? Was she trying to deny these emotions for my sake?

I can confirm the adage that birthdays and anniversaries are especially hard for the bereaved. Jillian was with me on January 16, 2005, when I turned sixty, my first birthday in thirty-five years without Barbara. As we were having breakfast, she told me that exactly one year earlier Barbara had tried to write a birthday note but couldn't complete it. I asked her if she could find the note, and within a few minutes she returned with a small sheet of paper filled with crossed out words. Several of the words were almost illegible, indicating her difficulty writing: "This is such a special day that I couldn't let it pass without writing. It's so difficult for me to combine letters and words. We've shared a spectacular life together, a love for one another that has only strengthened by time." These are, as far as I know, Barbara's last written words, and throughout the day I cried as I thought about what she had written. It was the best birthday gift I have received, a gift from the grave.

About that time I returned to St. Peter's Hospital to give copies of my newly published book *Empathic Teaching* to Fred Shapiro and Nancy Pettit, his scheduler, both of whom had taken a special interest in Barbara. Since I hadn't been in the hospital for ten months, I was expecting to be overwhelmed by wrenching memories. To my surprise, I felt emotionally in control, perhaps because Barbara had received such attentive and compassionate treatment from the nurses and doctors. A nurse named Ann recognized me and remarked that a few days earlier she had been inquiring about our family, wondering how we are doing. I expressed my gratitude to the many people who had helped us and said that I had many more positive memories than negative ones. Ann smiled and said that not everyone feels that way. "Some people never return here."

"After the first death, there is no other." Now I understanding the meaning of Dylan Thomas's observation in "Fern Hill" (112). It is impossible to lose a spouse to cancer without having one's attitude toward death change. Death no longer terrifies me, as it once did, and I am more accepting of its inevitability, perhaps because I have less to lose now that I have lost so much. I am sad rather than clinically depressed in every way but one. Who would not be sad in my situation? To the question, "Are you hopeful about the future?" I would say "no": hopelessness is one of the main signs of depression. But hope may return, as it has for countless bereaved throughout the ages. While reading Kay Redfield Jamison's *Exuberance*, I learned that Theodore Roosevelt's wife and mother both died on Saint Valentine's Day of 1884. "'You could not talk to him about it,' said a close friend. He drew a cross in his diary for the date of the fourteenth of February and wrote, 'The light has gone out of my life'" (9). Yet he immediately threw himself into his work and, despite his distress, he enjoyed life to the full, soon remarrying and beginning one of the great political careers in American history. Jamison's book is itself an example of exuberance: she dedicated it to the memory of her husband, Richard Wyatt, who died of cancer while she was writing it.

As the first anniversary of Barbara's death passed, I was struck by its lingering unreality. Despite the fact that there was no uncertainty over her death, it still seemed so unreal to me, and for the first time I could begin to fathom the far greater unreality of other types of loss, involving not death but absence, such as divorce. The major theoretical premise of Pauline Boss's study of unresolved grief is that "the greater the ambiguity surrounding one's loss, the more difficult it is to master it and the greater one's depression, anxiety, and family conflict" (7). If I still find myself looking into crowds of people to see if I can spot Barbara's face, or expect to hear her voice when the telephone rings, or call my cell phone to hear her voice, which is still on it, what must it be like for children of divorced parents, hoping that their parents will someday be together again?

I am also struck by the difficulty of letting go of sorrow. I brood over Washington Irving's statement, which I quoted earlier, about the eternal sorrow of the bereaved: "The sorrow for the dead is the only sorrow from which we refuse to be divorced." Can one hold onto grief or sorrow without being incapacitated? How much volition does one have in holding onto or letting go of an overwhelming emotional state? Does one *choose* to remain grief-stricken as an act of loyalty? "Those traumatized by extreme events," explains Dominic LaCapra in *Writing History, Writing Trauma*, "as well as those empathizing with them, may resist working through because of what might almost be termed a fidelity to trauma, a feeling that one must somehow keep faith with it." Part of this feeling, continues LaCapra, "may be the melancholic sentiment that, in working through the past in a manner that enables survival or a reengagement in life, one is betraying those who were overwhelmed and consumed by that traumatic past. One's bond with the dead, especially with intimates, may invest trauma with value and make its reliving a painful but necessary commemoration or memorial to which one remains dedicated or at least bound. This situation may create a more or less unconscious desire to remain within trauma" (21–22).

Friends have told me that it is time to let go of my grief. "I was sad to read that you are still immersed in the mourning process," Sophie Freud wrote to me eight months after Barbara's death. "But as you told me, you might find it difficult to 'let go' which is then a further loss. Perhaps the deep relationship Barbara and you had, which is so rare, and was so important and precious for both of you, can be celebrated as it was. You have been one of god's darlings to be selected out for such a good experience, and now clinging to it for ever and ever could be viewed as ungrateful. But perhaps completing the book will help."

Writing this book has indeed helped me to grieve, but as I approach its completion, I find myself needing to begin immediately another writing project. Writing about Barbara every day will be less difficult than *not* writing about her. I am already thinking about a new book, *Death in the Classroom*, a study of how personal writing can help college students memorialize their own losses. Just as writing has helped me, so will it help others. A letter I received from Gemma Cannon on June 30, 2005, affirms how my students' "risky writings" enabled her to complete a book on Longfellow and grief:

Dear Jeff

It's been almost two years since Barbara brought you to the Longfellow House in Portland. After the tour, you asked me a question *no one* asks (except a writing professor!): "What are you writing?"

I told you I'd started a piece on Longfellow and grief and you expressed interest in reading it when it was done. But my two-year-old daughter had just stopped taking naps, and I'd lost my daily time slot to write.

"I don't think I'll ever finish it," I sighed.

Then Barbara piped in, "You'll finish it. If it takes you ten years," she said, "you'll finish it."

A week letter you generously sent me a copy of your book *Risky Writing*. I put down my pen for a few weeks to re-evaluate. I realized I'd begun an intellectual approach to grief and Longfellow. It felt distant and safe but after reading your book, and the moving passages of your students, I knew I needed to take risks, too. I needed to get more personal (gasp!) And bring a "risky" approach to my work.

Through it all, I remembered Barbara's words to me. The calm sureness in her voice persuaded me to believe her and, in the intervening months, with her words in my heart, I grabbed an hour here and an hour there and scribbled away. And now it's done!

You graciously had asked to read it and so I've enclosed a copy for you. Keep it, Jeff, and use any of it with your class, if you think it would be

helpful. I also don't want you to feel obliged to read it if it's too emotionally difficult. Grief is an unpredictable force, and words, images, or
thoughts can paralyze us, leaving us emotionally immobile for days. If
you find "triggers" in these pages and you need to put them aside, and
cannot pick them up again, please know that I understand.

While writing about Longfellow and grief, I've thought often about
you and Barbara. I can't help but think that "something" inspired her to
bring you to the Longfellow House that day. Without her influence, I
wouldn't have received your book which guided me, and directly led to
the work enclosed. It's a gift you've both given me and it's now a gift I
can share with my family and, from that deep-beneath-me place, I thank
you both.

I look forward to hearing about your own work on grief and writing.
What a beautiful way to honor Barbara. I think of you often and hope
your family is well. What a gift to have daughters!

Again, thank you for everything.

Most sincerely,
Gemma Cannon

Gemma's book, "Relationships Don't End in Death: From Grief and Loss
to Comfort and Consolation," explores how Longfellow's response to the many
deaths in his life, including his two wives, helped her to mourn the premature
death of her sister-in-law from cancer. Gemma notes that rather than being
crushed by sorrow, Longfellow devoted his life to writing about it, discovering
that we can celebrate our continuing relationship with lost loved ones. Sorrow
is the catalyst behind so much art, as Longfellow and countless other artists
demonstrate. Writing is a way both to hold onto and let go of sorrow, helping
us to control grief rather than being controlled by it.

"The Jewish ideas about sorrow include the idea that sorrow has limits,"
states Leon Wieseltier. "The end of mourning is an essential part of the tradition of mourning. Ancient and medieval authorities are adamant that it is not
to exceed the period of a year. There must be no wallowing. The temptation
to nestle with nothingness must be resisted. The world has not died; only someone you love has died. The world awaits your return. There is work to be done
in the world" (546). I defer to the Jewish injunction not to mourn permanently,
not to be married to suffering, but this is easier said—and written—than done.
Sorrow cannot be magically willed away. As Wieseltier acknowledges, "Since
death is final, grief is final. Since death will never end, mourning will never
end. That is why the tradition must intervene to end it" (546). One can believe
in the necessity to circumscribe sorrow without believing in "closure," which,
as Wieseltier rightly points out, "is an ideal of forgetfulness. It is a denial of

reality, insofar as finality is never final. Nothing happens once and for all. It all visits. It all returns. But 'closure' says: once and for all. This is a misunderstanding of subjectivity, which is essentially haunted" (576).

And so sorrow's circumscription does not mean sorrow's ends; rather, life goes on, and one learns to live with death. Sorrow changes from an active, immobilizing force, with which one struggles mightily, to a passive, chronic feeling of sadness, a string of gray days in which the clouds unexpectedly part and the sun breaks through briefly and then vanishes. Barbara is now inside of me, part of my past, present, and future, a reminder of the joy and sorrow of life, a testament to the enduring power of love. A statement from the *Hebrew Union Prayer Book* affirms the only type of immortality in which I believe: "So long as we live, they too shall live, for they are now a part of us, as we remember them."

Some of my relatives have questioned my need to write this book. Barbara's suffering was so horrific that they have tried to forget the particulars of her illness. They cannot understand my testimonial obligation to record these details. Writing about Barbara's illness was like pulling the blanket off her, exposing her to public view. I have tried to reveal only what is necessary to depict her suffering, but for some readers I have exposed too much. They have been unable to complete the manuscript: it is simply too painful to read. Bearing witness to suffering is indeed painful, even traumatic. Nevertheless, writing has been lifesaving for me, and I hope that reading what I have written will be helpful to others.

I am glad that I started writing immediately after Barbara's death, for many of the details are now beginning to fade, a reflection, no doubt, of the passing of time. The grief immediately following her death was more intense than it is now. I do not think about her from the moment I wake up to the moment I fall asleep, as I did a year ago. Rereading the early chapters of this book, I am reminded how much I have adjusted to her death, as I feared I would not be able to do. These changes, I believe, are positive, demonstrating that we can survive a loved one's death and resume our lives. Recently I met at a literary reading two women whose husbands had died of cancer around the time of Barbara's death. We spoke lovingly about our spouses and remarked that now we are able to smile again.

I have lost my wife, but my daughters have lost their mother, and their sorrow is different from mine. In *Motherless Daughters*, Hope Edelman shows how a daughter's special closeness to her mother complicates the grieving process when her mother dies. "When a daughter watches a mother die, especially from an illness, she becomes aware of her own physical vulnerability as a female" (220). She quotes a statement by Naomi Lowinsky about the "horrific Catch-22" problem for the motherless daughter: "In order to fully identify with her femaleness, she's got to be in her body. But that also means identifying with her mother's body, and if she associates her mother's body with a terrible illness and an early death, it feels like the last place in the world she wants to go" (221). Edelman reports that the "fear of a foreshortened future is a common one among motherless women" (223), especially when the mother dies relatively young. Edelman was seventeen when her mother died of breast cancer at the age of forty-two, and she describes the "secondary loss" that reveals itself over time: "Twentysomething daughters often leap ahead to imagine the secondary losses—no one to help plan a wedding, no one to consult about child rearing, no grandmother for the kids—they envision as long-term effects of mother loss" (58).

Without being pollyannaish, Edelman observes that early mother loss has often served as a catalyst for a daughter's later success. She cites a 1979 study indicating that the "rate of mother loss among 'eminent' or 'historical geniuses' in the arts, the humanities, the sciences, and the military is as much as *three times* that of the general population, even after the mortality rates of earlier centuries are taken into account" (260; emphasis in original). Many famous women writers lost their mothers at a young age, including Anna Quindlen, who was nineteen when her mother died. "My mother's death made me a much happier and more optimistic person. People are always a little incredulous when I say that. I really felt that from this experience, you could take away one of two things. One is you could just think, 'What's the point? It's all over so quickly.' But the other is that you can look at life and think, 'my god. Every day that you have is so precious and so important'" (qtd. in Edelman, 274). Edelman concludes her book with an earned affirmation: "To be a motherless daughter is to be riddled with contradictions and uncertainties, but it is also to know the grit of survival, to hold an insight and maturity others did not obtain so young, and to understand the power of renewal and rebirth" (279).

I never fail to find Barbara in our children—in their appearance, in their achievements, in their goodness, and in their love for life. They resemble their mother in so many ways, and although they now live in different cities, they telephone me every day, and we see each other often. I used to think, when they were little, that they were clones of their mother. Now that they are older, they retain their similarities to Barbara but have their own personalities. The months immediately following Barbara's death saw many wonderful changes in their lives. Arielle received her Ph.D. in the spring of 2004, and she and Dave (along with Nate) moved to Connecticut, less than a mile from where my brother lives, where they are both clinical psychologists. Jillian and Alex moved from the Washington, D.C., area, where they worked in private law firms, to New York City, where they serve as federal prosecutors. Barbara would have loved to attend Arielle's commencement and Jillian and Alex's swearing in as assistant U.S. attorneys, as I did, my face beaming with pride. As I pen these final words on October 17, 2005—on what would have been Barbara's fifty-ninth birthday, eighteen months after her death—Arielle and Jillian are both pregnant, affirming life's age-old process of renewal. Before her diagnosis, Barbara and I would often say to each other that we were blessed in every way; after her diagnosis, we told each other that we were blessed in every way but one. Our children have been our greatest blessing, and they are a daily reminder of the ways in which Barbara increased the store of happiness in the world.

Only after Barbara died did I wonder about her influence on my teaching. She taught me to respect everyone's feelings, including those who rarely spoke in class. She did not easily verbalize her feelings, even when asked. I had to learn over time to draw her feelings out, gently and patiently. It was worth the effort because she taught me so much. In the same way, I try to draw my students' feelings out, gently and patiently, allowing everyone to be heard. A good class, I tell my students, occurs when everyone talks, and though this rarely happens in large classes, I always call upon as many people as possible. Over time students become more comfortable with speaking in class. When I come across students like myself, who love to speak in class but who may be unaware that they are preventing classmates from speaking, I tell them that they can speak again only after all their classmates have spoken. Sometimes this is met with grumbling, as I myself would have grumbled when I was an undergraduate, but most students comply with this policy.

Barbara's death has heightened my sensitivity to students' suffering. Before her death, I had a limited understanding of those students who have suffered grievous losses in their lives. Now I know the heartache that many of them feel. My eyes often well up with tears when students cry in the classroom or in my office, an example of pedagogical entrainment.

Barbara's main fear, apart from the fear of the process of dying, was that I would not do well after her death. I had to reassure her repeatedly that, with the love and support of my family and friends, I would be okay. It is still too early for me to contemplate a future without her. And yet by writing about her, first in the eulogy and now in this book, I have found a way to keep her close to me. Indeed, her presence is most palpable on the days when I write about her. I have spent hours each day reflecting on her and trying to find the words to capture her essence. Just as I often talked about her to my students when she was alive, I continue to talk about her in class, usually with a smile on my face. Both her life and death are noteworthy; she fought to remain alive, and I think she would approve of my efforts to make her death a subject for teaching.

Barbara has left me, but I have not left her. Her face is everywhere in my home and at the university, her timeless beauty preserved for all to see. I continue to wear my wedding ring. Scarcely an hour goes by without my thinking of her. Her name is still on our checks. I continue to use the first person plural pronoun, as in the preceding sentence. When my nine-year-old nephew,

Shane, asked me shortly after Barbara's death whether I was going to remarry, I was startled and didn't know how to respond. Hours later, after meditating on the question, I told myself that in the future I would say, "Yes, if I can find another Barbara." I will never find another Barbara, but she now lives within me. Wherever I am, she is, my beloved wife, friend, soul mate, and worrier-warrior.

APPENDIX

Upon completing *Dying to Teach*, I sent the entire manuscript to the students in Expository Writing who heard me read my eulogy for Barbara in March 2004. I invited them to share their responses to reading the book. I have not edited their letters except to correct misspellings and obvious typographical errors.

Dear ——,

I have completed a draft of my book *Dying to Teach: A Memoir of Love, Loss, and Learning*, and I am enclosing a copy. I have submitted the book for publication, but it will probably take a few months before I hear from my publisher.

I'm sending the MS to everyone in the spring 2004 Expository Writing course, of which you were a member. I hope that after you read the MS, you will write me a letter explaining your reactions to the book. I'm interested in the following questions:

How did you feel while you were reading the book?

Was there anything in the book that surprised you? Please explain.

Has reading the book changed your attitude toward death? If so, please explain.

Has the book motivated you to think about death? If so, in what ways?

Was it painful to read the book? Too painful? If it was too painful, please explain.

Have you spoken about the book to other people? If so, how did they react?

Has reading the book made it harder or easier for you to think about death?

Were your reactions to reading the book similar to or different from your reactions to hearing me read my eulogy in class?

Do you believe that "death education" would be a valuable part of a college curriculum?

You can respond to as many or as few of these questions as you wish in your letter. A suggested length of the letter would be 500–750 words. Please make sure the letter is as well written as possible. You can mail your letter to me at my home (I'm enclosing a self-addressed stamped envelope) or email it to me at jberman@albany.edu.

My plan is to include your letter and those of your classmates in the appendix of the book. Please indicate whether you give me permission to do so. Indicate whether you want me to use your name or not. There's no need to return the MS. As always, I appreciate your help.

Warmly,
Jeff Berman

You pick up a book every so often. You read it. You might even enjoy it. You put it down and someday soon after you'll pick up another one. I've always felt the greatest of books took you to places where you were scared to be. Jeff Berman's *Dying to Teach* takes you to a scary place but it brings you back with a greater sense of knowledge.

I picked up *Dying to Teach* after my waltz with death following a near-fatal car accident. I was hesitant to read it because of my own fear of death. After the fear diminished, my curiosity with death grew and *Dying to Teach* came back into my life. My curiosity arose from the fact that my near-death experience left me unscathed. My childlike invincibility returned through the help of psychotropic medicine and reflection upon memories past. I felt almost untouchable. Yet the fascination with death loomed over me. It was as if I had befriended a deadly snake that could take my life away at any moment.

My obsession began, so I picked up *Dying to Teach* and I read it cover to cover. A near-death experience brings you closer to death than you could ever imagine. *Dying to Teach*, however, brings you to the other side of death. It shows you the side of the living. Death is like watching someone go away and knowing you will never see them again. It isn't as simple as a bus ride to another state or a flight to another country, it's more. It's instinctive. As if the heart will have lost a spiritual part of itself. It will continue to operate the same but every other beat will cry out for that person you've lost in your life. The world in which you live will be different and difficult but tolerable. *Dying to Teach* explains everything in between and after death. The act of death may be as instantaneous as a bolt of lightning, but the gathering of the clouds and the clearing of the sky plays a huge role.

Dying to Teach isn't a book you can begin to explain to other people. Its complexity starts as difficult as tech support and ends as trying to explain to a child the beauty of love, life, loss, and an eternity together. You can only read it and take in all that it has to offer. I don't see it as a tribute only to a man's wife but rather an encompassing ride that shows you her life, her death, and her family. It shows you the complexity and fragility of life and death and how it affects all those around it. It encircles all lit-

erature that deals with death. I once compared Professor Berman's class
to a train ride. He conducts the direction in which we head but gives us
the pleasure to look around. *Dying to Teach* is the eyes of a soul into
which you can get lost. It will invoke something within yourself that will
make you view death differently. It may, at times, make you want to turn
away, but you will be caught in its gaze. Death is never welcome in anyone's home when all are healthy and well. However, when the one you
love suffers greatly, death is a guest whom you anticipate with each minute
but still find difficult to call and ask how far away it is from arriving.

I've never felt strongly about institutions because they never prepare
you for life. You're given lessons in your subject area and then you're pro-
pelled into the real world. Death is a personal experience which you will
encounter at least once in your life. The importance of death education
is a valuable one. There are plenty of other aspects to life that are never
covered in education; however, I feel death is a changing force that re-
shapes each person's world. With that in mind, it must be tackled in the
educational institution to at least give each person a bit of comfort when
they should confront it for themselves.

Dying to Teach has taught me to look at death as a natural course of
life. It is like a race. True, each finish line may be respectively different
to each person, but at some point, we all stop running.

Dying to Teach ran my emotions through each cycle like a washing
machine. Not to say I came out smelling clean and fresh, but rather soaked
with tears. The one part that will always reaffirm that love is never-
ending was when Jeff's daughter was able to find the birthday card that
Barbara had written for him. She wrote, "This is such a special day that
I couldn't let it pass without writing. It's so difficult for me to combine
letters and words. We've shared a special life together, a love for one another that has only strengthened by time." They were Barbara's last written words. It made me feel that even as she was passing away, you could
still see the fire of love for her husband burning brightly into death's darkness. I had to put the book down because I didn't want the ink to run.

Dying to Teach takes the reader beyond the teacher's podium. It isn't
a fictional story where you can only feel a certain amount of attachment
to the character. *Dying to Teach* is as real as life gets. It isn't a book worth
only reading but it's a book worth learning from.

—Kunal Arora

I haven't written an essay since I graduated college. Other than work-
related documents, I haven't read much either. The transition from college to the so-called real world is quite daunting. I don't carry that feeling
with me every day, but when I sit down and realize that I have a full-time

job and adult responsibilities, it's an eye-opener. When I received *Dying to Teach*, I felt excitement. This is rare because I don't usually get excited about reading, or writing, for that matter. But the topic of your manuscript held a special place in my heart: English 300, spring semester 2004. In that class, writing was no longer a chore; it was a pleasure. Reading other students' essays wasn't boring; it was intriguing. I can speak for most of my former English 300 classmates in saying that the level of comfort experienced in the classroom was the catalyst for an engaging and understanding classroom environment. Professor Berman preached empathy, he practiced empathy, and from his students, demanded the same.

Most of my anticipation in reading the manuscript came from wanting to see how my essay was used. I reveled in the idea that my words, my thoughts would be eventually published in a book that other people would read. I raced through every chapter, waiting to see where there would be mention of our class. More importantly, I wanted to find the response that I wrote to Professor Berman, after he read his eulogy to Barbara, because I didn't remember what I wrote exactly. I knew I would be able to identify it because I finished it with heartfelt words: Thank you. Thank you. I am sure that they were the most sincere and heartfelt words I have ever written in an essay. Everything I wrote in Professor Berman's class was sincere and heartfelt.

I didn't feel overwhelmed by the content of the book due to its nature; I was prepared to read about the intense subject matter, especially because it involved someone I knew. As I continued to read the manuscript, I felt as if I knew Barbara personally. The references to locations in Brooklyn that were familiar to me from my childhood; her desire to read *Possession* by A. S. Byatt surprised me. The surprise wasn't in the fact that she wanted to read it, but that I had read the book in an English class at the University, taught by Professor Randall Craig. Reading so many intimate and personal facts about someone who has passed is a surreal experience for me, particularly with Barbara.

I felt connected to this story in so many ways, through Barbara as well as Jeff. A few weeks ago, I spent nearly two weeks by myself at home. While my mother was away on vacation, I had to cook meals for myself every day, rather than the usual two or three times a week. I decided it would be much easier to make my favorite meal in bulk so that I could have dinner for an extended period of time without having to worry about making a meal every night. I smiled to myself when I read the portion of the manuscript that detailed the very same scenario. I then thought to myself that when the day comes when I am alone, I wish I could give the impression that everything was ok, just like Professor Berman did. In the spring of 2004 when I took his class, there was no way of me knowing that there was something wrong or that he was going through such an emotional roller coaster.

My reactions to reading the manuscript were very different than the reactions I had when hearing the eulogy you read in class. The eulogy took everyone by surprise; no one in the class knew what the subject of your essay was. You could probably label it as a "shock and awe" situation. Reading the manuscript, I was prepared for what I was going to encounter. I actually read it with feelings of anxiety and excitement.

As much as I enjoyed every aspect of English 300 in spring 2004, I am not sure if death education should be a part of a college curriculum. Obviously, it would have to be an elective/optional class, but I am not sure how most students would react to confronting death in the classroom. For the most part, it worked in our class but I think it would be very wishful thinking to believe that most students would have a positive reaction to this sensitive subject matter. I know that my experience with it changed me for the better, but did I really need it? That's debatable. But I don't regret the experience; I totally embrace it.

—Dia Daley

I have had four female relatives die of cancer within the past few years, all in my maternal family. The most recent loss was my Aunt Dee in July of this year. Similar to my other relatives, both her sickness and death were devastating, not simply because she was the latest cancer victim in our family, but because she died two weeks after her diagnosis.

The weekend before she died, I drove down to North Carolina where I met my parents, sister, uncle, and cousins at the hospital in which my aunt was staying. I seemed to be the calmest out of everyone. I felt odd because I seemed so unemotional, but I was unable to react any other way. I spent most of my time at the hospital either outside with some of my relatives, sitting on the bench and chatting about anything other than my sick aunt, or in the family lounge with my two cousins, ages seven and four, keeping them occupied with toys and coloring books while the rest of my family prepared for her death.

For the most part, my aunt was asleep. There were times when she would open her eyes, but it was clear that she rarely recognized anyone. She was usually unable to speak. She was fully conscious only twice during the entire weekend while I was in the room. The first time, she smiled at me. The second time, I held her hand and gave her a kiss. In the Brooklyn accent that she never lost despite not living there for forty years, she said, "Hey babe, how you doin'?" I left the room shortly after. That was one of the few times that I actually cried during her entire sickness and death. I knew that was the last time I would speak to her, and I was happy that she spoke to me in the accent that seems to be dying along with my family.

The day after we returned to New York, she died. I think I may have cried once for a few minutes, simply because she was gone forever. I would never hear her speak to me again. During the funeral service, I spent most of my time consoling everyone else. I never shed a tear.

Until I read your book, I felt awkward about my lack of emotion regarding my aunt's death. Had I grown so cold to death that I was unable to show a "normal" amount of emotion? I wish every day that I could travel back in time to spend just an extra five minutes with my family. I miss them immensely. While reading about your wife's illness and death, my thoughts kept returning to my aunt, and I felt at peace with her death. Here was the first death in the family that I was able to accept fully. Even though most of my time at the hospital was spent taking care of the children or taking my other family members' minds off of the situation, I felt that I had served a purpose. I was there for my aunt by being there for the rest of my family. While reading your book, I realized that, for the first time, I have no regrets with how I spent my time while one of my relatives was dying.

There were several times while reading your book that I felt you were discussing my past experiences. There were a few times when I found it difficult to read, and I had to skip ahead a few pages. While I feel at peace with my aunt's death, I am still not comfortable with the cancer that is killing my family. I still find many aspects of cancer disturbing. However, for those who have never experienced cancer, your book shows the struggles that a cancer patient and his or her family experiences from diagnosis to death and beyond. There is no "dying peacefully" when the sickness is so violent and the death is so premature.

While this book hasn't changed my attitude toward death or made it easier or harder for me to think about death, it made me realize how my outlook on death has changed. I'm not as avoidant as I used to be. I have found that death of a loved one needs to be faced. The longer you try to avoid it, the harder it will be when you are finally forced to face it. It is more devastating then, because you wish more that you had done things differently. I regret so much about how I treated my family members' illnesses in the past. When I received news of their cancer, I immediately went into denial. I refused to think about their illnesses and impending deaths. I went completely numb, refusing to feel anything. I refused to talk to anyone about their sicknesses. While I know I cannot change the past, I can still wish that I had acted differently.

This is when I am able to say, "If I had known then what I know now." Death education has the potential to be a valuable part of a college curriculum. However, talking about how to handle death and actually handling death are two different concepts. For some, death education would be extremely helpful. For others, like myself, it is impossible to prepare for such a devastating experience. Unfortunately, there is no textbook that is able to provide us with the perfect and least painful way to deal with the death of someone who was so close to you. A death education would be able to help some, though, so therefore, it would be very valuable.

Before ending this letter, I would like to thank you. Thank you for sharing Barbara's illness and death with me in class last year. Thank you for sharing your book with me. And thank you for allowing me to respond. My thoughts are still with you and your family.

—Kristen Darling

"He had me centered again by analogy—I'm now 20 feet from the edge of the cliff instead of 2 feet. I still have to deal with my anxiety in all aspects of life & claim myself." Barbara's Cancer Diary

Reading about death would seem, and often is, painful and anxiety provoking. Though I agree with Elaine Scarry's remarks on the unsharability of physical pain, it did not make the descriptions of Barbara's illness easy. Indeed for every mute ache that my imagination could not accurately translate, my awareness of the emotional suffering felt by Barbara and those close to her increased, and I felt the "sympathetic vibrations" that you recalled. Many times while reading your book, I felt pangs of sadness, and tears welled in my eyes. Emoting is something that I do not do well, but I do not find that this reaction is inappropriate when reading of tragic death or a meditation on grief. I was struck by the above quoted passage in Barbara's cancer diary, and its relevance to my feeling about your book. The analogy that Barbara's psychotherapist used for death—the distance, in this case, closeness to the edge of a cliff—explains not only the dangers, but also the benefits of reading your book.

The cliff of death is one that all are forced towards. The way in which we reach the edge indeed may differ. Some are dragged, trying to bargain for a reprieve. Others have the luxury of a slow stroll, perhaps even with moments of joyous repose. There are an intent few who have willingly run to its decisive rim, and jumped. It was painful to read this book, as I am one who knows that I cannot stop my journey towards the cliff, but have tried to find an ignorant solace in staring at my feet in hopes that I will not know where I am going.

Barbara's life, and your book, has shown another aspect of that cliff. With knowledge and acceptance of its existence, we may gain access to the view below. It is not one of the "valley of death" but of life. Barbara's willingness to remain active in not only her own life, but also the lives around her did not prevent her end, but did [show] how the acknowledgment of death affected the meaning of her life, and the lives of others after she died. The startling statistic mentioned in the book, that 80% of people in our culture die in an institution reveals a sterilization from death that I find unhealthy. Instead of protecting people, the partition between life and death creates anxiety out of mystery. *Dying to Teach* sets [out] to pick away at this wall, and do what you stated in your book dealing with death can do: reaffirm life.

—Matthew Davis

It took me a long time to get through your book. This is an odd way to start off a letter to you because it makes it sound as though I did not enjoy your writing, which I did, but let me explain. Death is something I have struggled with my whole life. One night, I tiptoed into my parents' bedroom and stood beside my dad. "Dad, you awake? Dad?" I asked him to come to my room with me and rub my back until I fell asleep. I was afraid to close my eyes and succumb to the dark. I was afraid of death. Only a few years before, I had been the young child sitting in a chair in temple, kicking my feet, whispering with my brother and giggling, despite the funeral service that was going on around me. My grandfather was dead, but I had no idea what dead meant. I did not understand my mother's tears.

That night in my bedroom, I told my dad about my fears. I told him that I could not sleep at night because I was scared to die. I was scared that my parents would die. He told me that I did not even have to begin thinking about his or my mother's death for many years, and that I would not have to think about my own death for many more years after that. He told me that everyone dies and it is something that I should not think about at such a young age. I took his advice. After that moment, I did not think about death.

I have realized that ever since that conversation, I have avoided death and dying in any way possible. Death made me angry. I did not know how to react to death and so I resisted reacting in any way at all. I hated when people would express their sorrow and go to funerals for people they were not close to. I grew hard when I heard people talk of the dead lovingly. I decided that in order to respect the dead you needed to leave the death alone and leave the grieving to those that were close to the deceased. I did not believe in forgiveness through death. I did not think it was right to talk about dead people as though they were saints. I chose, instead, to ignore death. Your book made me realize that this is an insensitive reaction. Honoring the dead and speaking nice words about the dead is not done for the person who has left the physical world. It is done for those who are still here. I regret not sending you the condolence card for your wife or attending the funeral, as I wanted to. I did not realize at the time that simple gestures like that can make a difference for someone.

For the first time in my life, in your class, I confronted death. I wrote my own essay about religion and the death of my grandmother. The words poured from me on to the page; I did not even have to think. I was thrilled at the ideas that I had come up with and knew that I had to read my essay aloud. While reading the essay in class, my voice faltered when I got to the section where I discussed the scattering of my grandma's ashes. Tears formed in my eyes. I could not finish the reading. This was a pivotal moment in my life. This was the first time I had publicly shed tears over a death. I had not cried at my grandma's funeral. I had not cried in front of my parents when they informed me of her death. I was haunted by her death, consumed by the feelings of guilt and anger that surrounded my decision not to face her demise head on. This public reading made me realize that I am human, more human than I thought. I am affected by death, and it is something that I will need to come to terms with during my life. However, despite this realization, I have continued to avoid thinking about death. That is, until I read your book.

It took me months to read your book. Hearing about the physical difficulties your wife had gone through horrified me. I was terrified by the mental and emotional difficulties both you and your wife encountered. I have not yet truly been in love. I do not wish to feel the passion for another that you felt for Barbara, only to have those feelings ripped from me by death. When you described the cancerous changes that your wife's body went through, all I could think about were the descriptions my father gave of my grandpa while his body was being ravaged by cancer. My dad told me about my grandpa's swollen feet. They were purple, fat. Like sausages. That description still chills me. I refused to go and visit him or think about the hardships he was going through. But I still remember my dad talking about his swollen feet. It is so hard for me to think about death through disease as anything but morbid and taboo. I feel that it is something no one should talk about. Your book scared me. Hearing you explain Barbara's death in such honest and unabashed ways made me contemplate ideas that I have been long avoiding. I did not want to think about my own death, which may be through cancer, as I have a long history of cancer in my family. I do not want to think about the day that my parents leave this world, leaving me to fend for myself. Your wife's death makes me feel as though I am afraid to fall in love, for fear that my love will one day have to end because of the ugliness of death.

Your book took me forever to finish because I had so much difficulty with the thoughts that emerged in my mind while I was reading. I resisted reading your book. I resisted writing this response. Right now, while writing this letter to you, I realize that I am dissatisfied with my words. They do not express what I mean to. All I can assure you of is that your book changed my view of death. It forced me to think about things that I have long been suppressing.

—Leslie DiPaolo

Jeff's manuscript is real. He has the courage to explore, expose, and even publish his most intimate thoughts. For these reasons, the manuscript is difficult to read. The reality of it is striking, and I began to experience deep emotions just by reading about his wife, whom I never got to meet. When he first read his wife's eulogy to our class, I felt selfish because I was taking for granted the privileges I had without even knowing it. Every day, we go through our routines without realizing that people around us may be dealing with the most heartbreaking tragedies of their lives. It is a difficult lesson to learn, but it is possibly the most valuable. Often, we don't even stop to think about our days, how we could make them better or how we are lucky that we have a home and a family to go to at the end of the day.

Jeff seemed to wonder if reading his wife's eulogy was too painful for us students, or if he "crossed the line" as a teacher. My answer to both of these questions is no. Unfortunately, there is no one right way to teach someone to deal with death and the process of dying. This seems strange as it is a reality that we must all face. Yet most people don't ever think about it, and we are never formally taught how to go through the motions of death as we are taught to go through life's routines.

Jeff showed us his way of dealing with death. It was difficult, but it was meaningful. He made us think and he made us feel. His humbleness, courage, and grace throughout a personal tragedy convinced me of his dedication to teaching and refreshed my own view of life.

—Amy Ferguson

Death is one of the most familiar, yet strangest, occurrences in life. It is expected; however, it is never expected. My eyes swell every time I think, see, or discuss it. I am so utterly disappointed by death I find that I am simply unable to deal with it. I have found that my attitude toward death has not changed much upon my completion of *Dying to Teach*. While it has intensified my appreciation for the fragility of life, the memoir has not helped calm my fears of death. Perhaps this is because I do not know the roots of these fears, thus, more than a shared experience with death is needed to conquer what lies behind my subconscious shadows. However, I have come to view death as a manageable experience. "I don't know what I would do without . . ." always comes to mind when I think about death. Contrary to this, you have conveyed the ability to learn how to get yourself through the next minute, the next hour, even the next year without someone you have had for the majority of your life. I am in awe of the courage in this book. *Dying to Teach* speaks genuinely with a naked vulnerability. The incredible lucidity in the analysis of emotion conveys the true therapeutic power of literature and writing.

At first, the number of literary references in the book surprised me. However, I quickly realized the use of these quotations were in part reflective of the central message of the memoir. Literature provides an array of characters, experiences, and emotions with which one can often identify. These similarities help pinpoint feelings and relay them in another voice through selective quotation, which can greatly clarify one's emotions for his knowledge and in this case for the knowledge of the reader. However therapeutic the act of reading literature or citing it, I found the most striking moments of the memoir were the allusions not to famous authors but to the authorial voices of my classmates, your daughters, your mother-in-law, and your wife.

Dying to Teach is dramatically set apart from other books and memoirs of death, in that, it conveys opinions from unique angles. The inclusion of your students in this remarkably personal experience is precisely what I found myself discussing with others while I was reading this book. I was on my break when I began a discussion with a coworker about the pressure on professors to publish and how this sometimes leads to a greater concern with research and publication than with students. I brought up *Dying to Teach* and how this memoir exemplifies the ability to merge the "advancement of knowledge" with its "human application." You have found ways, not just in this book but in the other books you have written, to include your students' ideas and opinions in your research and publications. Also, you continue this connection within your classroom, which keeps the process of theory and action closely tied together. The greatest failure of theory is in its inapplicability to human experience. I would go further to say that this is one of the leading hypocrisies within higher education: the teaching of theory but the failure to encourage or provide opportunity for action. You have demonstrated a definite link between life and the classroom with *Dying to Teach*. In fact, as one of my classmates put it, "I will view my professors differently." You have given yourself a human face with which most students can identity and that in and of itself has a shock value that keeps students engaged and most importantly inspired.

So the question is whether live application of theory discussed within the classroom should be taken to the next level with the inclusion of death education, or would this be too personal for academia? In my mind, there is a very important pro and con to this argument. The obvious con being that it would create an emotional atmosphere that would make students vulnerable and uncomfortable. However, this type of examination in the classroom might be deemed refreshing to students and interesting enough to escape the incessant drone of the mechanical note taking in lecture classes. Thus, there would have to be a delicate balance within the classroom to keep students wanting more. Provide "life-affirming" empowerment through the beauty of metaphor or allow for the mask of abstraction within artistic expression while creating an open atmosphere for any and all feelings associated with death. However, you have accomplished a similar atmosphere already in your expository writing classroom from which much of your material for *Dying to Teach* was fostered. Thus, I believe that a gifted individual such as you could not only make death education a valuable addition to a college curriculum but a life-changing experience for many students.

As I look at the several pages of notes that I have left out of this response, I realize that I could possibly write forever about this memoir. I have never felt so close to a book. While I did not know your family, I have known you as a professor and as a mentor for three of my four years at the University at Albany. You were the first person to validate my choice to be an English major and my inspiration for my choice to pursue a master's. I felt touched and honored to have read this work. In fact, as I approached the end of the book I kept thumbing through the last pages in disbelief that it was coming to an end so soon. But as I finished the last few lines I realized this was far from an ending. For every emotion buried in this memoir, you have birthed a new beginning for yourself, your family, and your students.

—Leanne Jwaskiewicz

I have to admit when I first received your manuscript I almost regretted telling you that I would read it and give you a response. I felt this way, not because I did not want to read it, but because I knew it would be about death, which is a subject I am not fully comfortable with. This is a reason why it has taken me so long to give you a response; that and the fact that I neglected to see there was a deadline. Although I am not comfortable with death I decided I was going to keep my word and respond to your manuscript. There were many reasons for my deciding to do so including the fact that I respect and admire you as a professor and it would be wrong for me to not keep my word to you after everything you have done for me. With this being said here is my response.

Once I actually started reading the book, I realized that it was not what I expected. I expected it to be all about Barbara and her death but you also included a lot of literary references, which broke up the book and made it not all about Barbara's death specifically, which I was happy to see considering my feelings about death. While I was reading the book I had a mixture of emotions. I felt sad when I read the chapter about Barbara's Cancer Diary and I saw the pain she was experiencing and the fact that at times she could not even get out of bed. I felt disappointed after reading the good news you and Barbara received from Fred about the PET scan and there only being some spots in her liver showing mild to moderate activity, which gave both of you hope that there was a chance for a cure only to find out later on that Barbara's condition eventually became worse. I would not necessarily say I was happy while I was reading the book as a whole, but I was happy with the end of the book where you talk about Barbara being embodied in your children. This gives me the idea that Barbara will be able to live on in your children.

There were a few subjects in the book that surprised me. The main idea, which I previously stated, was the usage of literary references. I did not expect to find anything that did not directly deal with Barbara's death in the book. Although I was surprised by your many literary references, I think you did a great job relating them to Barbara's death and how they helped you through the unfortunate ordeal. Another idea that surprised me, though small, was the fact that you did not want Jillian to participate in the CYO League because you were being prejudiced. With the open person you appear to be and the papers you had us write in class about prejudices and discrimination, I did not think you would ever be prejudiced against anyone but I guess no one is perfect. Although I was surprised by your actions I was happy that you admitted you were not proud of your opposition. Another surprising issue was the fact that Barbara did not want her parents to attend her funeral. I did not know why but after reading about Barbara's mother having Alzheimer's disease I guessed that had something to do with her decision; however I was surprised nonetheless.

I would not say reading the book changed my attitude toward death or made it harder or easier for me to think about death. I feel this way because like I stated earlier death is an uncomfortable subject for me. Although I know it is inevitable because everyone dies, it is still something I would rather not think about. After reading the book my feelings have not changed. It was not as painful to read the book as I thought it would be because it was not a detailed description of Barbara's death, which I was happy about. The literary references made it easier to get through the book because it was not all sad.

I feel "death education" may be a valuable part of a college curriculum. I know there are some people who, like me, do not like to think about death at all. I am sure there are others who are looking for different ways to cope with the death of a loved one or just death in general. The incorporation of "death education" in a college curriculum could possibly help those who do not like to think about death or have a fear of death get over that fear. "Death education" might also provide some answers to those trying to deal with death. College is the time in most people's lives where they start to actually think about and digest what is being taught to them. They become "adults" and start to think about life decisions which is why "death education" can be valuable in the college curriculum since they are actually able to understand and make sense of what is being taught to them.

Well I hope this letter finds you well. I am sorry once again that the response is late but I am happy that I am still able to contribute to your book.

—Vonetta Knox

It wasn't until midway through the book that I really began to understand the depth of your relationship with Barbara. It wasn't the actual death that made it so difficult to read your heartfelt memoir; it was the separation between you too. The emotional bond that was shared was intense and passionate, and throughout the entire ordeal you achieved touching strength in a time of continued adversity.

I recently took a family trip and on the plane ride home, I noticed a woman sitting with flowers on her lap. I put down your manuscript, and asked her why she so carefully carried the flowers through the five-hour trip. She responded by telling me that they were for her ailing grandmother, and that she was struggling to write a eulogy. As conversation progressed she asked if she could read some of the eulogies from your memoir. Her response was magical, it was as if she took your beautifully written words and transferred them into her own situation. Over the course of the next few hours she was able to write a heartfelt eulogy of her own, and claimed it was your work that inspired her. She said that the love for your wife flooded the pages with acute poignancy! I felt honored that your memoir could affect a stranger so strongly, as she seemed breathless after just a few pages. I later found out that evening that I had a death in the family, and needed to reread some of my favorite parts of the book, not only for insight on my own eulogy, but also strength and comfort in a time when I felt weak and lost. It was then that your memoir made me understand the complexity of death.

I was surprised to see you divulge not only the intensity of the disease, but also the amount of research that you did to know every aspect of the cancer. I was also surprised with the amount of quotes that related to the aspect of death and cancer. I did enjoy many of the quotes as I felt that they pertained well within the parameters of the book. On the subject of death education, I believe that it should be included in the college curriculum. It is impossible to ignore death in our everyday culture, especially considering that it encompasses everyone and everything on this planet.

The book was incredibly touching, which did also make it incredibly painful to read, and though I didn't know Barbara, I can still see the two pictures hanging in your office clearer than I can most college memories. In a memoir such as yours, I don't believe that you can be too painful, because mixing love with loss is a tender subject. I reacted differently in the chapters that described the classroom settings. The memory of the eulogy as well as other class moments involving Barbara was still very intense and difficult for me to read without pausing. I was touched deeply by many aspects of this book and believe that you had to include all of the hardest aspects of Barbara's passing. You had given your soul to Barbara, and it sapped you of all your emotional energy. Reading your last months with Barbara was especially difficult, because of the relationship that our class shared with you at the time.

After reading your memoir, I realized that you can't stop death or even prevent it, and I began to ask myself why do people die? Not in the physical sense, but in the emotional and metaphysical aspect of death. My conclusion was that people die to make life important. It is in death that the importance of life is clearly demonstrated. Thank you for the chance to once again be a part of Barbara's and your life, albeit through the loving and emotionally captivating text that you so beautifully inscribed. You are a loving father, a great husband, and most of all an incredible person.

—Johan Lang

Upon finishing the final words of *Dying to Teach* I felt as though I had traveled through your love and loss. As a member of your Expository Writing class in 2004, I was moved and brought to tears by the surprise reading of your wife's eulogy. However, it was not until reading this book that you revealed the raw experiences of such a loss. The detailed accounts of your family's battle with the vindictive cancer brought alive your wife's life before her illness and her courage throughout the pain.

You were wrong. As a professor you repeatedly denounced your abilities to master the art of "drawing a picture" through your literature. Your depiction of your wife both in life and death could not have been more descriptive. Perhaps the most powerful and clearest descriptions came upon reminiscing about your lives together and your love for one another. I found myself envious of the beautiful and real love you had painted. Her self sufficient lifestyle, her calm demeanor, her love for others, her intelligence, and her perfectionism were all portrayed through each memory you revealed to the reader. I was moved by your ability to reveal the complexities of her personhood through every word.

While reading *Dying to Teach* I felt relief for you. I don't entirely know why. I divided the pages of the book up to fit inside my bag in an effort to read them during my commute to work. On the Long Island Railroad, miles away from Albany and you, Barbara came alive to this twenty-two-year-old postgraduate. Upon arriving at Penn Station I would stuff the draft back into my bag and wonder if you knew how your words, your life were floating around in my mind. Looking back, I guess I felt such relief because you had managed to keep a part of your beloved wife alive to others.

As I read the book I was neither disturbed nor surprised at any point. I found your detailed honesty to be incessantly sad, however entirely necessary. The details of her physical and mental torture, however "disturbing," were the realities of how the disease had ravaged both her life and yours. While this disease did not define Barbara's life, it was a defining factor of her end. As a result, it was important for you to accurately represent the mercilessness of its wrath upon her body.

Upon concluding the book, you began to acknowledge the unanswerable questions that are left in death. You list the many things, after Barbara's death, which you simply will never know: "I don't know when Barbara uttered her final words or what they were . . . . I don't know when the essence of her life or spirit passed." It is because of this that I am uncertain whether or not a course in "death education" would be entirely possible. Death seems to me to be an indefinable end that we, in life, can never truly comprehend. How then, could death be taught? Instead, perhaps a course on loss and/or grieving may more accurately represent the suffering the living endure in death.

The inclusion of Barbara's journal entries and letters had a prevailing impact. These documents allowed her, as the subject of the book, to achieve a first-person voice. Through her words the reader gained a slightly greater understanding of this beautiful and loving woman. Moreover, I was struck by the critical role her documented thoughts and experiences played upon you after her death. I realized then, writing is necessary not only for oneself but for those who we will leave behind. Upon closing *Dying to Teach* I picked up a notebook and wrote the first journal entry of my entire life. While writing has been a significant part of my existence,

I could never bring myself to write candidly about my own life. Your book has convinced me of the importance of such self disclosure, both for the writer and the unknown future interpreter.

Professor Berman, your candid work has moved me in a way that words cannot describe. I hope that the writing of this book was a therapeutic experience for you. I feel privileged to have been given a slight peek into a fraction of Barbara's incredible spirit. I hope that life finds you, your daughters, and your grandson at peace and filled with beautiful memories of Barbara. Thank you, as always, for allowing me to grow from your life.

—Catherine Lennon

P.S.—Excuse my grammar, it has been quite a few months since I have taken your course!

The arrival of your manuscript could not have come at a worse time in my life, but I was compelled to read it. On the last day of finals this past spring (2005), after a battle of nearly 20 years with HIV/AIDS, my uncle died. He was only 53. I tried to look at it positively—he lived longer than all the doctors had predicted. He taught me to appreciate life, to live each day to the fullest. Yet as I read the manuscript, I found myself becoming angry. I was angry that with each page I read, death was thrust into my face and I was forced to confront it. I was angry at my uncle for losing the battle. I was angry that he, an alumnus of the University at Albany, wouldn't get the chance to see me graduate, or that he wouldn't watch me marry, or that he wouldn't be there for me to call when I just wanted to talk. I cried through most of the book, which was a completely different reaction compared to when I first heard Barbara's eulogy read during class in spring of 2004.

When you disclosed that your wife was ill and that you had written her eulogy, I was shocked. Students often forget (or choose not to acknowledge) that professors have lives outside of the classroom. I felt terrible for your family; no one should have to suffer that way. But I wasn't one of the students in the room who broke down and cried. I felt disconnected from the issue of death. I've seen friends and family lose loved ones, but I had never lost someone whom I couldn't picture life without. As much as I tried to be empathetic, I couldn't grasp the concept until I was forced into the situation.

I believe that many people feel similarly to me on the issue of death. For this reason, I don't believe that "death education" would be a valuable part of a college curriculum. I have read a number of the novels that you discussed in the chapter "Barbara's Death." In class, we looked at the various deaths and how the other characters reacted. I found the novels interesting, but they didn't teach me about death or even cause me to wonder about the issue. In order for "death education" to be helpful, the student must be emotionally invested in the subject. It would be unfair to group together students who do not have the same experiences about death.

Sometimes I forget that my uncle is gone because of the love I still have for him and all the memories that I will hold onto forever. Just as you said you find yourself looking into crowds to try and spot Barbara's face, I expect him to walk through the door when I'm at his house. But these memories keep him alive in my heart, just as Barbara will always be in yours.

—Jennifer Lonschein

I recently finished your manuscript. I had been anticipating it since I read the early draft toward the end of our expository writing class in the spring of 2004. When I first read the original draft, I had hoped that your ideas would develop into another book dealing with the pedagogy of self-disclosure. When the manuscript arrived in my mailbox, I jumped at the chance to read it.

As a student in your expository writing class, I became interested in the concept of writing as a form of therapy. Having carefully read the course requirements, I knew the class would be trying, both academically and emotionally. However, it was a challenge I was willing to accept. Throughout the semester, my papers grew more personal, and I challenged myself by reading my most personal essays aloud. While many of the students' disclosures were moving, no revelation affected me more than your reading of Barbara's eulogy.

Dying to Teach fascinated me because of how much it covered. As a memoir, this is the ultimate self-disclosure. When you read the eulogy aloud in class, I deeply admired you for it. Not only was your courage astounding, but you gave back to your students. Many of our self-disclosures were incredibly difficult, but your courage was doubtlessly transferred to us, giving us the level of comfort necessary in such a classroom environment. Your inclusion of Barbara's cancer diary surprised me, but I felt it made an excellent contribution to *Dying to Teach*. It was difficult for me to read because of the immense pain she was going through. However, given her refusal to throw anything away, as well as her undying love for you, I'm certain she would not object to its presence in your book.

Aside from the many gripping self-disclosures, the chapter "Barbara's Death" was very enlightening for me. Death is one of the only certainties in life; sooner or later, we must all come to terms with our mortality.

Many people don't have a stomach for such material, but death education can be very insightful for those choosing to study it. Many of the books you discuss are titles I plan to read.

The concepts of assisted suicide and euthanasia remain controversial, yet they permeate [classical] literature as well as contemporary literature. My reading of D. H. Lawrence's novel *Sons and Lovers* reminds me of a discussion I had with a friend of mine after watching Clint Eastwood's latest film, *Million Dollar Baby*. I was fascinated that a film dealing with assisted suicide could win the Academy Award for Best Picture. After seeing this film, I discussed *Dying to Teach* with a few friends of mine.

Many of my friends were intrigued with tales from my expository writing class. Some aspired to take the class, but were disappointed they couldn't as they weren't English majors. I discussed your manuscript just as I had discussed your expository writing course, and again my conversations were met with fascination. Once *Dying to Teach* is published, my copy will immediately be going on loan to a number of friends that find the material intriguing.

I have made an important insight based on my discussions with others. Despite the depressing nature of death education, one can walk away with a very positive experience. Is death education for everyone? No. Some would prefer not to have such emotions invoked, and that is perfectly understandable. However, there is no denying that there is much to learn both in literature and in life from death education.

Your syllabus for expository writing listed empathy as the only prerequisite. Everyone who registered for the course was aware that it would be very personal and emotional. You assured us on the first day of class that there would be many more laughs than tears. You were right. You connected with your students, an accomplishment I cannot say for many others at a large university. Many believe that student-teacher relationships shouldn't be so personal, but this is merely a matter of preference. If the student and the professor both agree to empathic self-disclosures, there is much to be learned through emotions, as well as difficult subjects such as death, suicide, or any other risky topics.

Jeff, it was an honor for me to read *Dying to Teach*. Your expository writing class helped me to grow as a writer, a student, and an individual. The pedagogy of self-disclosure has immensely grasped my interests over the past two years, and I hope to further explore writing as a form of therapy. I truly believe that this book contributes significantly to your studies, because you are practicing what you have been so passionately teaching. I wish you the best of luck with its publication.

—Matthew O'Connell

When I received the manuscript several months ago, I carefully opened the envelope and set the mass of paper in the center of the coffee table. My intent was to read it from beginning to end within the week and have a response to you shortly thereafter. I read through the introduction and part of chapter one before I decided to put it aside. I'll go back to it in a few days, I thought. I didn't. I couldn't. I wasn't sure if I wanted to endure it again. I picked it up months later and couldn't stop reading until I had finished. Two of my dogs had just had a terrible disagreement, which resulted in some bloodshed, some stitches, and a long discussion about whether or not it was prudent for them to continue living in the same house. I was inconsolable for two days, and I recalled a moment in Barbara's eulogy that read, "She believed that she could never love a child as much as she loved our dog." I feel the same way.

That is when it occurred to me that when my father died, I could not cry. I did not shed a single tear. But now that there was an issue with my dogs, the tears wouldn't stop. How backwards and peculiar. Throughout the reading of the manuscript, I mostly felt detached and cold, as though I was standing outside in the snow and was watching the words unfold through a foggy clearing that I had made with my mittens in a frosty window pane. I felt childish and a little ashamed, like I was reading something I shouldn't; this was not meant for my eyes. I read it anyway, unable to stop staring and unable to turn away. I couldn't find anything that surprised me; numbness knows no surprises. I imagine that I've become so good at insulating myself from death and suffering that it has become an automatic response. "This might hurt, so brace yourself."

Reading the book has not changed my attitude toward death. I would still prefer to avoid it, but more than that, I would like my husband to avoid it. I have long assumed that I will outlive him (his father died of a heart attack in his fifties), and it terrifies me. We have a very devoted relationship and cherish every moment we spend together (with rare exception). Reading about the closeness of your relationship with Barbara puts an exclamation point on what I already knew: life is too short and often too hard, so spend every minute carefully and always say, "I love you."

I have not spoken about the book to anyone. I'm not sure how one would broach the topic. My husband knew the book was there, and several friends and family members have been through my house and must have seen it on the coffee table. The title would have given an intimation of what the book is about, but no one asked about it. That's odd. How often do you see a stack of paper that high on a coffee table? A friend of mine is a high school English teacher. He didn't ask about it either, although I'm sure he read the title and perhaps a few pages when I stepped out of the room. No one said a word.

I can't say that the book made it easier or harder to think about death. I am still both obsessed and repulsed by it, like driving by an accident scene. I still work very hard at concentrating on living, which on many days is difficult enough without overshadowing it with thoughts of death. It is similar to how I felt about hearing the eulogy in class. I prefer to distance myself as much as possible. Perhaps my past relationship with depression makes me more guarded than most, but I feel an immediate need to withdraw when confronted with an unavoidable sadness. I know that sadness is not the intent of the text, but the written word impacts each reader differently and it is impossible to anticipate every possible reaction. I do believe that "death education" could be a valuable part of the college curriculum. It did and does make me very uncomfortable. I still find it unsettling. I'm nervous even as I sit here writing. But a college education should be about more than just guidelines, textbooks, and tests. A college education should include exploration and self-discovery even if it is uncomfortable, or perhaps especially so.

—Erin Schambach

I have completed my reading of *Dying to Teach*. Though my prior knowledge of your wife was limited, it made me anxious to read the manuscript. I was not disappointed. My experience with the book was a little different from my reactions to the eulogy. The eulogy was read to me while I was an undergraduate; I have now graduated. I was able to read the book at my own pace (which was quick) and then think about what I just read. As I read the book, I continuously looked forward to any mention of your wife. I found that learning about her was the most enjoyable aspect of the book. (This should make you happy, because you were successful in your ability to convey in your writing precisely what you wanted: an everlasting image of your wonderful wife.) Though I did notice all the literary citations, I enjoyed the references to *One True Thing* the most. I am most familiar with that novel and, therefore, I could grasp the correlations you made between this novel and yourself better than any other work you used.

The book was focused on the subject of death. It was not painful to read the book. On the contrary, I found the experience enjoyable. I am not trying to say that I find death enjoyable; I can't imagine anyone would. But the book was able to commemorate a woman, while employing honesty and love. I am not ashamed to say that during the reading of the eulogy I cried. I was one of the girls coming out of the bathroom every few minutes. Likewise, I cried at times during the reading of the book. After hearing the eulogy, I questioned why people live, if just to die. Yet, I admitted I would not have traded living for not having lived. The book only enforced my notion that life is better, even if it must end. We all know that it must.

It is not harder or easier for me to think about death. But reading the book has made me realize that one can truly mean everything to another. It was never a secret to me that you and your wife shared the type of relationship that people can only hope for. Your eulogy was evidence of that. But the book showed the reader so much more; it showed the love that you feel for your wife. Perhaps the book made it easier for me to think about life after death. I could tell by the information you shared in the manuscript that life is not easy for you. But the fond way in which you spoke about your wife and how privileged you felt to have been married to her indicates that memories will do their best to sustain you. Life after death does not sound easy. At times, it seems unbearable. But I have learned that my life could impact other persons so strongly that they would not change having known me for not. In addition, I may be so impacted by another that they may be able to leave their mark on me, visibly or invisibly, and I will never be the same. Because of your book and honesty, I believe this impact can begin with something as innocent as an arranged meeting of two young people. Hopefully, my future husband and I will share this impact.

I still think that death is terrible. I still wonder why people live if they will only eventually die. And, I still wish that I could believe in an afterlife where we can rejoin our families and friends. But I have begun to think that maybe a life without any life-altering experiences with death is the saddest life. If death cannot alter one's life, then maybe it means one has never truly loved another; if there is not love, then there can be no loss. Perhaps one cannot exist without the other. In my mind, solace does not exist because of a paradise, though often I wish it did. The book has shown me that even those who do not have a religious explanation to turn to can find solace. They are able to find solace in memories, in future miracles and gifts, and family members. Most of all, they can find solace in just having had the privilege of having known a person. They find solace in the realization that the time they shared together was a gift, the best gift of their own lifetime.

I strongly believe that "death education" would be a valuable part of a college curriculum. I think talking about death is perhaps the most taboo of all subjects in our society today. The best place to open the forum for this type of discussion would be to undergraduates in college. They are at an age where they take everything in and feel good about becoming knowledgeable adults. With the right teacher and proper guidelines, educating about death openly and with empathy can be an unforgettable, positive experience for college students.

I would like to thank you for allowing me, my classmates, and fellow readers of this book to take a glimpse into a real-life love story of two wonderful people. I have never forgotten my experiences in Expository Writing, or your Thomas Hardy–D. H. Lawrence course, and I doubt I ever will. I regret not being able to take all of your courses but feel lucky to have been in the two I did take, especially Expository Writing. I know all your writing sections are special because of the carefully selected topics discussed, but I can't help but feel that our section was extra special. Maybe all sections feel that way. But I am sure most of the students from my class, if not all, felt that you enhanced their college experience more than a majority of their professors. It was my pleasure to read this book and to respond to it. I hope all goes smoothly with the publishing.

—Dimitra Voulkidis

I find it difficult to remember a true emotion. I define "true emotions" as the feelings I have at the exact moment it affects my disposition. True emotions hurt, confuse, and aggravate both my body and my mind. Even happiness can be confusing and aggravating, especially when one is accustomed to contentment. A happy pessimist is never at ease.

Commenting on a manuscript is a hard task, but recalling how I felt throughout our Expository Writing class is nearly impossible. After an unexpected death, I become shocked and sensitive to the subject. Once those feelings subside, I avoid the topic in an attempt to feel more comfortable. The loss may have devastated me at first, but later I can rein in my scattered emotions. When I wrote my expository essays, I was in a particular state of mind for each piece. Rereading my own writing is interesting; I am surprised by my own words, and I felt so differently about certain topics then.

When my friend's mother died in March 2004, the semester I took your course, writing about it was so soothing. At least that is how I feel about the process *now*, but when I was writing the essay it was painful and complicated. I only can recall my emotions at the time because I still have that essay, that time capsule of sensations. I remember writing it in the open basement of my dormitory, streaking the ink with my uncontrollable emotions. I remember how my sinuses felt like they were imploding, and how grateful I was that no one bothered me.

I remember this, yet while reading your manuscript I couldn't determine which excerpts I had written. I couldn't remember how I felt listening to Barbara's eulogy. I imagine I must have been surprised. I know I was one of the few who did not cry, although it was upsetting. There was a feeling of discomfort in the class; most of the students awkwardly stared at the floor. It was an unexpected moment since we were not aware of your wife's condition. But the raw yet refined draft (if such a description makes sense for an emotionally open essay) opened a new door for our class and for everyone's relationship with you. It wasn't too personal; it wasn't uncomfortable or disturbing to learn more about your life as we shared intimate details of our own.

I find it fascinating how other people deal with death and loss, but I would not be motivated by a death to study methods of coping. I have never read about death and eulogies in such detail before. I know from experience, and from your study, that people attempt to avoid confronting the issue (for example, people partaking in small talk in front of an open casket). You were brave to accept her disease as terminal. You didn't pretend she was healthy or that she wasn't dying.

You taught us in class how to write about our lives, which involves writing on death, love, prejudice, abuse, and more. I cannot understand why professors think they must exclude complex subjects like death from the curriculum when it plays such an integral role in life. But a professor only takes his or her students and course curriculum as far as he or she is willing to go. You showed me that it is possible to maintain appropriate relationships with students while divulging personal details of your life. I am still unsure how you manage to bridge the student-professor gap with such ease. Your course was unique, as is your outlook on writing, teaching, life, and death. People will discover new ideas in this text, and I know one day your Expository Writing course will be taught in universities across the country. Anonymity will no longer exist in the college classroom.

—Amanda Zifchak

I finished reading *Dying to Teach* this past week, and I wanted to allow myself a few days to sleep on it and think about it before responding. While I read the book, I felt both sad and curious: my heart went out to you, your family, and those who were close to Barbara, and at the same time I wanted to read further and further to learn more about her life. Your descriptions of the kind of daughter, mother, and wife she was, as well as the experiences you shared, made me care about her, even though I had never met her. The biggest surprise in this book was its biographical nature. However, after thinking about it for a few days, it seems obvious that a book about a person's death should also be very much about her life. If you go on to write a biography about her, I would be interested in reading it.

Reading the book has motivated me to think about the death of my parents, because Barbara's death is inconsistent with the assumptions my parents have about their own deaths. The book offered excellent points to discuss with my parents, and it motivated me to discuss death with them soon so that we can come to an understanding before the time comes. It also caused me to be concerned about living so far from them when they need a caregiver. The book also motivated me to think about the prevention of cancer and other illnesses. It made me wonder how many other people I see on a daily or weekly basis also suffer from the loss of a loved one to a terminal illness. Reading the book did not change my attitude toward death.

I spoke to my grandmother on the phone on one of the days I was reading the book. I told her why I was reading the manuscript, and I began to cry when I read the title to her. I told her the story, and we cried together over the phone. Her reaction was that she was sad that a beloved woman died so young, and she remarked that she imagined that it must have been terrible for you to read the eulogy to our class.

It was difficult, rather than painful, to read the book, but I did not find it too difficult. I wanted to finish this book, and I did. The content weighed on my heart, and at times reading it made me feel like I was reliving the tragedy in place of you and your family. Reading the book has made it easier for me to think about death because I feel more prepared now. My reactions to reading the book were similar to my reactions to hearing you read your eulogy in class. Because the book told so much more about Barbara's life than the eulogy did, I felt the same sense of making discoveries about her life as I did when I heard the eulogy. A major difference was that we had about a minute to get used to the idea that day in class before you started reading, whereas we have had over a year to think about this before reading the book. However, that did not make the book any less effective.

Yes, I believe that "death education" would be a valuable part of a college curriculum, because I greatly value any form of preparation for events that arise in life. I appreciate it when a more experienced person warns me about how an experience may be or is able to answer the questions I have before I experience something. I believe it could be a valuable part of a high school curriculum.

Professor Berman, you have the deepest condolences not only for the loss of your dear wife, but for the sadness you are experiencing in your life without her. I wish I could do something to help. I will keep you and your family in my thoughts and prayers.

—Anonymous

WORKS CITED

Abbruzzese, James, and Ben Ebrahimi. *Myths and Facts about Pancreatic Cancer*. Melville, New York: PRR, 2002.

Aberbach, David. *Surviving Trauma*. New Haven: Yale University Press, 1989.

Abrams, Meyer. *A Glossary of Literary Terms*. 4th ed. New York: Holt, Rinehart and Winston, 1981.

American Psychiatric Association. *Diagnostic and Statistical Manual of Mental Disorders*. 4th ed. Washington, D.C.: American Psychiatric Association, 1994.

Arendt, Hannah. *The Human Condition*. Chicago: University of Chicago Press, 1958.

———. "Remembering Wystan H. Auden." In *W. H. Auden: A Tribute*, edited by Stephen Spender, 181–87. New York: Macmillan, 1975.

Ashenburg, Katherine. *The Mourner's Dance: What We Do When People Die*. New York: North Point Press, 2002.

Astrow, Alan. "Thoughts on Euthanasia and Physician-Assisted Suicide." In *Facing Death: Where Culture, Religion, and Medicine Meet*, edited by Howard Spiro, Mary McCrea Curnen, and Lee Palmer Wandel, 44–51. New Haven: Yale University Press, 1996.

Attig, Thomas. *How We Grieve*. New York: Oxford University Press, 1996.

Atwood, Margaret. *Negotiating with the Dead: A Writer on Writing*. Cambridge: Cambridge University Press, 2002.

Austin, J. L. *How to Do Things with Words*. Cambridge: Harvard University Press, 1962.

Bain, Ken. *What the Best College Teachers Do*. Cambridge: Harvard University Press, 2004.

Battin, Margaret Pabst. *The Least Worst Death*. New York: Oxford University Press, 1994.

Bayley, John. *The Character of Love*. New York: Collier, 1963.

———. *Elegy for Iris*. New York: St. Martin's Press, 1999.

Beauchamp, Tom, and James Childress. *Principles of Biomedical Ethics*. 5th ed. New York: Oxford University Press, 2001.

Becker, Ernest. *The Denial of Death*. New York: Free Press, 1975.

Behar, Ruth. *The Vulnerable Observer*. Boston: Beacon Press, 1996.

Belenky, Mary Field, Blythe McVicker Clinchy, Nancy Rule Goldberger, and

Jill Mattuck Tarule. *Women's Ways of Knowing*. New York: Basic Books, 1986.

Benjamin, Jessica. *The Bonds of Love*. London: Virago, 1990.

Berman, Jeffrey. "Compassion of Hospice Eases a Trying Time." Letter to the Editor, Albany *Times-Union*. June 1, 2004.

———. *Diaries to an English Professor: Pain and Growth in the Classroom*. Amherst: University of Massachusetts Press, 1994.

———. *Empathic Teaching: Education for Life*. Amherst: University of Massachusetts Press, 2004.

———. "'The Grief That Does Not Speak': Suicide, Mourning, and Psychoanalytic Teaching." In *Self-Analysis and Literary Study: Exploring Hidden Agendas*, edited by Daniel Rancour-Laferriere, 35–54. New York: New York University Press, 1994.

———. *Joseph Conrad: Writing as Rescue*. New York: Astra Books, distributed by Twayne Publishers, 1977.

———. *Risky Writing: Self-Disclosure and Self-Transformation in the Classroom*. Amherst: University of Massachusetts Press, 2001.

———. *Surviving Literary Suicide*. Amherst: University of Massachusetts Press, 1999.

Bishop, Wendy, and Amy Hodges. "Loss and Letter Writing." In *Trauma and the Teaching of Writing*, edited by Shane Borrowman, 141–55. Albany: State University of New York Press, 2005.

Boker, Pamela. *The Grief Taboo in American Literature*. New York: New York University Press, 1996.

Bollas, Christopher. *The Shadow of the Object*. New York: Columbia University Press, 1987.

Book of Job. In *The New Oxford Annotated Bible*. Edited by Michael Coogan. 3rd ed. New York: Oxford University Press, 1989.

Bosco, Ronald, and Joel Meyerson. *Ralph Waldo Emerson: A Bicentennial Exhibition at Houghton Library*. Harvard Library Bulletin 13, n.s., fall–winter 2003.

Boss, Pauline. *Ambiguous Loss: Learning to Live with Unresolved Grief*. Cambridge: Harvard University Press, 1999.

Bracher, Mark. *The Writing Cure: Psychoanalysis, Composition, and the Aims of Education*. Carbondale: Southern Illinois University Press, 1999.

Breger, Louis. *Freud: Darkness in the Midst of Vision*. New York: Wiley, 2000.

Brock, Dan. "Physician-Assisted Suicide as a Last-Resort Option at the End of Life." In *Physician-Assisted Dying*, edited by Timothy Quill and Margaret Battin, 130–49. Baltimore: Johns Hopkins University Press, 2004.

Brodkey, Harold. *This Wild Darkness: The Story of My Death*. New York: Metropolitan Books, 1996.

Burns, David. *Feeling Good: The New Mood Therapy*. New York: Avon Books, 1992.

Butler, Sandra, and Barbara Rosenblum. *Cancer in Two Voices*. San Francisco: Spinsters Book, 1991.

Byock, Ira. *Dying Well: Peace and Possibilities at the End of Life*. New York: Riverhead, 1997.

Caine, Lynn. *Being a Widow*. New York: Penguin, 1988.

Cannon, Gemma. "Relationships Don't End in Death: From Grief and Loss to Comfort and Consolation." Typescript.

Cassell, Eric. *The Nature of Suffering*. 2nd ed. New York: Oxford University Press, 2004.

Cavell, Stanley. *Pursuits of Happiness: The Hollywood Comedy of Remarriage*. Cambridge: Harvard University Press, 1981.

Chekhov, Anton. "Lights." In *The Oxford Chekhov*. Vol. 4, *Stories, 1888–1889*, translated and edited by Ronald Hingley. Oxford: Oxford University Press, 1980.

Chodorow, Nancy. *The Reproduction of Mothering*. Berkeley: University of California Press, 1978.

Colum, Padraic, ed. *The Arabian Nights*. New York: Macmillan, 1923.

Conrad, Joseph. *The Nigger of the "Narcissus."* In *The Portable Conrad*, edited by Morton Dauwen Zabel. New York: Penguin, 1976.

Cottle, Tom. *A Sense of Self: The Work of Affirmation*. Amherst: University of Massachusetts Press, 2003.

Couser, G. Thomas. *Vulnerable Subjects: Ethics and Life Writing*. Ithaca: Cornell University Press, 2004.

Craig, Randall. *Promising Language: Betrothal in Victorian Law and Fiction*. Albany: State University of New York Press, 2000.

Csikszentmihalyi, Mihaly. *Creativity*. New York: HarperCollins, 1996.

Datta, V. N. *Sati*. New Delhi: Manohar, 1988.

Derrida, Jacques. *The Gift of Death*. Translated by David Wills. Chicago: University of Chicago Press, 1995.

———. *The Work of Mourning*. Edited by Pascale-Anne Brault and Michael Naas. Chicago: University of Chicago Press, 2001.

Deutsch, Eliot. "Loneliness and Solitude." In *Loneliness*, edited by Leroy Rouner, 115–23. Notre Dame, Indiana: University of Notre Dame Press, 1998.

Dickens, Charles. *Great Expectations*. Harmondsworth, Middlesex, Eng.: Penguin, 1965; rpt. 1985.

Dickinson, Emily. *The Poems of Emily Dickinson*. Edited by Martha Dickinson Bianchi and Alfred Leete Hampson. Boston: Little, Brown, 1931.

Didion, Joan. *The Year of Magical Thinking*. New York: Knopf, 2005.

Dowbiggin, Ian. *A Merciful End: The Euthanasia Movement in Modern America*. New York: Oxford University Press, 2003.

Draper, Maureen McCarthy. *The Nature of Music*. New York: Riverhead, 2001.

Eckstein, Jerome. "An Atheist's Bible." Typescript.

———. *The Deathday of Socrates*. Frenchtown, N.J.: Columbia Publishing, 1981.

———. *Metaphysical Drift: Love and Judaism*. New York: Peter Lang, 1991.

Edelman, Hope. *Motherless Daughters: The Legacy of Loss*. New York: Delta, 1995.

Edson, Margaret. *Wit*. New York: Dramatists Play Service, 1999.

Eggers, Dave. *A Heartbreaking Work of Staggering Genius*. New York: Vintage, 2000.

Einstein, Albert. *The World as I See It*. Translated by Alan Harris. New York: Philosophical Library, 1979.

Eliot, George. *The Mill on the Floss*. Edited by Gordon Haight. Oxford: Clarendon Press, 1980.

Emmons, Robert. Introduction. In *The Psychology of Gratitude*, edited by Robert Emmons and Michael McCullough, 3–16. New York: Oxford University Press, 2004.

Emmons, Robert, and Michael McCullough, eds. *The Psychology of Gratitude*. New York: Oxford University Press, 2004.

Felman, Shoshana, and Dori Laub. *Testimony: Crises of Witnessing in Literature, Psychoanalysis, and History*. New York: Routledge, 1992.

Fitzgerald, F. Scott. *The Crack-Up*. New York: New Directions, 1945.

Frankl, Viktor. *Man's Search for Meaning*. Translated by Ilse Lasch. Boston: Beacon Press, 1962.

Freud, Sigmund. *Beyond the Pleasure Principle*. In *The Complete Psychological Works of Sigmund Freud*. Translated by James Strachey. Standard Edition. Vol. 18. London: Hogarth Press, 1955.

———. "Mourning and Melancholia." In *The Complete Psychological Works of Sigmund Freud*. Translated by James Strachey. Standard Edition. Vol. 14. London: Hogarth Press, 1957.

Ganzini, Linda. "The Oregon Experience." In *Physician-Assisted Dying*, edited by Timothy Quill and Margaret Battin, 165–83. Baltimore: Johns Hopkins University Press, 2004.

Gay, Peter. *Freud: A Life for Our Time*. New York: Norton, 1988.

Gaynor, Mitchell. *Sounds of Healing*. New York: Broadway Books, 1999.

Gilbert, Sandra. *Inventions of Farewell: A Book of Elegies*. New York: Norton, 2001.

Gilligan, Carol. *In a Different Voice*. Cambridge: Harvard University Press, 1982.

Glaser, Barney, and Anselm Strauss. *Time for Dying*. Chicago: Aldine, 1968.

Glick, Ira, Robert Weiss, and Colin Murray Parkes. *The First Year of Bereavement*. New York: Wiley, 1974.

Goleman, Daniel, ed. "Afflictive and Nourishing Emotions: Impact on Health." In *Healing Emotions*, 33–46. Boston: Shambhala, 1977.

Greenberg, Sidney, ed. *A Treasury of Comfort*. New York: Crown, 1954.

Groopman, Jerome. *The Measure of Our Days: A Spiritual Exploration of Illness*. New York: Penguin, 1997.

Hall, Donald. *Without*. Boston: Houghton Mifflin, 1998.

Hardy, Thomas. *The Return of the Native*. New York: Norton Critical Edition, 1969.

Harpham, Edward. "Gratitude in the History of Ideas." In *The Psychology of Gratitude*, edited by Robert Emmons and Michael McCullough, 19–36. New York: Oxford University Press, 2004.

Harris, Jill Werman, ed. *Remembrances and Celebrations*. New York: Pantheon Books, 1999.

Harris, Judith. *Signifying Pain: Constructing and Healing the Self through Writing*. Albany: State University of New York Press, 2003.

Hartman, Geoffrey. *Scars of the Spirit: The Struggle against Inauthenticity*. New York: Palgrave Macmillan, 2004.

Hatfield, Elaine, John Cacioppo, and Richard Rapson. *Emotional Contagion*. Cambridge: Cambridge University Press, 1994.

Heilbrun, Carolyn. *Writing a Woman's Life*. New York: Ballantine, 1988.

Hemingway, Ernest. *Death in the Afternoon*. New York: Scribner's, 1932.

———. *A Farewell to Arms*. New York: Scribner's, 1929.

———. *For Whom the Bell Tolls*. New York: Scribner's, 1940.

Herman, Judith. *Trauma and Recovery*. New York: Basic Books, 1992.

Hobhouse, Janet. *The Furies*. New York: New York Review of Books, 2004.

Holland, Norman N. "The Brain and the Book." Typescript.

Hooper, Judith. "Beauty Tips for the Dead." In *Minding the Body*, edited by Patricia Foster, 107–37. New York: Doubleday, 1994.

Hyman, Stanley Edgar. *The Tangled Bank*. New York: Atheneum, 1974.

Jamison, Kay Redfield. *Exuberance: The Passion for Life*. New York: Knopf, 2004.

———. *Touched with Fire: Manic-Depressive Illness and the Artistic Temperament*. New York: Free Press, 1993.

Janoff-Bulman, Ronnie. *Shattered Assumptions: Towards a New Psychology of Trauma*. New York: Free Press, 1992.

Jones, Ernest. *The Life and Work of Sigmund Freud*. 3 vols. New York: Basic Books, 1953–57.

Jordan, Judith V., Alexandra G. Kaplan, Jean Baker Miller, Irene P. Stiver, and Janet L. Surrey. *Women's Growth in Connection: Writings from the Stone Center*. New York: Guilford Press, 1991.

Kimsma, Gerrit, and Evert van Leeuwen. "Assisted Death in the Netherlands: Physicians at the Bedside When Help Is Requested." In *Physician-Assisted*

Dying, edited by Timothy Quill and Margaret Battin, 221–41. Baltimore: Johns Hopkins University Press, 2004.

Kirmayer, Laurence. "Landscapes of Memory: Trauma, Narrative, and Dissociation." In *Tense Past: Cultural Essays in Trauma and Mastery*, edited by Paul Antze and Michael Lambek, 173–98. New York: Routledge, 1996.

Kübler-Ross, Elisabeth. *On Death and Dying*. New York: Macmillan, 1970.

Kushner, Harold. *When Bad Things Happen to Good People*. New York: Avon, 1983.

LaCapra, Dominick. *Writing History, Writing Trauma*. Baltimore: Johns Hopkins University Press, 2001.

Laub, Dori. "An Event without a Witness: Truth, Testimony, and Survival." In *Testimony: Crises of Witnessing in Literature, Psychoanalysis, and History*, by Shoshana Felman and Dori Laub, 75–92. New York: Routledge, 1992.

Lepore, Stephen, and Joshua Smyth. *The Writing Cure: How Expressive Writing Promotes Health and Emotional Well-Being*. Washington, D.C.: American Psychological Association, 2001.

Lessing, Doris. *A Small Personal Voice*. New York: Vintage, 1975.

Levinas, Emmanuel. *Entre Nous: On Thinking-of-the-Other*. Translated by Michael Smith and Barbara Harshav. New York: Columbia University Press, 1998.

———. *Is It Righteous to Be?* Edited by Jill Robbins. Stanford: Stanford University Press, 2001.

Lewis, C. S. *A Grief Observed*. San Francisco. HarperSanFrancisco, 1961.

Long, Judy. *Telling Women's Lives*. New York: New York University Press, 1999.

Lowinsky, Naomi. *The Motherline*. Los Angeles: Tarcher, 1993.

Luna, Alina. *Visual Perversity: A Re-articulation of Maternal Instinct*. Lanham, Md.: Lexington Books, 2004.

Martin, Terry, and Kenneth Doka. *Men Don't Cry . . . Women Do*. Philadelphia: Brunner/Mazel, 2000.

McAdams, Dan, and Jack Bauer. "Gratitude in Modern Life: Its Manifestations and Development." In *The Psychology of Gratitude*, edited by Robert Emmons and Michael McCullough, 81–99. New York: Oxford University Press, 2004.

McNally, Richard. *Remembering Trauma*. Cambridge: Harvard University Press, 2003.

Mermann, Alan. "Learning to Care for the Dying." In *Facing Death: Where Culture, Religion, and Medicine Meet*, edited by Howard Spiro, Mary McCrea Curnen, and Lee Palmer Wandel, 52–59. New Haven: Yale University Press, 1996.

Miller, Nancy K. "Memory Stains: Annie Ernaux's *Shame*." In *Extremities: Trauma, Testimony, and Community*, edited by Nancy K. Miller and Jason Tougaw, 197–212. Urbana: University of Illinois Press, 2002.

Miller, Nancy K., and Jason Tougaw. "Introduction: Extremities." In *Extremities: Trauma, Testimony, and Community*, edited by Nancy K. Miller and Jason Tougaw, 1–21. Urbana: University of Illinois Press, 2002.

Moller, David Wendell. *Confronting Death: Values, Institutions, and Human Mortality*. New York: Oxford University Press, 1996.

Morris, Virginia. *Talking about Death Won't Kill You*. New York: Workman Publishing, 2001.

Nabokov, Vladimir. *Lolita*. London: Weidenfeld and Nicolson, 1965.

Nash, Robert. *Liberating Scholarly Writing*. New York: Teachers College Press, 2004.

Nelson, Judith Kay. *Seeing through Tears: Crying and Attachment*. New York: Routledge, 2005.

Nietzsche, Friedrich. *Human, All Too Human*. Translated by Gary Handwerk. Stanford: Stanford University Press, 1995.

Nuland, Sherwin. *How We Die*. New York: Vintage, 1993.

Nussbaum, Martha. *Upheavals of Thought: The Intelligence of Emotions*. Cambridge: Cambridge University Press, 2001.

O'Brien, Sharon. *The Family Silver: A Memoir of Depression and Inheritance*. Chicago: University of Chicago Press, 2004.

O'Conner, Patricia. *Woe Is I*. New York: Riverhead Books, 1998.

Oxford English Dictionary. 2nd ed. Oxford: Oxford University Press, 1989.

Parkes, Colin Murray. *Bereavement: Studies of Grief in Adult Life*. 3rd ed. Madison, Conn.: International Universities Press, 1998.

———. "What Becomes of Redundant World Models?" A Contribution to the Study of Adaptation to Change." *British Journal of Medical Psychology* vol. 48 (1975): 131–37.

Parkes, Colin Murray, and Robert Weiss. *Recovery from Bereavement*. New York: Basic Books, 1983.

Patchett, Anne. *Truth and Beauty*. New York: HarperCollins, 2004.

Pearlman, Robert, and Helene Starks. "Why Do People Seek Physician-Assisted Death?" In *Physician-Assisted Dying*, edited by Timothy Quill and Margaret Battin, 91–101. Baltimore: Johns Hopkins University Press, 2004.

Pennebaker, James. *Opening Up: The Healing Power of Expressing Emotions*. New York: Guilford Press, 1997.

Pickering, George. *Creative Malady*. New York: Dell, 1974.

Pincus, Lily. *Death and the Family*. New York: Pantheon, 1974.

Plath, Sylvia. *Collected Poems*. Edited by Ted Hughes. New York: Harper and Row, 1981; HarperPerennial, 1992.

Quill, Timothy, and Margaret Battin, eds. *Physician-Assisted Dying*. Baltimore: Johns Hopkins University Press, 2004.

Quindlen, Anna. *One True Thing*. New York: Dell, 1994.

Robinson, Ray, ed. *Famous Last Words*. New York: Workman Publishing, 2003.

Rosenblatt, Paul. "Cross-Cultural Variation in the Experience, Expression, and Understanding of Grief." In *Ethnic Variations in Dying, Death, and Grief: Diversity in Universality*, edited by Donald Irish, Kathleen Lundquist, and Vivian Jenkins Nelsen, 13–19. Washington, D.C.: Taylor and Francis, 1993.

Roth, Philip. *The Dying Animal*. Boston: Houghton Mifflin, 2001.

———. *Patrimony*. New York: Simon and Schuster, 1991.

———. *The Professor of Desire*. New York: Farrar, Straus and Giroux, 1977.

Rouner, Leroy, ed. *Loneliness*. Notre Dame, Ind.: University of Notre Dame Press, 1998.

Russo, Richard. *Straight Man*. New York: Vintage, 1997.

Salzberg, Sharon, and Jon Kabat-Zinn. "Mindfulness as Medicine." In *Healing Emotions*, edited by Daniel Goleman, 107–44. Boston: Shambhala, 1997.

Sarton, May. *The Small Room*. New York: Norton, 1961.

Scarry, Elaine. *The Body in Pain*. New York: Oxford University Press, 1985.

Schimmel, Solomon. "Gratitude in Judaism." In *The Psychology of Gratitude*, edited by Robert Emmons and Michael McCullough, 37–57. New York: Oxford University Press, 2004.

Sedgwick, Eve Kosofsky. "Off My Chest." In *Extremities: Trauma, Testimony, and Community*, edited by Nancy K. Miller and Jason Tougaw, 186–96. Urbana: University of Illinois Press, 2002.

Seligman, Martin. *Learned Optimism*. New York: Knopf, 1991.

Selwyn, Peter. "Before Their Time: A Clinician's Reflections on Death and AIDS." In *Facing Death: Where Culture, Religion, and Medicine Meet*, edited by Howard Spiro, Mary McCrea Curnen, and Lee Palmer Wandel, 33–37. New Haven: Yale University Press, 1996.

Showalter, Elaine. *Teaching Literature*. Oxford: Blackwell, 2003.

Siegel, Bernie. *Love, Medicine, and Miracles*. New York: Perennial Library, 1988.

Silin, Jonathan. "After a Loss, Silence." *Chronicle of Higher Education*, March 18, 2005, B16.

Solomon, Robert. Foreword. In *The Psychology of Gratitude*, edited by Robert Emmons and Michael McCullough, v–xi. New York: Oxford University Press, 2004.

Spargo, R. Clifton. *The Ethics of Mourning: Grief and Responsibility in Elegiac Literature*. Baltimore: Johns Hopkins University Press, 2004.

Spiro, Howard. "Facing Death." In *Facing Death: Where Culture, Religion, and Medicine Meet*, edited by Howard Spiro, Mary McCrea Curnen, and Lee Palmer Wandel, xv–xx. New Haven: Yale University Press, 1996.

Sprengnether, Madelon. *Crying at the Movies*. Saint Paul, Minn,: Graywolf Press, 2002.

Stearns, Ann Kaiser. *Living through Personal Crisis*. New York: Ballantine, 1985.

Steinbock, Bonnie. Introduction. In *Killing and Letting Die*. Edited by Bonnie Steinbock. Englewood Cliffs, N.J.: Prentice Hall, 1980, 1–19.

Stewart, Garrett. *Death Sentences: Styles of Dying in British Fiction*. Cambridge: Harvard University Press, 1984.

Stowe, Harriet Beecher. *Little Foxes*. Boston: James Osgood, 1873.

Styron, William. *Darkness Visible*. New York: Random House, 1990.

Theroux, Phyllis, ed. *The Book of Eulogies*. New York: Scribner, 1997.

Thomas, Dylan. *The Collected Poems of Dylan Thomas*. New York: New Directions, 1953.

Tillich, Paul. *The Courage to Be*. New Haven: Yale University Press, 1952.

Tolstoy, Leo. *The Death of Ivan Ilych*. Edited by Irving Howe. Classics of Modern Fiction. New York: Harcourt, Brace and World, 1968.

Tougaw, Jason. "Testimony and the Subjects of AIDS Memoirs." In *Extremities: Trauma, Testimony, and Community*, edited by Nancy K. Miller and Jason Tougaw, 166–85. Urbana: University of Illinois Press, 2002.

Warren, Robert Penn. *All the King's Men*. New York: Bantam, 1973.

Watkins, Philip. "Gratitude and Subjective Well-Being." In *The Psychology of Gratitude*, edited by Robert Emmons and Michael McCullough, 167–92. New York: Oxford University Press, 2004.

Wieseltier, Leon. *Kaddish*. New York: Knopf, 1999.

Wildman, Wesley. "In Praise of Loneliness." In *Loneliness*, edited by Leroy Rouner, 15–39. Notre Dame, Ind.: University of Notre Dame Press, 1998.

Wolfenstein, Martha. *Disaster: A Psychological Essay*. Glencoe, Ill.: Free Press, 1957.

Wolff, Tobias. *Old School*. New York: Knopf, 2003.

Woolf, Virginia. *Mrs. Dalloway*. Edited by G. Patton Wright. The Definitive Collected Edition. London: Hogarth Press, 1990.

———. "On Being Ill." In *Collected Essays*. Vol. 4. New York: Harcourt, 1967.

Younoszai, Barbara. "Mexican American Perspectives Related to Death." In *Ethnic Variations in Dying, Death, and Grief: Diversity in Universality*, edited by Donald Irish, Kathleen Lundquist, and Vivian Jenkins Nelsen, 67–78. Washington, D.C.: Taylor and Francis, 1993.

Index

A

Abbruzzese, James, 57
Aberbach, David, 207
Adams, Barbara, 170
Adams, Ted, 209–210
Adler, Morris, 215
"Adonais," 105
"After Great Pain," 5, 57
AIDS, 13, 127, 253
Albert, Arielle, 3, 5, 16–17, 33–36, 42–44, 45, 54, 68, 72–73, 80, 90, 103, 141, 166–167, 172, 173–177, 183, 185–186, 194, 214, 220, 223, 234–235
Albert, David, 3, 42, 103, 223, 234
Albert, Nate, 7, 44, 58, 104, 141, 169, 220, 234
All the King's Men, 8
Allen, Woody, 200
Althusser, Louis, 106, 107
Alzheimer's disease, 3, 220–221
American Cancer Society, 20, 187, 209, 219
anticipatory grief, 56–57
Anuar, Gabe, 61
Anuar, Karen, 3, 5, 45, 48–52, 61, 68, 165, 166, 177–178, 183, 185–186, 201, 218
Anuar, Shane, 235–236
Arora, Kunal, 238–239
Arrow of Gold, The, 203
Ashenburg, Katherine, 139, 187, 190
assumptive world, 1–2, 5, 6, 15
Astrow, Alan, 85–86
attachment theory, 2, 19, 228
Attig, Thomas, 217
Atwood, Margaret, 14

Auden, W. H., 183
Austin, J. L., 215
Autobiography of a Face, 176
Azzai, Ben, 179

B

Bach, Johann Sebastian, 30
Bain, Ken, 115
Baker, Alice, 128–129, 218
Barber, Samuel, 185
Barthes, Roland, 106
Battin, Margaret Pabst, 84, 86, 93
Bauer, Jack, 217
Bauer, Kim, 210
Bayley, John, 3, 74, 104
Beauchamp, Tom, 119
Becker, Ernest, 15
Beethoven, Ludwig van, 30
Behar, Ruth, 119, 130
Bel Canto, 59
Belenky, Mary Field, 19
Benjamin, Jessica, 134
bereavement, 55–56, 70, 105, 114, 188, 190, 215, 217, 232–233
Berman, Barbara
    and ability to fix almost anything, 94, 101–102, 168; as an absent presence, 222–223; and acceptance of death, 55, 67, 103; Arielle Albert's eulogy of, 173–177; and attitude toward religion, 108–109; and attunement to her family and friends, 19; and awareness of loss, 17–19; and being "not Barbara," 76, 87; and birth of Arielle, 33–36,

Berman, Barbara (*continued*)
  101; and calm demeanor, 177; and
  cancer diary, 4, 7, 11–61, 189, 249; and
  career as a computer analyst, 168,
  172, 178, 210; and career as a teacher,
  34, 100, 177–178; and catastrophizing,
  26, 102, 176; and chemotherapy,
  11–12, 15, 21 passim, 31–32, 43–44, 53;
  and comments about Arielle's wedding gown, 14; and confusion and
  disorientation, 87, 129; and "courage
  to be," 16; and creativity, 94, 101, 177;
  and dehydration, 90–91; and devotion
  to her family, 179; and diagnosis of
  terminal pancreatic cancer, 1–2, 8,
  11–12, 102–103; and early relationship
  with Jeff, 99–102; and end of speaking days, 88; and excellent health before diagnosis, 11, 103; and existential
  anxiety, 15–16; and external catheter,
  47, 68; and fear of death, 15, 40,
  54–55; and feeling tortured, 79, 103,
  141; and funeral, 185–186; and the
  Golden Rule, 179, 184; and gratitude,
  218; and growing up in Brooklyn, 167,
  171–172; and inability to read, 59; and
  interest in the past, 13; and jaundice,
  53; Jerry Eckstein's eulogy of,
  178–184; Jillian Berman's eulogy of,
  166–172; and Jillian's wedding, 39,
  201; and "juicing," 29; Karen Anuar's
  eulogy of, 177–178; and last entries
  in cancer diary, 59; and last written
  words, 229, 239; and leave-taking, 53,
  60; and letter to Arielle on her thirtieth birthday, 33–36; and letter to
  her father on his ninetieth birthday,
  48–52; and letter from her mother,
  41–42; and letter about Pandora, 4,
  17–19; life after, 209–236; and living
  life to the fullest, 169, 177; and long-
  lived relatives, 1, 11; and love for her

children, 33–36, 101; and love for col-
  lecting, 13, 102, 175; and love for dogs,
  4, 14, 18–19, 20, 100–101, 211; and love
  for friends, 4, 19, 60, 94, 179; and
  love for life, 12, 169; and love for
  music, 29–31; and love for parents,
  14; and love for traveling, 168–169,
  174–175, 177; and need for antipsychotic medication, 76, 129; and
  need for painkillers, 52–53, 57–58, 77,
  87–90; and need for survivor stories,
  8, 20; and need to teach her family to
  survive without her, 97, 201; and negative blood tumor markers, 24; and
  not looking like a statue when she
  died, 71–74; and pain management,
  77, 90; and panic attacks, 21, 27 passim, 33, 42, 53, 141, 197; and paralyzed
  vocal cord, 14–15, 109; and parents,
  Morris and Jean Kozinn, 14; and
  peaceful death, 71–74, 165–166; and
  perfectionism, 101–102, 112, 139,
  168–169; and physical pain, 57–59, 71,
  77, 79, 90, 141; and pride in her body,
  60; and protectiveness of her children, 155; and psychotherapy, 26–27,
  37, 39–40, 54–56; and remaining alive
  for eleven days without water, 90;
  and request for all her pain medication, 87–89, 92, 95–96; and response
  to dogs' deaths, 16–17; and response
  to pancreatic cancer vaccine, 22 passim, 59, 67; and response to thalidomide, 44, 59, 141; and retirement
  from work, 27, 60; and silence, 60,
  87–88; and sister, Karen Anuar,
  177–178; and speaking for, 109; and
  throat surgery, 15; and use of complementary therapies, 28–29; and use of
  psychopharmacological drugs, 27 passim, 33, 129, 197; and vaccine booster,
  47–48, 53; and wasting away of her

body, 59, 97, 165–166; and will to live, 165–166, 169; and wish to be remembered, 61, 178, 201–202; as a "worrier-warrior," 176, 236

Berman, Courtney, 42

Berman, Elliot and Debbie, 60

Berman, Jeffrey, "Eulogy for Barbara" the aesthetic pleasure of writing the, 8, 137–138, 140, 190; the attempt to be faithful to the ethics of mourning in the, 4, 107–108; Barbara's reluctance to read the, 104, 200; and the bridge between the living and dead, 129; and creating a "natural critical learning environment," 115; creating a verbal portrait of Barbara in the, 4, 113, 138; and emotional contagion, 200; as an expression of pain, 127, 139; and the fear of bursting into tears, 189; as a flow experience, 139; as a form of "obsessional review" and "distancing," 189; and intersubjectivity, 127; maintaining composure at the funeral while reading the, 4, 112, 186; motives for writing the, 2, 111, 129, 138, 190, 207; and the narrativization of trauma, 127, 208; and narrowing the distance between teacher and students, 5, 134; as a performative act, 115; reading aloud the, 117–118; and remembering the dead, 107; as a reminder of mortality, 132, 195; and respecting privacy, 124; and the sacred duty to the other, 129, 140; speaking for the other in the, 4; striking the right tonal balance in the, 103, 168; students' reactions to, 4–5, 117–141, 191–200, 208; and the value of talking and writing about death, 134, 204; writing the final draft of the, 99; writing the first draft of the, 4, 99; writing truthfully in the, 124

Berman, Jillian, 3, 5, 16, 17, 32–33, 37–39, 54, 68, 72–73, 80, 90, 103, 141, 166–172, 174, 183, 185–186, 194, 201, 214, 220, 223, 224, 228, 229, 234–235, 249

Beyond the Pleasure Principle, 205–206

Bishop, Wendy, 36

Blanton, Smiley, 206

Blue Sky, 59

Boker, Pamela, 70

Bollas, Christopher, 54

Book of Elegies, The, 105

Bosco, Ronald, 190

Boss, Pauline, 230

Bowlby, John, 2

Bracher, Mark, 112

Brahms, Johannes, 29–30

Breger, Louis, 206

Breitenstein, Geraldine, 3, 56, 94–96, 165, 218

Brock, Dan, 85

Brodkey, Harold, 61

Bronte, Emily, 100

Brown, Cailin, 115

Browning, Elizabeth Barrett, 207

Burns, David, 45

Butler, Michele, 22

Butler, Sandra, 16

Byatt, A. S., 59, 240

Byock, Ira, 84, 85, 86, 97

C

Caine, Lynn, 114

Camus, Albert, 176, 183

cancer
and acupuncture, 28; and cancer research, 66–68; and chemotherapy, 11–12, 15, 21 passim, 31–32, 43–44, 53; and complementary therapies, 28–29; and CT scans, 24–25, 32, 46–47; and depression, 26–27, 57;

cancer *(continued)*
   and gene therapy, 23; and GM-CSF, 47–48; and group therapy, 39–40; and healing power of music, 29–31; and "immortality in culture," 65; and the immune system, 26, 28–30; and immunotherapy, 22–24; and interferon, 47; and the "juvenile delinquents of cellular society," 110; and maintaining hope, 25–27, 67–68; and mortality rate of pancreatic cancer, 11; and nonspecific symptoms of pancreatic cancer, 20; and optimism versus pessimism, 26–27; and pain management, 52, 57–58, 71, 77, 83–88, 141; and pain of pancreatic cancer, 57, 141; and pancreatic cancer, 11–12, 20 passim; and pancreatic cancer vaccine, 3, 12, 13, 21–26, 31–32, 59, 67–68, 103; and pancreatic cancer vaccine "booster," 47–48, 53; and PET scan, 32; and physicians' high death anxiety, 65; psychological challenge of, 25–27; and radio frequency ablation, 29; surveillance theory of, 26; and thalidomide, 44; and therapeutic touch, 28–29; and visualization, 28–29
Cancer in Two Voices, 16
Cannon, Gemma, 45–46, 55, 231–232
caregiving
   and anticipatory grief, 56–57; and being "tested," 78–79; and "compassion fatigue," 128–129; the difficulty of, 64, 75, 87, 103–104; and difficulty of letting go of loved ones, 91; and end-of-life care, 91–93; as an expression of love, devotion, and reverence, 97; and the feeling that one is dying for the other, 129; the gift of, 97; and home-care hospice, 128–129; and learning

about death; and the "look of controlled suffocation," 135; and need to maintain hope, 25–27, 78; and physician-assisted suicide, 92–93; and physical and psychological exhaustion, 77, 128–129; responsibility of, 128; and speaking on behalf of the dying, 4
Cassell, Eric, 13, 88
catastrophizer, 26, 102, 176
Cavell, Stanley, 74
Chance, 203
Character of Love, The, 74, 104
Chekhov, Anton, 13
Childress, James, 119
Chodorow, Nancy, 19
"Claire de Lune," 185
Coffin, Rev. William Sloane, 69
Colum, Padraic, 214
Community Hospice of Albany County, 219
complementary therapies, 28–30
conclamatio mortis, 73
Confronting Death, 65
connected knowledge, 19
Conrad, Joseph, 7, 74, 78, 129, 202–204
Cook, David, 14
Corrections, The, 59
Cottle, Tom, 133
counterphobic motivation, 202–207
Couser, G. Thomas, 119
Craig, David, 103, 213–215
Craig, Randy, 43, 60, 103, 213, 215, 224, 227, 240
Creative Malady, 207
crying, 37, 54–55, 79, 89, 112, 121–124, 127, 131, 185, 187, 193, 194, 221–222, 227–228
Crying at the Movies, 227
Csikszentmihalyi, Mihaly, 139

D
Daley, Dia, 239–241
"Dance of the Blessed Spirits," 185
Dante, 224
Darkness Visible, 29, 112, 176
Darling, Kristen, 241–243
Darwin, Charles, 207
Datta, V. N., 56
Davidman, Joy, 70
Davis, Matthew, 243–244
death
    accepting, 55, 67, 103, 228–230; books about, 110–111; and changed attitude toward, 5, 12, 229–230, 242, 246; cross-cultural attitudes toward, 55–56; and "Death with Dignity Act," 93; and death education, 237–261; and the "death instinct," 205; and the death rattle, 72; and death rituals, 73, 186–187; and death scenes, 63, 97; and denial, 141; and difficulty of talking and writing about, 2, 9, 201; and dying trajectories, 12; and end-of-life care, 83–88, 91–97; and the euphemism of "passing," 108; and existential anxiety, 15; and the gift of, 16; and impossibility of saving a person from death, 16; the lingering unreality of, 230; and loss of dignity, 110–111; and making the dead part of our lives; as the muse of art, 191, 207; mystery of, 72–73, 88; and the need for a "last touch," 73; premature, 104; and right-to-die movement, 83–88, 91–97; and silence, 88; speaking personally about, 141; and stage theory of dying, 55
Death in the Afternoon, 224
Death and the Family, 58
Death of Ivan Ilych, The, 3, 54, 63, 74, 141, 176

Deathday of Socrates, The, 179–180
Debussy, Claude, 185
dehydration, 90–91
de Man, Paul, 106–107
depression, 176, 205–207, 257
Derrida, Jacques, 16, 106–107
Descartes, 14
des Pres, Terrence, 200
Deutsch, Eliot, 225
Diagnostic and Statistical Manual of Mental Disorders, 95
Diaries to an English Professor, 2, 115–116, 204
Dick, Ed, 3, 39–40, 47, 53–54, 95, 165
Dickens, Charles, 63, 76, 104, 139, 222–223
Dickinson, Emily, 5, 57, 114
Didion, Joan, 190
Dinesen, Isak, 112
DiPaolo, Leslie, 244–246
"Do Not Go Gentle into That Good Night," 74
Doka, Kenneth, 55, 204
Donne, John, 64–67
double effect, 83–88, 96
Dougan, Clark, 210
Dowbiggin, Ian, 85, 93
Dranoff, Glenn, 3, 21 passim, 43–44, 47, 67, 89, 109, 186–187, 210, 226
Draper, Maureen McCarthy, 29
Dying Animal, The, 17
Dying Well, 85

E
Eastwood, Clint, 255
Ebrahimi, Ben, 57
Eckstein, Jerry, 5, 165, 178–184
Eddy, Mary Baker, 207
Edelman, Hope, 7, 233–234
Edson, Margaret, 4, 63–68, 120

Efron, Art, 219–220
Eggers, Dave, 6–7
Einstein, Albert, 216–217
elegy, 105–106
Elegy for Iris, 3
Eliot, George, 72
Eliot, T. S., 33
Emerson, Ralph Waldo, 187, 190,
    210–211
Emmons, Robert, 217
emotional contagion, 22, 200
Empathic Teaching, 2, 121, 130, 227, 229
empathy, 19, 21, 76, 125, 128, 200, 217,
    219, 230, 235, 240, 255, 258
Empire Falls, 59
endorphins, 90
energy centers, 28–29
entrainment, 30–31, 222, 235
Entre Nous, 129
eulogy, 4, 99–105, 111–112, 115–116,
    165–184, 250
euthanasia, 4, 80–97, 255
existential anxiety, 15–16
external catheter, 47, 67
Extremities, 208
Exuberance, 29, 230

F
Family Silver, The, 112
Famous Last Words, 73
Farewell to Arms, A, 4, 68–72, 80, 96–97
Faure, Gabriel, 30
Feeling Good: The New Mood Therapy, 45
Felman, Shoshana, 122–123
Ferguson, Amy, 246
"Fern Hill," 229
Fiddler on the Roof, 220
First Year of Bereavement, The, 189
Fitzgerald, F. Scott, 74, 139
Fliess, Wilhelm, 206
Florer, Julia, 212

flow, 139
For Whom the Bell Tolls, 68
Forster, E. M., 139
Foucault, Michel, 106
Fourth Great Obituary Writer's
    Conference, 108
Frankl, Viktor, 113
Franzen, Jonathan, 59
Freud, Sigmund, 3, 38, 54, 205–207
Freud, Sophie, 231
frozen emotion, 70
Furies, The, 25

G
Ganzini, Linda, 93
Garber, Eugene, 211
Gay, Peter, 206
Gaynor, Mitchell, 30–31
Gift of Death, The, 16
Gilbert, Sandra, 105
Gilgamesh epic, 225
Gilligan, Carol, 19
Glaser, Barney, 11, 56, 73
Glick, Ira, 189
Gluck, Christoph Willibad, 185
Golden Notebook, The, 54
Golden Rule, 179–184
Goleman, Daniel, 26
Golijov, Oswaldo, 43
Gootblatt, Ellen, 60–61, 175, 229
Gorer, Geoffrey, 8–9
gratitude, 217–219
Grealy, Lucy, 52, 176
Great Expectations, 76, 222–223
Greenberg, Sidney, 215–216
Grief Observed, A, 70–71
Grief Taboo in American Literature, The,
    70
grieving patterns, 55, 208
Griffiths, Gareth and Caroline, 60
Groopman, Jerome, 109

H
Halberstadt, Sophie, 206
Hall, Donald, 3, 74, 223
Hallman, Ted, 28
Hamlet, 2, 12
Hannan, Maryanne, 211, 214
Hardy, Thomas, 37, 74
Harpham, Edward, 217
Harris, Jill Werman, 111
Harris, Judith, vii, 111–112
Hartman, Geoffrey, 200
Hatfield, Elaine, 122
Heart of Darkness, 78, 203
Heartbreaking Work of Staggering Genius, A, 6
Hebrew Union Prayer Book, 233
Heilbrun, Carolyn, 74
Hemingway, Ernest, 4, 37, 68–72, 74, 203, 224
Herman, Judith, 95
Hillel, 178–179, 182
Hilton, Conrad, 74
Hobhouse, Janet, 25
Hodges, Amy, 36
Hogan, Carrie, 218
Holland, Norman, 115, 139, 205, 207
Holocaust, 113–114, 166, 179, 182–183
Hooper, Judith, 61
Hope, A. D., 3
Hospice, 53, 56, 71–73, 93, 96, 108, 128–129, 218–219
How We Die, 110–111
human research, 119
Huygens, Christian, 30
Hyman, Stanley Edgar, 58

I
In a Different Voice, 19
Inferno, 224
In Memoriam, 105
Institutional Review Board, 119

intersubjectivity, 19
Inventions of Farewell, 105
Irving, Washington, 215, 230
Is It Righteous to Be?, 130
Iverson, Jill, 218

J
Jaffee, Elizabeth, 21
James, Alice, 73
James, Henry, 69, 73
Jamison, Kay Redfield, 112, 207–208, 230
Janoff-Bulman, Ronnie, 1, 15
Janzow, Joel, 72–73, 218
Job, 2, 109–110
Johnson, Samuel, 59
Jones, Ernest, 206
Jordan, June, 19
Joseph Conrad: Writing as Rescue, 202–204
Josselson, Ruthellen, 119
Jung, Anne, 165
Jung, Carl, 54, 206
Jwaskiewicz, Leanne, 246–248

K
Kabat-Zinn, Jon, 28
Kaddish, 186, 188
Kafka, Franz, 130
Kaufman, Michael and Debra, 60
Keats, John, 105, 139, 222
Kenyon, Jane, 3, 74
Kevorkian, Jack, 64, 81, 92
Kierkegaard, 58
Killing and Letting Die, 85
Kimsma, Gerrit, 91–92
"Kindness," 111
King Lear, 37, 58
Kirmayer, Laurence, 96
Knox, Vonetta, 248–250

Kozinn, Morris and Jean, 14, 40–43, 48–52, 108, 167, 170, 173, 220–221, 249
Kozinn, Howard and Janice, 60
Kress, Jack and Susan, 38, 60
Kubler-Ross, Elisabeth, 3, 17, 55, 72
Kushner, Harold, 1–2

L
LaCapra, Dominic, 230
"Lady Lazarus," 103
Lamott, Anne, 59
Lang, Johan, 250–251
language of condolence, 5, 209 passim
La Rochefoucauld, 217
Laub, Dori, 122–123
Lawrence, D. H., 37, 74, 255
learned helplessness, 26–27
Learned Optimism, 27
Least Worst Death, The, 84, 86
Leeuwen, Evert van, 92
Lennon, Catherine, 251–253
Lepore, Stephen, 112
Lessing, Doris, 54
Levi, Primo, 176
Levinas, Emmanuel, 106, 129–130
Lewis, C. S., 70–71
life script, 1
Lolita, 104
loneliness, 224–225
Long, Judy, 19
Longfellow, Henry Wadsworth, 45–46, 231–232
Lonschein, Jennifer, 253–254
Lord Jim, 78, 203
Love, Medicine and Miracles, 26
Lowinsky, Naomi, 233–234
Luna, Alina, 19
Lundell, Ellen and Ed, 34, 211
"Lycidas," 105
Lyotard, Jean-Francois, 106, 107

M
Macbeth, 112
"Maid with the Flaxen Hair," 185
Malamud, Bernard, 205
Man Who Mistook His Wife for a Hat, The, 220
Mankes, Karen and Russ, 23
Mann, Horace, 73
Man's Search for Meaning, 113–114
MapQuest, 228
Martin, Terry, 55, 204
Marx, Karl, 58
McAdams, Dan, 217
McCullough, Michael, 217
McNally, Richard, 95–96
Measure of Our Days, The, 109
Men Don't Cry . . . Women Do, 55
Merciful End, A, 85
Mermann, Alan, 66, 86
Metaphysical Drift, 179–180
metaphysical loneliness, 179–180
"Michelangelo" phenomenon, 133
Mill on the Floss, The, 72
Miller, Nancy K., 208
Million Dollar Baby, 255
Milton, John, 105
mind-body connection, 26–27
Moller, David Wendell, 65
Montaigne, 180
Morley, Sandy, 211
Morris, Virginia, 8, 71, 90, 114
Motherless Daughters, 233–234
Mourner's Dance, The, 139, 187
mourning, 106–107, 205–208
"Mourning and Melancholia," 205–206
mourning sickness, 224–228
Mozart, Wolfgang Amadeus, 30, 185
Mrs. Dalloway, 40
music, 29–31, 185, 220
mutual recognition, 134
Myths and Facts about Pancreatic Cancer, 57

N
Nabokov, Vladimir, 104
Nadel, Alfred and Sybil, 23, 43
Nash, Robert, 14
Negotiating with the Dead, 14
"natural critical learning environment," 115
Nelson, Judith Kay, 228
Nicholas Nickleby, 104, 139
Nietzsche, Friedrich, 8, 37–39
Nightingale, Florence, 207
Noonday Demon, The, 112
Nostromo, 78, 203
Nuland, Sherwin, 85, 92–93, 110–111
Nussbaum, Martha, 55

O
Oates, Joyce Carol, 35
O'Brien, Sharon, 112
obsessional review, 189
O'Connell, Matthew, 254–255
O'Connor, Patricia, 108
"Ode to Melancholy," 139
Old Curiosity Shop, The, 63
Old Man and the Sea, The, 69
Old School, 120–121
"On Being Ill," 12
On Death and Dying, 3, 17
On Meanings of Life, 179
One True Thing, 3–4, 75–89, 96–97, 120, 227, 257
Opening Up, 112
Orris, Edward, 47
Othello, 221
Ovid, 70
OxyContin and Oxycodone, 52

P
pain and suffering, 12–13, 58–59, 109–110
Parkes, Colin Murray, 1, 56, 69, 70, 114, 188, 189, 190

Patchett, Ann, 52, 59
Patient and Family Guide to Hospice Care, A, 90
Patrimony, 188
"Pavane for a Dead Princess," 185
Pearlman, Robert, 88
Pennebaker, James, 112
Pettit, Nancy, 229
Phaedo, 180
Physician-Assisted Dying, 86, 92
physician-assisted suicide, 83–89, 91–97
Pickering, George, 207
Pincus, Lily, 58, 189–190
Plague, The, 176
Plath, Sylvia, 103, 111, 203
Plato, 179–181, 215
Platonic Method, The, 179–180
Port, Len, 16, 87–89, 95, 100, 116, 204
Possession, 59, 240
"Prelude to the Afternoon of a Faun," 185
Proust, Marcel, 207
PSYART, 115
Psychology of Gratitude, The, 217–218
psychoneuroimmunology, 30
Pursuits of Happiness, 74

Q
Quill, Timothy, 86
Quindlen, Anna, 3–4, 75–89, 120, 234

R
Rancour-Laferriere, Daniel, 204
Raskin, Sherman, 188
Ravel, Maurice, 185
Reiter, Howard, 139
Remembering Trauma, 95
repetition-compulsion principle, 205–206
Reproduction of Mothering, The, 19

Return of the Native, The, 37
"Reverie," 185
Rilke, Rainer Maria, 30
Risky Writing, 2, 117, 127, 200
Robinson, Ray, 73
Rodgers and Hammerstein, 37
Roosevelt, Theodore, 230
Rosen, Jon and Anna, 60
Rosenberg, Steven, 68
Rosenblatt, Paul, 56
Rosenblum, Barbara, 16
Roth, Philip, 17, 188
Rouner, Leroy, 225
Russo, Richard, 59
Ryan, Karen and Peter, 24, 60

S
Sachs, Oliver, 220
Salzberg, Sharon, 28
Sarton, May, 227
Scarry, Elaine, 12–13, 243
Schambach, Erin, 256–257
Scheherazade, 214–215
Schiavo, Terri, 93
Schimmel, Solomon, 217
Schwartz, John, 93
Secret Agent, The, 203
Sedgwick, Eve Kosofsky, 64
Self-Analysis in Literary Study, 204
self-blame, 89, 95, 204,
Seligman, Martin, 26
Seneca, 217
Sewall, Richard, 114
Sexton, Anne, 203
Shadowlands, 70
Shakespeare, William, 58, 112, 221
Shamai, 178, 182
Shapiro, Fred, 3, 20, 21, 44, 47, 67, 229
Shelley, Percy Bysshe, 105

Showalter, Elaine, 114
Siegel, Bernie, 26, 29
Signifying Pain, 111–112
Singer, Mark, 108
Silin, Jonathan, 114–115, 134
Silver Palate Cookbook, 224
Small Personal Voice, A, 54
Small Room, The, 227
Smyth, Joshua, 112
Socrates, 179–181
Solomon, Andrew, 112
Sonnet to Orpheus, 30
Sons and Lovers, 255
Sopranos, 200
sorrowfuljoy, 7
Sounds of Healing, 30
South Pacific, 37
Spargo, R. Clifton, 107–108
Sparks, Helene, 88
speech acts, 215
Spiegel, David, 26
Spinoza, 113
Spiro, Howard, 9
Sprengnether, Madelon, 227
Stearns, Ann Karen, 70
Steinbock, Bonnie, 85
Stewart, Garrett, 63
Stowe, Harriet Beecher, 228
Straus, Ida, 73
Strauss, Anselm, 11, 56, 73
St. Peter's Hospital, 219
Styron, William, 29, 112, 176
suicide, 16, 78, 80–97, 100, 103, 114–116, 180–181, 200, 202–207, 221, 255
surveillance theory of cancer, 26
survival stories, 8, 20
Survival in Auschwitz, 176
Surviving Literary Suicide, 2, 130, 200
Surviving Trauma, 207
survivor guilt, 16, 89

suttee, 56
Symposium, 215

T
"talking back," 4, 27, 63
Talking about Death Won't Kill You, 90
Tanglewood, 43–44
Teaching Literature, 114
Telling Women's Lives, 19
Tennyson, Alfred Lord, 105
Testimony, 122–123
Them, 35
Theroux, Phyllis, 105, 108
This Boy's Life, 120–121
This Wild Darkness: The Story of My Death, 61
Thomas, Dylan, 74, 105, 229
Thousand and One Nights, 214–215
Tillich, Paul, 15–16
Time for Dying, 56
Tolstoy, Leo, 3, 54, 141, 176, 195
Touched with Fire, 207
Tougaw, Jason, 13, 127, 208
trauma, 5, 7, 94–96, 127, 200
Trauma and Recovery, 95
traumatic forgetting, 94–96
Treasure of Comfort, A, 215–216
Truth and Beauty, 52

U
Under Western Eyes, 78, 203
Unquiet Mind, An, 112, 207

V
Vacco v. Quill, 93
Vanity Fair, 227
Verdi, Giuseppe, 30

Victory, 78, 203
Voulkidis, Dimitra, 257–259
Vulnerable Observer, The, 119, 130

W
Warren, Robert Penn, 8
Washington v. Glucksberg, 93
Waste Land, The, 33
Watkins, Philip, 218
"Wave Riders" grief program, 136
Weisburgh, Herb, 28, 165
Weiss, Joyce, 29
Weiss, Robert, 70, 114, 189
Werther effect, 200
When Nietzsche Wept, 59
Whitman, Walt, 105
widow-burning, 56
Wieseltier, Leon, 58, 186, 188, 228, 232–233
Wilde, Oscar, 63
Wildman, Wesley, 225
Williams, Ralph Vaughan, 185
Willscher, Alex, 32–33, 37–39, 42–43, 103, 228, 234
Willscher, Claire and Garth, 32, 42
Willscher, Lynn, 32, 38, 42–43, 45
Willscher, Max, 38
Wit, 4, 63–68, 97, 120, 227
Without, 3
Wolfenstein, Martha, 204–205
Wolff, Tobias, 120
Women's Growth in Connection, 19
Woolf, Virginia, 12, 37, 40, 203
Work of Mourning, The, 106–107
World as I See It, The, 216
"worry time," 45–46
writing
    as an affirmation of existence, 14; as an antonym for silence, 13; as a bridge connecting past, present, and

writing (*continued*)
  future, 14, 19; as a death ritual, 188; as an expression of love, 19; as a form of self-anesthesia, 190; as a form of "obsessional review" and "distancing," 189; as grief work, 2, 5, 188–191, 204, 231; and healing, 2, 111–116, 204, 133; and human research, 119–120; and letter writing, 36; and mourning, 111–116, 138–139, 231; as problem solving, 2, 113; as a quest for a lost beloved, 14; as rescue, 7, 129, 202–204; and self-disclosure, 112, 115–141; therapeutic nature of, 2, 7, 133, 204; as a way to memorialize loss, 188–191

Writing Cure, The (Bracher), 112
Writing Cure, The (Lepore and Smyth), 112
Writing History, Writing Trauma, 230
Writing a Woman's Life, 74
Wuthering Heights, 100

Y
Yalom, Irvin, 59
Year of Magical Thinking, The, 190
Younoszai, Barbara, 109

Z
Zifchak, Amanda, 259–260

Scheneffell